MUTING ISRAELI DEMOCRACY

THE HISTORY OF
COMMUNICATION

Robert W. McChesney
and John C. Nerone, editors

*A list of books in the series
appears at the end of this book.*

AMIT M. SCHEJTER

Muting Israeli Democracy

HOW MEDIA AND
CULTURAL POLICY
UNDERMINE
FREE EXPRESSION

UNIVERSITY OF ILLINOIS PRESS

URBANA AND CHICAGO

Library of Congress Cataloging-in-Publication Data

Schejter, Amit.
Muting Israeli democracy : how media and cultural
policy undermine free expression / Amit M. Schejter.
p.   cm. — (History of communication)
Includes bibliographical references and index.
ISBN 978-0-252-03458-9 (cloth : alk. paper)
ISBN 978-0-252-07693-0 (pbk. : alk. paper)
1. Broadcasting—Law and legislation—Israel.
2. Freedom of expression—Israel.
3. Broadcasting policy—Israel.
I. Title.
KMK1067.S34   2009
343.569409'94—dc22   2009009442

Contents

Preface

> If I have a worry, it is almost exposed; if I have love,
> it will quietly disappear; if I have roots, they are
> slowly growing.
> —Rachel Shapira

One afternoon in 1993, as my dissertation adviser, Jorge Reina Schement, and I were strolling along College Avenue in New Brunswick, New Jersey, I was finally able to put into words something that had been bothering me for years. I had just returned from a year in Israel, during which time I had served as senior adviser to Minister of Education and Culture Shulamit Aloni. Although I had never been a member of a political party or any other established power group in Israeli society (with the exception of the Scouts, if you consider the Scouts to be an established power group), once I assumed this high-profile position, I kept running into people whose names I recognized only from the media but who seemed to know who I was. They also knew my father, even though he had immigrated to Israel from Argentina in the 1950s and was a professor of biochemistry (not an overly powerful position). They knew my professors in law school, and they knew the partners in the law firm I had been affiliated with before going to graduate school. In fact, it was one of the partners in this law firm who initially put me in touch with the minister and whose recommendation helped get me the job.

"Jorge," I said, "I have just spent a year, being 'part of the immediate scene in which the drama of the elite is enacted,'" in the words of C. W. Mills. Indeed, I had become one of the "captains" of the Israeli power elite's "higher thought and decision." And during that year, I had taken part in an extraordinary drama "centered in the command posts of the major institutional hierarchies."[1] But what amazed me most about that revelation was how naturally and easily I had slipped into that role and how naturally and easily I had been accepted by all those already there. On second thought, wasn't it only natural that an Ashkenazi Jewish sabra[2] male like myself, with all the right credentials and pedigree, was part of this self-selected group?

During my years of mingling with Israel's power brokers, I also noticed how much we shared culturally. Working in the Ministry of Education and Culture and then for the national broadcaster—the Israel Broadcasting Authority—I took part in meetings, debates, and discussions that addressed the very nature of Israel's cultural DNA. And whether it involved attending hearings at the Supreme or District courts; participating in Knesset committee sessions; sitting or chairing public committees; observing cabinet meetings devoted to issues of education, culture, and media; or just chatting with my fellow power brokers on and off the job, it seemed there were values we all shared and accepted and never argued about.

My instincts told me there must be an explanation for this phenomenon in the field of study that has intrigued me since I was a teenager: the study of cultural industries and the artifacts they produce. The things we shared were rooted in cultural products that had become an integral part of my identity and that I loved dearly—Hebrew songs, literature, theater, and film. They were also part of the organized rituals and ceremonies held on Independence Day, Memorial Day, and Holocaust Memorial Day that have always moved me to tears, whether I was attending them in person or watching them on television on the other side of the world. At that point, in the early 1990s, I was already a doctoral student in communications policy as well as a lawyer, and my professional involvement in law making and media policy was to provide further validation to my observations.

I was once told that a person's intellectual development begins with the first paper he or she writes in college. Indeed, the first major paper I wrote as a law student at the Hebrew University of Jerusalem was about the role of legislative history in the interpretation of law. Whether this paper was in the back of my mind or not at that time, I started studying the history of Israeli media law. My dissertation touched on two laws— the public broadcasting law of 1965 and the commercial broadcasting law of 1990—and the way the cultural obligations they set over broadcasters were interpreted by secondary regulators and implemented by the respective broadcasters.

I learned much about the ideological origins of media law when I worked for the Israel Broadcasting Authority and later on, when I became involved, in various capacities, in Israeli media policymaking. For fifteen years now, I have been exploring the impact of media law and policy on the development of Israeli culture. As my knowledge of social and legal theory expanded, I began to feel I was in a position to write authoritatively about how Israeli media were being molded to serve a particular image as well as to critique what I was seeing. A number of my findings have been published over the years in academic journals and law review articles, and when I arrived at Penn State University and joined the College of Communications there, I found an atmosphere that supported my interests and my desire to incorporate my observations into this book.

This intellectual and personal odyssey across continents, professional affiliations, and personally challenging (though mostly gratifying) circumstances would not have been possible without Judy, my wife and companion of more than sixteen years; the mother of our four children, Matan, Tamar, Iddo, and Ye'ela; and the editor and final authority on any and all of my academic and professional work. Judy read the manuscript and edited it and made important suggestions that shaped its final form significantly. She also made sure that no one distracted or disturbed me while I was writing.

The final act of compiling this book together took place in the summer of 2007 in Israel. In those crucial three months, I put together fifteen years of work into what I hope is a comprehensive thesis on democracy and hegemony in Israel. This could not have been accomplished without the daily support of my wonderful parents, who hosted our entire family for three months. From the morning, when my mother prepared my oatmeal breakfast, to the evening, when my father carefully chose the right Cabernet for dinner, and all the hours in between, when both took charge of the children, my parents provided the environment that enabled Judy and I to concentrate on our creative endeavors. This book is therefore dedicated to my family.

My dear friend and colleague, Professor Dafna Lemish of Tel Aviv University, graciously invited me to spend those three months at the university, providing me with a comfortable office, an Internet connection, a spectacular view of the Tel Aviv skyline, and a noisy air conditioner that silenced all outside disturbances. Penn State's College of Communications, Dean Doug Anderson, and Associate Dean for Graduate Studies and Research John Nichols provided me with a summer research stipend that helped fund this adventure. Two up-and-coming scholars of Israeli media law, my former student and current collaborator and friend Moran Yemini, a doctoral candidate at the University of Haifa, and my friend Zohar Kadmon Sella, a Ph.D. candidate at Columbia University, read the manuscript and made insightful and eye-opening comments. This book is therefore also dedicated to my friends.

I am also grateful to all the people at the University of Illinois Press who believed in this book, submitted it for review swiftly, and made the acquisition process so painless. In particular, I owe thanks to Bob Mc-Chesney and John Nerone, editors of the History of Communications series; to two anonymous reviewers who provided me with valuable feedback; to Dawn McIlvain, the associate editor charged with its production; to Kate Babbitt, the meticulous and creative copyeditor, who has made this book much better, more accurate, and more approachable, and to Senior Acquisitions Editor Kendra Boileau, who has marshaled me through the different stages leading to production with productive advice and support (and a great sense of humor).

I also want to dedicate this book to the State of Israel, since my passion for this subject developed out of my own deep love for Israel and for Israeli culture. Although my research demonstrates the distorted power structure within Israeli society and the oppressive nature of the policies that guide the media system that serves it, I am a true believer in the Zionist ideal of an independent homeland for the Jewish people based on principles of justice. I also ascribe to the purportedly naïve notion that offering a mirror to a loved one is the best way to promote self-reflection and change.

State College, Pennsylvania, July 2008

Introduction

THE MAKINGS OF A MUTED DEMOCRACY

" . . . and all the people answered with one voice"
—Exodus 24:3

Democracy became the descriptor of the political system of dozens of countries in the final quarter of the twentieth century (Schrader 2002) and at an unprecedented pace (Huntington 1991). The term "democracy" means different things to different people, however, and as democracies proliferated so did their typologies. Smooha (1997) has identified four types: liberal, *Herrenvolk*, consociational, and ethnic, based on the relationship between the ethnic groups composing these societies. Another typology identifies the disparities or tries to reconcile the differences between democracy as social choice theory and deliberative democracy (Dryzek and List 2003), basing the analysis on the political decision-making process. Yet another attempt to classify models of democracy identifies the levels of freedom in electoral processes as a central criterion (Schedler 2002). All of these attempts to uncover the meaning of the term "democracy" share a common element: they each include the idea that a democracy espouses a structure that allows the people to rule through their representatives and a value system that ensures the people can still be heard.

In this book I analyze the media system of a particular society that purports to be a democracy. This analysis is rooted in the belief that the media of mass communication offer members of a society the opportunity to have their voice heard by other members of that society and participate in a discourse at the societal level. This discourse bridges many of the physical barriers that generate societies that are merely "imagined," as Anderson (1983) describes them. The "mediated" expression of the "imagined" society is the modern-day opportunity to engage in this discourse. However, when the media in a given society are designed to provide a platform for some voices to be heard over others, then democracy is muted. In a muted democracy, the central media of mass communications, and in particular the electronic media, are designed to serve a power structure that promotes a hegemonic interpretation of that society's culture and identity. The façade of a free system that adheres to democratic principles covers the fact that the system is actually designed to produce a message that serves a particular image of that society, muting competing interpretations that may challenge it. Is Israel a muted democracy?

This question may seem surprising, since Israel generally emerges in international comparisons as a democracy that practices a policy of free press. Indeed, Freedom House, a Washington, D.C.–based nonprofit organization that conducts comparative studies of press freedom around the world, singles Israel out as the only country with a free press in the Middle East and North African region and ranks it in 59th–64th place among the world's 194 countries.[1] WorldAudit.org, an international not-for-profit organization based in England, ranks Israeli press freedom 37th in the world among the 150 nations with a population of more than 1 million and gives it a score of 1 on a scale of 1 to 7, with 1 being the "most free" regarding "the degree to which people can participate in the political process of their country."[2] Reporters Without Borders, an international nonprofit organization registered in France, concluded that the Israeli press are "the only ones in the region that had genuine freedom to speak" and ranked Israeli press freedom as 50th in the world among the 168 countries it ranks.[3] Muted, however, does not mean silent, and a muted democracy may provide the illusion that it is far more supportive of free speech than it really is. Israel is no exception to this rule.

Almost needless to say, Israelis perceive their press as free and believe in fundamental individual civil rights, including freedom of expression (Andsager, Wyatt, and Martin 2004). As early as 1953, the Israeli Supreme Court declared that the laws governing the political institutions in Israel indicate that it is a state based on democratic foundations (*Kol Ha'am v. The Minister of Interior* [1953]).[4] The court was required to make this declaration because Israel did not at the time have a formal constitution guarding basic freedoms (and it still does not). The Israeli Supreme Court has often cited the principle of free speech and implemented it while defending hate speech on television (*MK Rabbi Meir Kahane v. IBA* [1987]), commercial speech on radio (*Kidum Entrepreneurship and Publishing Ltd. v. IBA* [1994]) and television (*Mayo Simon Marketing and PR Ltd. v. Second Authority for Radio and Television* [1996]), freedom of speech for perceived enemies of the state on public broadcasting (*Zichroni v. IBA* [1983]), and freedom of speech in reporting on wrongdoing in the security forces (*Schnitzer v. Chief Military Censor* [1989]). The result is a thick legal corpus that attests to the fact that indeed the media enjoy a high degree of freedom. One might even say that this freedom is strengthened by the judiciary. This freedom, however, is not guaranteed by a firm constitutional backbone that could prevent legislation and enforcement of laws that are undemocratic because they curb freedom of expression by infusing the sphere of the media with an ideologized version of culture.

The lack of a formal constitutional commitment to free speech has mostly affected Israeli media by allowing the imposition of severe restrictions on media, both print and electronic. The publication of a newspaper, for example, requires a license, and Article 19 of the Press Ordinance authorizes the minister of the interior to shut down newspapers that publish materials that may endanger "the public peace."[5] This ordinance has been widely used even years after it was limited in scope by the *Kol Ha'am* case, in particular against newspapers in Arabic serving Palestinians living in Israel. The Supreme Court on occasion approved the use of Article 19 (e.g., in *Omar International, Inc. v. Minister of the Interior* [1982]) as well as the use of the Defense Regulations, which grant authorities similar powers to take sanctions against the media,[6] although the Court has noted the limitations on government power to restrict freedom of the press (*Walid Muhi a-din Asli v. Superintendent of Jerusalem* [1983]). Media, communication, and legal scholars as well as local and international watchdog organizations have pointed out these and other systematic deviations from freedom of the press in Israel. The existence of an active military censorship, with which the media maintain quite willingly a "marriage of convenience" (Goren 1976; Nossek and Limor 2001; Segal 1990), has been a major theme of such critiques, as have developments in media ownership, whose concentration in the hands of a few have tended to promote self-censorship among reporters fearing for their job security (Negbi 1998). Moreover, the suppression of free speech in the areas occupied by Israeli military forces since the 1967 war with its neighboring countries—in particular the West Bank of the Jordan River and the Gaza Strip—has had a long-lasting effect on the development of press freedoms in the Palestinian Authority (Jamal 2000).

In this study, however, I identify a distortion in Israeli democracy in general and media freedom in particular that is only tangentially associated with Israel's ongoing state of war with most of the Arab world. I do not attempt to argue that Israel is not a democracy in form; in fact I argue the opposite. Ever since the establishment of the State of Israel, its Jewish majority has been engaged in a lively discussion about its identity and purpose, with the media facilitating, engaging in, and serving as an important conduit in this discourse. Rather, I argue that the dominant culture, which has never fully committed to the basic tenets of democracy, allowed laws to be enacted that structure Israeli electronic media in ways that effectively limit the boundaries of the purportedly lively public discourse. This legal structure, which serves a particular self-image of Israeli society that it is also meant to preserve, is instrumental in creating and sustaining a muted democracy. While Israel's institutions may be democratic and while the enforcement of these policies may seem to have but a limited effect, I argue in this book that free speech in Israel is institutionally muted to ensure the continued domination of the Jewish majority's preferred interpretation of what Israel means as a Jewish-democratic state. This deliberate limitation of public debate is achieved by policies of two kinds: policies that allow the government to control the flow of news and policies that allow the government to dictate a cultural agenda to electronic media.

Israeli media law is a product of a political system that aspires to exercise rigorous controls over the electronic media. One of the most dramatic manifestations of this regulatory culture is the forced inclusion of content that serves a self-prescribed statist order, national order, and cultural order. The Israeli media operate within a closed and highly regulated regime that aims to fulfill cultural objectives dictated by dominant groups within the Jewish majority who are bent on preserving their particular interpretation of Zionism. The broadcasting system that emerged in Israel aspires to serve statist cultural goals by limiting the scope of messages deemed "proper" to broadcast and artificially enhancing messages it deems desirable to further national goals. Through laws, regulations, and court rulings, the electronic media—though "free" to discuss every aspect of political life and to expose corruption at the highest ranks of government, including the military—are limited to expressing an interpretation of national culture that fulfills the need to maintain the existing power structure. While individual participants in television and radio programs are free to express any views they wish and critique the operations of the state, the system is structured in a way that renders the media agents in perpetuating national rituals designed to promote a dominant, hegemonic interpretation of culture and avoiding a critique of the self-prescribed notion of what constitutes the nation.

The fact that Israeli policymakers have adopted such an interventionist approach to broadcasting is not coincidental. Policy is a reaction to a real or perceived social need rooted in the belief patterns underlying the system of regulation (Redford 1969). Regulation of media in democratic societies has more often than not come about as a reaction to the emergence of new technologies and the desire to guarantee that all have access to new media. But lawmakers and governments have been known to add provisions to media policies that were not directly aimed at solving technological problems or obtaining a more efficient allocation and use of public resources. Many of these regulations and policies have focused on the cultural opportunities technology presents. This regulation of culture is particularly at play when a national culture is forming, a challenging phase that most post-colonial regimes have faced. Indeed, once they complete the task of establishing social and political institutions, new nations tend to turn their attention to issues of identity. Geertz (1973), who identified this process in all nations established between 1945 and 1968, recognized two "towering abstractions" that needed to be balanced in the pursuit of uniqueness and distinctiveness: "essentialism," defining tradition, culture, and national character; and "epochalism," placing the accomplishment of creating a nation in its proper historical context. Both concepts view the creation of a national culture in a newly formed state as a process aimed at serving and legitimizing the political apparatus that is the state itself. At times, this is achieved through the creation of a "national identity" that is identified with the state, even though the "nation" it creates does not include all citizens of the state. This process is not unique to Israel and has been identified across the globe.

Using the electronic media to advance these cultural goals is rooted in a theory of the relationship between media and culture and the underlying assumptions of the role of governments in directing culture. These policies, which I call media-culture policies, cease to exist as technology-regulating policies and become what Tatalovich and Daynes (1988) call social-regulatory policies, those policies that exercise legal authority in order to preserve community values, moral practices, and norms of interpersonal conduct or to modify and replace them with new standards of behavior.

A media-culture policy study requires an analysis of the theories and values underlying the policy. This analysis examines the belief systems and ideological biases of policymakers and how policymakers perceive the relationship between mass media and culture and the role governments play in this dynamic. This goes beyond the mainstream questions that policy research addresses, which generally concern how effectively social programs are delivered. A systematic analysis of legal documentation relevant to a particular issue helps identify motivations that may be legitimate within a specific social order (at least formally). But the fact of formally justifying government action through laws obscures their real political importance in serving a dominant ideology (Cotterell 1992, 212). These distortions become apparent when the preferential treatment a government gives to one demographic group stands at odds with the liberal values that system claims to uphold or, in the case of this book, when one dominant interpretation of culture that serves one group over others is exposed.

The evolution of the media in Israel has been a subject of fascination for communications scholars over the years. From Elihu Katz's essay "Television Comes to the People of the Book" (1971) to Gabriel Weimann's article "Zapping in the Holy Land" (1995), the obsession of Israelis with the media and its effects on Israeli society has been extensively studied and documented. Research on the subject has focused on issues as diverse as how Israelis use the media (Katz, Haas, and Gurevitch 1997) even when it is on strike (Cohen 1981), how Israeli audiences adapt to foreign programs ranging from *Teletubbies* (Lemish and Tidhar 2001) to *Who Wants to Be a Millionaire?* (Hetsroni 2004), and how the Israeli media function during times of war (Liebes 1992), terror attacks (Weimann 1990), and peace celebrations (Liebes and Katz 1997).

The structural aspects of Israeli media, however, have garnered less attention. Three books recently published in English have discussed this phenomenon: Caspi and Limor (1999) document the history and organization of Israeli print and broadcast media, Oren (2004) focuses on the formative years of Israeli television, and Peri (2004) delves into the media's role in molding Israel's political and social scene. More focused studies, published as journal articles, such as those undertaken by Gandal (1994) and Levi-Faur (1998), have traced the development of the cable and telecommunications industries, respectively.

The legal documents used to support the case made in this book include Israeli media laws, regulations drafted by the various media regulators, committee reports that served as the basis for laws and regulations, protocols of debates in the Knesset (parliament) and its committees, Supreme Court rulings that interpreted media laws, protocols of resolutions made by regulatory bodies that were never officially published but were posted electronically, legal opinions of the attorney general and legal advisers of the different media outlets that were either made public or acquired through archival research, and news reports regarding all of the above. The documents span from the report of a United Nations committee on television in Israel, published in 1961 to decisions made by the Cable and Satellite Council in 2007.

I argue that Israeli media law and policy have been designed to serve an interpretation of Israeli culture that supports the perpetuation of non-egalitarian structures built into Israeli society. The techniques used to support this effort include limiting participation in the creation of culture and regulating the type of messages that will enter the media sphere. The policies regarding both are intertwined. In chapter 1, I provide some theoretical background regarding the term culture. In this book, I use the term "culture" to mean the symbolic order of a given group that is created by forming a group memory through perpetuating an ideologized version of the group's myths and rituals. The media, I contend, serve as electronic shrines in which these myths are maintained by incorporating the civil ceremony, the ideologically adapted form of the ritual, into the media fare.

In chapter 2, I identify the basic elements of the Zionist story as the building blocks of official Israeli culture and trace its incorporation into the hegemonic dogma of *mamlakhtiyut,* which identifies Israel as exclusively Jewish and Western. Since the 1980s, Israel's official identity has come to include capitalist-individualist values that have led to the promotion of the dyad "Jewish and Democratic" as its sole descriptor. It is illegal to contest this identity in political expressions: political parties whose platform denies either the democratic or the Jewish character of the state are banned. I describe the detailed legislative, administrative, and judicial effort to maintain this descriptor of Israeli culture as the only legitimate one. Laws and administrative acts institutionalize myths and rituals, and court actions protect the interpretation of these myths and rituals.

Chapter 3 focuses on the connection between Israeli political culture and Israel's media space. I claim that understanding the infatuation of Israelis with media technology—as demonstrated by their adoption patterns—helps explain why Israeli law and policymakers are so keen to control the content of this media. I discuss two of the defining features of Israeli political culture—a strong belief in the media's powerful effect and a general indifference to the public interest—and claim that they serve as the basis for designing media institutions so that their content serves the need of the government.

Chapter 4 surveys the evolution of Israel's electronic media, describing how they have developed into a closed system that is subject to many controls. I demonstrate a pattern by which the introduction of a new electronic media outlet may seem at first to be a step toward fewer controls but eventually ends with the introduction of governmental oversight of the new medium.

In chapter 5, I discuss the laws pertaining to broadcasting in Israel and analyze the "goals" for broadcasting as delineated by the law, court rulings, and regulatory acts. Television, which was introduced in Israel as a propaganda tool in 1968, continues to fulfill its original function despite the development of commercial television since then. To show how media law and regulation are designed to serve the state's ideological objectives, I compare the public broadcasting law of 1965 and the commercial broadcasting law of 1990 and the regulations enacted under them.

In chapter 6, I describe the development of multichannel television in Israel. Although policymakers initially envisioned a small-scale venture that would be regional in focus, multichannel television has blossomed into a huge industry that also serves the interests of the country's reigning cultural groups. The chapter traces four stages in the evolution of policies for cable and direct-to-home satellite television from 1986 to the present, showing how a system designed to provide choice and viewing alternatives (albeit limited) emerged into a system that eventually exercised control over Hebrew- and Russian-language content in order to serve the interests of the country's Jewish majority.

Fears about propaganda from across the border influenced the design of policies that affect the flow of news and information. Chapter 7 focuses on the ban on transborder broadcasts that target Israeli audiences for commercial purposes. I especially emphasize the legal structure of this ban and ongoing efforts to use it to block foreign broadcasts that present a version of reality that differs from the official line.

Chapter 8 looks at the electronic media rights of the Palestinian minority living within Israel's internationally recognized borders. Although the marginalization of the Palestinian minority is a recurring theme in this book, here I systematically review the rules and regulations of electronic media that pertain to the needs of this population. Neither *mamlakhti* nor commercial nor multichannel television is required by law to truly serve this population. The chapter looks at laws, regulations, and minutes of Knesset committee and plenum meetings as well as at several legal cases that demonstrate how this minority group is perceived in Israel as an "enemy within" and therefore deemed worthy of receiving only propaganda in the way of media offering.

Finally, the conclusion draws together all the evidence presented in the book to argue that although many "mouths" have been created by the system, their voices are often muted by that system in the interest of preserving the dominant culture. A homogeneous and harmonized establishment has created a vast web of laws and regulations to proactively maintain a non-egalitarian undemocratic order. While Israeli media enjoy much freedom to speak, I argue, the extent of their expression is limited and confined. Thus, while they contribute as vocal participants to the management of daily democratic functions, they are muted when it comes to contributing to the creation of an egalitarian culture. Having been packed with uniform hegemonic content has led the electronic and even the print media to acquiesce with the dominant culture to the extent that the role they purportedly play as democracy's watchdog is compromised as well. Hence Israel is a muted democracy.

1 *Culture*

FEATURES AND INSTITUTIONS

In order to identify the dominant elements of Israeli culture in the legal landscape in which the electronic media operate, I describe my understanding of the meaning of the term "culture" in this chapter. I discuss how myth and ritual, the building blocks of culture, are subordinated to serve a dominant group in society as they are transformed into their rational and institutional format in the form of ideology and ceremony, which help establish collective memory and identity. The infusion of ideology and ceremony into the legally prescribed media fare is one of the mechanisms by which dominance of a particular interpretation of culture is preserved and by which democracy is muted.

The Building Blocks of a Culture

Culture can be defined as both the story people tell themselves about themselves and the mental-intellectual connection among a group of people that makes their lives possible (Geertz 1973, 448). It is both the whole way of life and its common meanings as well as the arts and learning (Williams 1989, 4). A culture is a set of beliefs and assumptions developed by a given group in order to cope with the external process of adaptation and the internal process of integration (Inglehart 1990, 4). It is "the stock of knowledge from which participants in communication supply themselves with interpretations as they come to an understanding about something in the world" (Habermas 1984–1987b, 138). And because culture serves as the basis for understanding social reality, the development of a national culture is essentially the outcome of a power struggle. Carey (1992) describes culture as a process of "the making of meaning . . . of wording the world together" (57) that involves struggle and conflict. He points to two social arenas in which this conflict plays out (although he acknowledges that the process "suffuses social space") and that he identifies as "particularly important": the mass media and the educational system. Lasswell (1948), Wright (1960), and McQuail (1987) argue that one of the functions of mass media in society is the process of transmitting culture, or "socialization." McQuail refers to socialization as "continuity" and sees it as a process by which generations communicate what they perceive as important within the culture to the young.

This approach also involves analyzing communication in terms of power. Because the meanings expressed through myth and ritual are subjective, power plays an important role in the creation of an individual's perception of culture. According to Keesing (1974, quoted in Aronoff 1983), culture not only refers to the belief system of the individual and what he or she believes about his or her world but also to what he or she theorizes about the beliefs of others, beliefs that may contribute to an individual's image of the state of public opinion and to his or her reasons for expressing ideas opposed to it (Noelle-Neuman 1974). The symbolic forms of myth and ritual serve as the building blocks of culture and help the individual determine what these beliefs are (Aronoff 1983, 4).

Theoretical descriptions of this power struggle differ. Gramsci's theory of hegemony argues that the study of the cultural product provides evidence that it represents an unconscious ideological bias favoring the ruling class, a result of the subordination of the subconscious of the working class (McQuail 1987). Hegemony is a condition that Gramsci perceives to be separate from actual visible political power. Because it lies in the subconscious, it determines what is truly the ruling class. The ruling class's control of government is a consequence of the legitimacy to rule that is achieved by reaching a hegemonic status (Forgacs 1988, 422–424). Hutchinson offers a different analysis in his theory of cultural nationalism, which he defines as a movement to recreate a distinctive national civilization (Hutchinson 1987, 16). According to Hutchinson, cultural nationalism is independent of political nationalism and can be seen as a bottom-up effort to revive what binds a nation together. This process originates from the people as individuals instead of from what the state defines as social order. Cultural nationalism has a different goal than political nationalism: It seeks the moral regeneration of the national community rather than the achievement of an autonomous state. Historical memory serves to define the national community. Cultural nationalism arises from a crisis of identity and function, is embraced by secular intellectuals and the intelligentsia, and is generated by the formation of the modern state. (It may also inspire an assault on that very same state.)

Regardless of whether the Israeli experience is a top-down hegemonic process or a bottom-up creation of cultural nationalism, it clearly is an example of the institutionalization of culture, a process that derives its content from both rational and nonrational cultural resources. Aronoff (1983) identifies the prominent nonrational cultural resources as myth and ritual, while he identifies ideology and secularized forms of civil ceremony as culture's rational components (7). Myth and ideology are a culture's reservoir of symbols; ritual, civil ceremonies, and memory are the tangible formats through which a society maintains these symbols.[1] Communications are the avenue over which these symbols travel.

According to Connerton, myth is a collective symbolic text that constitutes a reservoir of meanings that can be used in different structures and contexts (Connerton 1989, 53–56). Myth provides members of a culture with a fundamental model of society that gives practical meaning to values and beliefs. It is a taken-for-granted aspect of everyday life (Bennet 1983). The use of myth, according to Habermas (1984–1987a, 46), provides a "gigantic mirror-effect, where the reciprocal image of man and the world is reflected"; as a result, "everything can be explained using a symbolic order." Like myth, ideology is a symbolic representation, and like myth, ideology can be understood within the contexts of defined groups. However, unlike myth, which seems to "emerge," ideology is a symbol system that is created for a purpose and embraced by only some of the members of the culture. At the same time, ideology is also history-bound and can be understood only by studying the historical events of the time when it was created (Althusser 1969).

If myth is a "gigantic mirror," ideology is the terrain on which people become conscious of their social position. Ideology is a function of the relation of an utterance to its social context (Eagleton 1991). It can be used, therefore, as a tool (Gramsci 1988) that serves a specific group in society. If it is a class-based society, ideology serves the ruling class, but in a classless society, it serves everyone (Althusser 1969, 235). Althusser argues that because it exists in every society, ideology can be equated with the unconscious as a phenomenon that exists but cannot be physically identified. Althusserian thinking, therefore, supports a theory of society and culture in which no understanding of social reality and experiences is "real" because these understandings are always seen through prisms that exist in the unconscious (Hall 1986). On the other hand, Giddens

(1979) argues that there is no such thing as ideology, only ideological aspects of symbolic systems; any type of "idea-system" may be ideological (187). To examine ideology, in his eyes, is to look at how "structures of signification are mobilized to legitimate the social interests of hegemonic groups" (188). He identifies a "peculiarly universal" trait of such groups: maintaining the existing order of domination. Giddens identifies ideological forms that are used to establish domination: the representation of sectional interests as universal ones, the denial or transmutation of contradictions, and the naturalization of the present or the preservation of the status quo (193–195).

Ritual, which should be differentiated from myth, is a technique, a behavioral routine through which symbols are applied to everyday life (Bennet 1983). Myths are associated with ritual, just as beliefs are associated with action (Silverstone 1988). A ritual is an enactment of a myth. Rituals establish and display the social principles embodied in the myth, and participation in ritual can be perceived as embracing a particular interpretation of the myth. Ritual plays a role in invoking social memory. Through ritual, the participant's attention is drawn to objects of thought and feeling of special significance (Connerton 1989, 44). Although ritual can be identified in a particular time and place, especially when it appears in the form of a ceremony, it is not limited in its effect to the ritual occasion. The ritual itself has significance beyond the information being transmitted in its process. Kertzer (1983) identifies five roles that ritual serves in the political process: meeting the need of political organizations to exist by using symbols, providing legitimacy to the social order, providing diverse segments of society with a sense of solidarity with and loyalty to the political system, inspiring people to action, and fostering a particular cognitive view of the world. Change within a political system comes about when ritual fails to prevent questioning and criticism of ideology (Hegland 1983).

Myth, ideology, ritual, and civil ceremony all contribute to the creation of a social identity, "a 'production' that is never complete, always in process, and always constituted within representation" (Hall 1990, 222). The creation of identity—the process through which an individual searches for a unity of existence—depends on the existence of communication.

Communicative action, the purposive action through which culture is created, facilitates the formation of personal identities (Habermas 1984–1987b, 138). It also facilitates the creation of group identities. This process leads to the formation of one of two "cultural identities." One identity implies the existence of a shared culture among people with a shared history and ancestry and reflects that "commonness" through stable, unchanging, and continuous frames of reference and meaning. The other identity is in the process of *becoming* "one" (rather than the process of *being* one). In this second instance, "meaning continues to unfold beyond the arbitrary closure that makes it possible" (Hall 1990, 223–230).

Memory is one of the basic tools used to track the formation of identity. Since it is physically impossible to acquire tangible qualities of the unity of oneself, memory, an idea one can share only with oneself, is what creates the uniqueness of an individual. While it is impossible for a person to become part of another individual and share his or her memory, it is possible for a person to join a group and acquire its common memory in order to reflect his or her group identity. In this sense, the difference between personal identity formation and group identity formation lies in the indefinable number of participants capable of willfully acquiring an existing identity.

Just as memory knits together an individual's identity over his or her lifetime, an imagined form of memory, what we could call social memory, preserves the unity of group identity. Controlling a society's memory is a process largely conditioned around the hierarchy of power (Connerton 1989). A society's perception of the past affects how it lives in the present; the interpretation and meaning given to current events depend upon how knowledge of the past is constructed. For both individuals and societies, present factors influence recollections of the past, and past factors influence experience of the present (4–6). Connerton, however, also observes that images of the past have a legitimizing effect and may serve as the basis for legitimizing the present social order. Connerton's presupposition is that shared memory by the social actors underlies any social order. A society's images of the past and recollected knowledge of the past become the subject that forms its myths. Thus culture-building is an ongoing process. Myth becomes ideologized through ceremony, which in turn contributes to social memory that produces new ideological mythic artifacts for public consumption. The media play a central role in this process.

The Role of Policies Regarding Media and Culture in Building a National Culture

While "the specific contours and outlines of [collective] memory are open to interpretation . . . that we are forming through the media a common recollection of [an] era seems self-evident" (Nerone and Wartella 1989, 85). Maurice Halbwachs first introduced the concept of collective memory in 1925 (Hoskins 2004). As Katz and Wedell (1977) have observed, the promotion of national integration—that is, creating a sense of belonging to a new nation-state (171)—was among the incentives for introducing electronic media in developing countries. Studying social memory can become, therefore, an exploration of the social impact of communication technologies (Kansteiner 2002, 179). The primary means for providing a collective identity is to create a "shared" past through narrative (Olick and Robbins 1998). How a group's history is represented, contend Liu and Hilton (2005), is central to the construction of the group's identity, norms, and values; the representation of its history provides the group with a sense of what it has been in the past and what it should aspire to be in the future (537). Anderson (2000) rejects the consensus among both historians and media critics that television is an unsuitable medium for constructing history and argues that American television, at least, has "virtually since its inception sustained an extremely active and nuanced engagement in the construction of history" (15). The role television and film play in constructing history (and the contributions of these media to social memory) has been documented, among other places, in Hong Kong (Ma 1998), China (Farquhar and Berry 2004), Japan (Fujitani 1992), and Israel (Peri 2001).

Dayan and Katz (1992) demonstrate how this process takes place (although indirectly) when discussing the role of media events in the creation of history. Media events, as they define them, are grand-scale interruptions of everyday life, when all media focus on a single event they have not organized that serves some need for a ceremony to mark an event. In their list of such events, which include Pope John Paul II's visit to Poland, Egyptian president Anwar Sadat's visit to Jerusalem, and the annual broadcasting of the International Bible Quiz on Israeli television, civil ceremony, the "rational" expression of cultural activity, comes to life via television production. These pre-planned events of "civil ceremony" have become possible only since the introduction of broadcasting. Dayan and Katz observe that "media events" mark holidays of "civil religion" and perform functions similar to those of religious holidays, noting that "media events are electronic monuments" (207, 211).

Merelman (1991) argues that popular culture, which he defines as a "consciously contrived, deliberately produced media form" (36), is the elaborator of democracy's cultural dimensions and the means by which the transmission of cultural models is made possible from the political elite to the generally passive public. Popular culture reproduces the individual/group, the static/dynamic, and the egalitarian/hierarchical elements of liberalism and links them in an attractive narrative format. He sees popular culture as a creator of a "system of discourse" that provides diverse groups in society with a sense of how they relate to other groups and helps them adapt to the demands other groups present. It also defines which forms of political conflict are acceptable. Indeed, scholars view popular culture as an arena where the struggle for hegemony is played out (Gitlin 1980) because "in the twentieth century, the language of popular culture has displaced an older language of political analysis, and popular culture media have displaced political parties as the principal link between the people and the politicians who run their government" (Edsforth 1991, 21).

The role of policymakers in advancing a self-serving culture should not and cannot be diminished. While it is common to focus on the economic and business aspects of cultural policy (i.e., Heilbrun and Gray 1993; Throsby 1999; Footer and Graber 2000), cultural policies can and have been analyzed in the context of their functions of creating and promoting symbols. An example is Sassatelli's (2002) description of how certain European Union policies have contributed to the creation of an "imagined" European community.

Social regulatory policies, the focus of this study, are differentiated in the literature from policies based on economic reasoning per se because they entail the exercise of legal authority to modify community values, moral practices, and norms of interpersonal conduct; replace them with new standards of behavior (Tatalovich and Daynes 1988); or preserve existing standards. Using media to propagate social and cultural understandings is a specific type of cultural policy and at the same time a social regulatory policy.

Although they both involve the relationship between symbolic representation and issues of national and civic identity (McGuigan 2004), media and cultural policies are rarely considered in the same breath (Hesmondhalgh 2005). The relationships between media, media products, and culture serve, therefore, as an introduction to the ensuing discussion of the attributes of Israeli culture, Israeli cultural policies, and the role media policy plays in their design, which is the focus of this book.

2 The Building Blocks of Official Israeli Culture

The process by which imagined (Anderson 1983) or mediated (Poster 1999) communities are created is linked to the development of communications (Thompson 1995, 62). National television has been identified as a powerful force that pushes a society toward the creation of a national identity (Schudson 1994, 40). The creation of Israel's "imagined community," as Anderson notes (1983), has transpired in two separate phases in which two "imagined" entities were created: an imagined "nation" and an imagined "state." This took place (first) through the creation of the Zionist movement that established the Jewish people as a nation and (second) through the establishment of the State of Israel (136). The Zionist ethos and narrative serve as the ideological basis for the State of Israel, establishing a challenging coexistence between "nation" and "state." However, the state presents them as seamlessly intertwined to the citizens of Israel. Formal media policy has played a key role in this effort.

Zionism

While the historic connection between Jews and the land of Israel and their yearning to return to this land has been a subject of the Jewish liturgy for ages, the political manifestation of this bond and its translation into a practical plan that called for the establishment of an independent state governed by Jews and for Jews—which required that Jews be recognized as a nation and not just as a religious group—did not exist before Theodor Herzl founded the Zionist movement in the mid-1890s (Laqueur 2003). This development coincided with the British empire's colonization of the Middle East; for a while, Britain allowed limited Jewish immigration to the colony of Palestine, where a Jewish homeland was to be established.

Whether Zionism should be seen in the context of a national liberation movement or as a colonial movement (i.e., Peled and Shafir 2005), its existence mandated the creation of a new culture, virtually from scratch. The Zionist story is an "essential" story that replaced a variety of blurred entities with a constant clear entity that has become a "tradition" only as a result of its invention (Ram 2006). As Shavit (1996) notes, Zionism created a new national culture to address the need to provide itself with a cultural content that would shape its identity. The evolving narrative told the story of a "people with no land" arriving in a "land with no people," a narrative that encompasses a number of mythical elements. In order to fuse the myth of the historical connection with the land, Hebrew names were assigned to all topographical sites (mountains, riverbeds, valleys, etc.) (Benvenisti 1997). The myth of "pioneering" (Eisenstadt 1967), embodied in the myth of the young Israeli sabra (Almog 2000), was created, even though the description fit only a tiny minority of the population. However, the myth had an enormous cultural impact, as it depicted a courageous agricultural-settler of European origin fighting off primitive Arabs who strove to undermine Zionist efforts to make the desert bloom.

This myth was perpetuated, for example, in the story of Tel Hai, which assumed legendary proportions (Zerubavel 1996), and the eventual celebration of Tel Hai Day, a civil ceremony commemorating a mythical battle between heroic Jewish settlers and deceitful Arab infiltrators. The sabra myth served as a basis for turning Zionism into a "civil religion" and as the basis for the formation of a Jewish collective identity that adopted the characteristics of an *ethnie* (Shimoni 1996)—a group that has a common name, a common descent, common historical memories, a shared culture, shared territory, and a sense of solidarity. The shared elements of this evolving culture, according to Smooha (1993), are the Jewish religion; Jewish nationalism; the Hebrew language and written culture; the Israeli ethic that emphasizes skills, achievement, hard work and competitiveness; and Western values such as democracy, materialism, a middle-class lifestyle, and mass culture. In the fundamental Zionist perception, Israel and Zionism are the only legitimate form of Jewish existence—an existence that has proven superior to the Diaspora option and, in fact, negates it (Shapira 2004, 69), even though the Zionist movement itself has in recent years embraced living in the Diaspora as a legitimate choice as long as it is aligned with a deep political (and often financial-philanthropic) commitment to Israel. Negating the exile is an integral part of the myth of redemption, which, together with revolt and replacing an image of weakness with one of strength, have become the pillars of the Zionist narrative (Shalit 2004). Indeed, the Zion-Diaspora dichotomy is so deeply engrained in the Zionist myth that it is often cited to explain why pre-state Zionists did not take greater measures to alert the world about the Holocaust (Sternhell 1998, 329).

Mamlakhtiyut

Zionism became the civil religion of Israel. The state formed by the Zionist movement adopted its cultural narrative, and the Zionist-statist hegemony was manifest in the concept of *mamlakhtiyut* (Kimmerling 2004), a dogma conceived of by Israel's first prime minister, David Ben-Gurion.[1] It has been described as "an instrument of ethnocentric particularity" (Peleg 1998, 234) because it regards the state as both a political entity and a "social and cultural integrating agent" (Kedar 2002, 129). *Mamlakhtiyut* highlights three sub-transitions undertaken by the Jews in their evolution from a people to rulers of a state: a transition from a focus on sectoral interests to a focus on the common good; a transition from semi-voluntarism to clearly defined duties; and a transition from foreign rule to national sovereignty (Peled and Shafir 2005, 38). As such it is designed to seem like an egalitarian endeavor, while in fact it promotes a dogma that serves only a portion of society. The basic elements of this dogma are that the State of Israel is the embodiment of the generations-long yearning of Jews to form anew an independent political entity; that Israel is the state of the Jewish people; that Israel belongs to all the Jewish people, not just to its citizens; and that Israel is a modern "Western"-style nation that requires Jews who do not share "Western" values to "modernize" through "melting-pot" apparatuses. *Mamlakhtiyut* is the basis for the civil religion that became an inherent part of the culture that preserved and reproduced the Zionist-Ashkenazi (European) hegemony (Kimmerling 2004, 150–151).

As a ruling ideology, *mamlakhtiyut* also has legal ramifications that institutionalized it into civil ritual. This is especially relevant to the two social arenas (Carey 1992) in which the power struggle for national identity plays out: education and media. The enactment of the Mamlakhti Education Law in 1953 dismantled the pre-state ideological educational organizations and established a national system entrusted with *mam-*

lakhti educational goals. When broadcasting was about to be transferred from the hands of the government to a nongovernmental institution—namely, the Israel Broadcasting Authority (IBA)—the law stipulated that the new authority should maintain broadcasting as a *mamlakhti* service (and the lawmakers refrained from using the term "public broadcasting service," which the European broadcasters it was designed to imitate use to describe themselves). Among other things, the IBA was formed to serve the needs of the *mamlakhti* educational system. Hence, in legal terms, *mamlakhtiyut* means both nonsectarian and independent. However, an analysis of the cultural missions of the educational system and the IBA, as stipulated by law, provides evidence that the mission of *mamlakhtiyut* was to serve a preconceived hegemonic order.

While the popular and institutional usage of *mamlakhtiyut* implies a form of national unity, differentiation and conflict have become so constant a factor in Israeli identity that they are referred to as inherent to Israeli society. Indeed, the question is not whether they exist but instead how they can be utilized as an integrative force rather than a fracturing one (Kahane 1992). The description of Israeli identity as fractured may be interpreted as a sociological theory that serves the establishment (Ram 1993), as an idealization of a troubled reality, or as a justification for the tendencies of hegemons to overcome conflict by imagining that consensus is achieved by imposing the goals of *mamlakhtiyut*.

Since its inception, Israel has been involved in wars along its borders and has been a target of recurring violent attacks aimed at civilians and centers of population. The outcome of the 1948 and 1967 wars was the eventual domination of an Arab minority by a Jewish majority. Israeli Arabs, according to the Zionist narrative, do not have a national identity—which Israeli Arabs describe as "Palestinian"—but rather belong to an amorphous undefined Arab nation that has many territories and countries in which to determine its Arabness. Recent political agreements that provide Palestinians in territories occupied in the 1967 war with a certain degree of political autonomy and even political statements by Israeli leaders that recognize the need for a two-state solution in the disputed land do not undermine the basic Zionist perception that Palestinians are "Arabs" and that their Palestinian identity is self-constructed to serve political goals. Indeed, the Jewish-Palestinian conflict over Israel and Palestine and the ensuing cultural policies developed in Israel regarding its Palestinian minority are crucial for obtaining a full understanding of the arguments made in this book. I discuss the history of Israel's relationship with its Palestinian minority and the media policies it affects in greater detail in Chapter 8.

Israel's geopolitical predicament notwithstanding, the conflict among the different ethnic Jewish groups is a result of the massive waves of Jewish immigration the country has experienced. During the 1950s, a Jewish population of only 600,000 absorbed more than 1 million immigrants, mainly from North Africa and Iraq. In the 1990s, following the collapse of the Soviet Union, more than 1 million immigrants from the former Soviet republics found their way to Israel, whose population had swollen to 5 million by that time. Together with the steady trickle of immigration over the years, these massive influxes of newcomers has been the backdrop for most of the social tension among Jewish Israelis over the years. Some of this tension is the almost natural outcome of a struggle over resources; the old timers, mostly of European descent (also generally referred to as Ashkenazi), settled the newcomers of the 1950s, mostly of Middle Eastern descent (also generally referred to as Mizrahi), in neighborhoods and towns removed from the affluent center. Another element of this tension is cultural. The Ashkenazi Jews, who played a central role in the Zionist movement and controlled the establishment of the state in its founding years, identified Israel as a Western country based in Western culture and refused to include Middle Eastern Jewish traditions in the emerging secular-statist hegemonic culture. Katz and Gurevitch (1973) viewed the confrontation between secular nationalism and the traditional religious identity of the Jewish community as the country's most obvious source of tension (17). Decades later, however, Yiftachel and Kedar (2000) identified the source of conflict as a three-layered ethnocratic structure in Israel peopled by Ashkenazi Jews, Mizrahi Jews, and Arabs (or Palestinians) that allows the dominant Ashkenazi group to sustain its power by controlling cultural hegemony.

Mizrahi Jews, in fact, began immigrating to Palestine before the Zionist movement was founded. When the first Zionists began arriving in Palestine in 1882, Mizrahi Jews constituted 60 percent of the Jewish population of the land (Smooha 1978) and their share among the immigrants was higher in the pre-state years than their share among total world Jewry. In contrast, since the inception of the state, Mizrahi Jews have found themselves in the role of "back-seat drivers" in the Zionist revolution. Not only was their historical contribution to Zionism largely ignored, but they were also isolated geographically and concentrated in "development towns" located in the periphery of the country where a "discernible low status 'ethno-class'"(Yiftachel 2000) emerged, of which they constituted the majority. This demographic planning effort reflected what Yiftachel and Kedar (2000) have called the "settling ethnocracy," a political system based on a combination of ethnonational expansion and ethnoclass stratification. The same approach was evident in the educational system, in which Mizrahi Jews, stigmatized as "backward," were relegated to segregated vocational high schools (Dahan and Levy 2000). Their cultural heritage, at first shunned, has been gradually introduced in the schools, but only after it had been deemed unthreatening (Smooha 1993, 182).

Shohat argues that "Zionist historiography pays little attention to the history of the Jews in the Muslim world" (1999, 6). The marginalization of the Mizrahi contribution to the Zionist endeavor is an outcome of the dominant ideological construct. Since it is inconsistent with Zionism's Western orientation and with the interpretation of Jewish existence as a uniform experience shared by all Jews, the Mizrahi contribution to culture contradicts the dominant Zionist ideological narrative. This dominant description was predominantly Ashkenazi in focus (Chetrit 2004, 309), and Mizrahi Jews were seen as a threat to the veracity of this cultural narrative (Smooha 1993, 182). The story of the Mizrahi Jews and their relationship to the state was, therefore, reformulated to fit the mold of the dominant Ashkenazi story (Shenhav 2004, 155).

The isolation of Mizrahi Jews from positions of power was a product of the political culture that evolved in Israel in its formative years. When the state was founded, Israel's political leaders discussed the possibility of appointing a token Mizrahi to the twelve-member cabinet (Shohat 1988). The first Mizrahi to serve in the Israeli cabinet held the insignificant post of police minister. The judicial system was also bereft of Mizrahi representation. It was not until 1962—fourteen years after the founding of the state—that the first Mizrahi Supreme Court justice was appointed and a designated seat for Mizrahi justices was created. This seat was called the Sephardi seat (because Mizrahi Jews follow the religious traditions associated with the Jews who were expelled from Spain, which is called in Hebrew Sepharad) and was set aside on the court as a measure of affirmative action (Levitsky 2006, 112). As Lahav (2001) contends, the first two Mizrahi justices left no enduring impression on Israeli jurisprudence and are remembered best for endorsing opinions written by other justices. Shohat (1989) analyzes the prejudiced portrayal of Mizrahi Jews in Israeli film and demonstrates how the portrayal of Mizrahis in popular culture has suffered from equal stigmatization. Avraham (2003) describes how the Mizrahi population's geographical distance from the major centers of power has contributed to the negative image of the overwhelmingly Mizrahi development towns in Israeli media.

Jewish, Democratic, and Neoliberal: Israel since the Mid-1980s

Since the 1980s, the dominant Israeli story has undergone a transformation and has adapted to a changing ideological, technological, and economic reality. Indeed, since the political upheaval of 1977, when the Labor Party was ousted from power after running the state since its inception, Israel has made the transition from a "developmental state to a competition state" (Levi-Faur 2000). It has rapidly changed from "developing country to post industrial country" and has skipped a period of stabilization (Sharkansky 1987). In the process, it has changed "from a Socialist-inspired mixed, highly centralized, highly planned state-centered, protectionist economy to a much more decentralized and international-oriented neo-liberal one" (Aronoff 2001). These changes—in the state's institutional structure, in its industrial infrastructure, in the organization of its labor force, in the distribution of its wealth, in the nature of its welfare state, and, of course, in its media, all under the guise of adopting a new counterhegemonic (and at the same time neohegemonic) ideology— took place without any substantial ideological opposition and practically swept along the entire state and its citizenry (Filc 2006, 227).

The political impact of these changes has been dramatic. For one thing, the principles of social democracy, upon which the state was founded, were gradually replaced (Aharoni 1998). Since the mid-1980s, capitalist jargon has been adopted by both liberal and conservative governments (Ben Bassat 2002), and Israeli policymaking in general has shifted away from a communal-socialist ideology toward a pluralist-capitalist one (Ben Yisrael 1994). Hirschl (1997, 1998, 2000) traces the "institutional disregard for subsistent social rights" (2000, 1087) in Israel to the narrow "neo-liberal" and "individualist" (1998, 428) worldview illustrated by what has been called "the constitutional revolution" since 1992.

Indeed, the most dramatic expression of this change in the value system that underlies Israeli law and policymaking was demonstrated in 1992 when the Knesset added two constitutional building blocks to the legal corpus—Basic Law: Human Dignity and Liberty and Basic Law: Freedom of Occupation.[2] These laws formally defined the state as Jewish-democratic and made these twin elements the founding principles of legal interpretation, although one describes national identity and the other the state's political system. A political party, for instance, cannot be formally established if it negates in its platform the idea that Israel is "Jewish-democratic," and a party promoting such a platform cannot compete for seats in the Knesset.[3] Thus, every "assault" on the state's "Jewishness" can be legally silenced—a questionable procedure in a democratic state—because it is seen as an attack on the inseparable dyad of Judaism and democracy and the very essence of the state. Examples of "defensive" or "militant" democracies that enacted laws to combat assaults on their democratic nature include post–World War II Germany and France and postfascist Spain (Lowenstein 1937; Minkenberg 2006; Comella 2004). The unique attribute of the Israeli experience is that the narrow, exclusive, and nondemocratic descriptor of the state's identity has become as sacred as democracy itself. Tamir (1993) contends that "the liberal tradition with its respect for personal autonomy reflection and choice, and the national tradition with its emphasis on belonging, loyalty and solidarity, although generally seen as mutually exclusive, can indeed accommodate each other" (6), and Gavison (1999) contends that a state that describes itself as belonging to one ethnic group can be democratic. But other commentators are skeptical (i.e., Peleg 2007 calls the dyad a "flawed" and "illiberal" form of democracy), and some (i.e., Gontovnik 2004, 641) conclude that Israel's cultural policies do not fit those of a "liberal" society, although it may identify itself as such. Some (i.e., Kremnitzer 2004) go so far as to state that preventing a free discussion of Israel's Jewishness is "entirely implausible" (163). Yet others believe that these policies are rooted in the oppression of the Palestinian people both within Israel's borders and beyond them (Barzilai 2002). Thus, views of Israel as "non-liberal" (i.e., Doron 1998, 165) or "neo-liberal" (i.e., Hirschl 1997, 137; 1998, 428) emerge from the realization that the state has recently shifted its focus from promoting social, cultural, and collective rights to promoting individual rights in order to advance dominant cultural understandings that serve the state's self-determination as both "Jewish" and "democratic," a determination that is at best contradictory and at worst cannot be settled. The transition in the underlying value system is reflected in law and policymaking, most pointedly in cultural policies.

Cultural Legislation in Israel

MAMLAKHTI EDUCATION

Mamlakhtiyut, which is the basis for the dominant interpretation of culture and the national cultural agenda, was first articulated in the decision to dismantle the partisan educational system, a remnant of the pre-state era, and combine all Israeli schools into a *mamlakhti* system. The *mamlakhti* education system set as its goal in the 1953 Mamlakhti Education Law:

to base education in the State on the values of Israel, and the achievements of science, on the love of the homeland and loyalty to the State
and the people of Israel, on training in agricultural work and craftsman-
ship, on pioneer training, and on the ambition for a state based on liberty,
equality, tolerance, mutual help, and love of fellow people.[4]

This narrative, which lays out the basic myths of Zionist culture and
serves as the basis for the Zionist ideology, was first amended in 1980
to include in its goals "awareness of the memory of the Holocaust and
the heroism."[5] In 2000, the entire law was amended. The new goals of
mamlakhti education, demonstrating the changes in the state's ideological stance, are as follows:

1. To educate a person to be person-loving, love his people and love
   his land, a loyal citizen to the State of Israel, honoring his parents
   and family, his heritage, his cultural identity and his language;
2. To instill the principles of the proclamation on the establishment
   of the State of Israel and the values of the State of Israel in a Jewish democratic state and to develop a sense of respect for human
   rights, basic liberties, democratic values, obedience to the law, the
   culture and views of fellow people, and to educate to the quest for
   peace and tolerance in the relations between people and between
   nations;
3. To teach the history of the Land of Israel and the State of Israel;
4. To teach the Jewish Bible, the history of the Jewish people, the
   heritage of the People of Israel and the Jewish tradition, to instill
   the memory of the Holocaust and the heroism, and to educate to
   honor them. . . .
11. To recognize the language, culture, history, heritage and unique
   tradition of the Arab population and other population groups in
   Israel, and to recognize the equal rights of all citizens of Israel.[6]

The 2000 Mamlakhti Education Law aimed to make the goals of the
mamlakhti educational system more universal and reflect an acceptance
of and internalization of universal values. The wording and prioritiza-
tion of the goals, however, leaves little doubt as to what the hegemonic
interpretation of the culture is and what the ideology it serves aims to
achieve through its educational system: Jewish heritage is one that should
be "taught," while the language, culture, history, and heritage of the Arab
population (which constitutes 18 percent of the population) is merely to
be "recognized." In fact, the word "Arab" appears in the text of the law
only in article 2(11), the section cited above. It can be presumed from
reading the law, therefore, that the State of Israel requires even members
of the Palestinian minority in Israel to "learn" the Jewish Bible, while
it merely "recognizes" the language Palestinians speak and write. The

usage of the term "Arab" to describe the Palestinian minority is in itself an expression of the Zionist narrative that denies the existence of a national Palestinian identity (a point to which I return in Chapter 8).

THE FLAG, THE ANTHEM, INDEPENDENCE DAY, AND MEMORIAL DAY

In addition to the cultural values that are to be introduced through the educational system, Israeli law has instituted specific symbols. The flag and the state emblem were instituted by law in 1949; desecrating them carries a penalty of up to one year of imprisonment.[7] The flag is the flag of the Zionist movement and the emblem depicts the menorah as it is engraved on the columns of the Titus Gate in Rome, where it is being carried by Roman soldiers in 70 A.D. Both these symbols serve the ideological understanding that the Jewish state is a continuation of the historic Jewish kingdoms of antiquity. Amendments to the Flag and Emblem Law were not made until the 1980s. One amendment, enacted in 1986, requires government buildings, including "the administrative buildings of the institutions of higher education," to display the flag.[8] A similar obligation was imposed in 1997 on all recognized schools.[9] The draft of the bill explains that the goal of the amendment is to raise consciousness of and to imbue Israeli students with the values of the state and its symbols. Thus, civil ceremony plants ideological constructs in the physical public sphere. The draft also cites the fact that it is customary to do so in many countries, including the United States, thereby providing this nationalistic act with a "Western-democratic" stamp of approval. In 2004, the anthem of the Zionist movement, "Hatikva" ("The Hope"), which has become the national anthem and begins with the words "As long as deep in the heart; the soul of a Jew yearns," was added to the flag and national emblem as part of the law.[10] This institutionalized it as the state's anthem, yet it strengthened the Jewish-democratic dyad in a way that excludes non-Jewish citizens from partaking in civil ceremonies.

National memorial days have provided opportunities to institute more civil ceremonies with ideological constructs. Independence Day Law was enacted as early as 1949, and Independence Day celebrations were designed to reflect collective values that represent national and state objectives (Dominguez 1989).[11] Official symbols were created for special Independence Day celebrations held in 1968 and 1973. A Memorial Day for the Fallen Soldiers of Israel was created by law in 1963.[12] Interestingly, this law was enacted as a result of a tradition that emerged in the early years of the state that commemorated Israel's fallen soldiers on the day preceding Independence Day.[13] While the legislation seems to have been ceremonial and a response to a demand from the grassroots, it was not without an underlying political message, dictated by Ben Gurion's ruling majority, which sought to influence the official interpretation of history. The law of 1963 named the day as Memorial Day for the Fallen of the War of Independence and the Israel Defense Forces in order to exclude from national memory pre-state underground organizations that defied Ben Gurion's orders. Only in 1968, after opposition leader Menachem Begin—the leader of the pre-independence Irgun organization that fought the British occupation and the Palestinian population and paramilitary organizations in the pre-state years in defiance of Ben Gurion and his Haganah organization—joined a national unity government were all of Israel's war casualties included and the official prayer amended to include the pre-state underground members.[14] The law was not officially amended until Begin's tenure as prime minister (1977–1983).[15] Begin proposed compressing all the national memorial days into one and marking them on Tisha B'Av, the day commemorating the destructions of the First Temple in 586 B.C.E. and the Second Temple in 70 A.D. This initiative, however, met with considerable opposition, and it was decided that each day of memorial would be marked separately in order to preserve and emphasize its unique character.

Tisha B'Av itself, however, did become an official day of mourning. The Prohibition Over Opening of Sites of Enjoyment on Tisha B'Av Law of 1997 states that Tisha B'Av is a mourning day for the Jewish people commemorating the destruction of the Temple and authorizes all municipalities to institute regulations that enforce a prohibition on the opening of cafes, restaurants, and all other places of "public enjoyment" on the eve of this day. Interestingly, the prohibition does not cover the day itself, when religious people traditionally fast; it remains a regular working day.[16]

In 2000, the government decided (without amending the law) to include in the Memorial Day for the Fallen Soldiers a memorial day to mark the memory of victims of terrorist attacks. This was seen as a major political statement because it drew a parallel, through civil ceremony, between the status of civilian victims of terrorism and fallen soldiers, who hold a sacred place in the collective national memory. An organization representing widows and orphans of fallen soldiers contested this decision in court, but the Supreme Court ruled that the government's decision was reasonable and within its jurisdiction (*Organization of IDF Widows and Orphans v. the Prime Minister of Israel* [2000]). When a resident of the city of Haifa who had lost a brother in the 1973 war and his wife in a more recent suicide bombing protested against the city holding both ceremonies at the same time, since this prevented him from paying his respects to both his relatives, the district court refrained from intervening subject to the understanding that the mayor of Haifa would rethink his position about the timing of the ceremonies (*Zilberstein v. Mayor of Haifa* [2005]).

On Memorial Day, designated cable channels are not allowed to broadcast advertising, and during both Memorial Day and Independence Day, the family channel and the children's channel must carry a minimum of two hours of locally produced programming on the "theme of the day," including programs that express the "Israeli experience and Jewish tradition."[17] Telephone services during Independence Day are to be provided at a holiday rate. Moreover, discounts on regulated landline telephone services are provided only during the Jewish Sabbath and Jewish holidays.[18] Choosing Independence Day as a day for discounted rates, a day that Israel's Palestinian minority marks as the Naqba—a day of mourning for the destruction of the Palestinian dream of independence— is yet another demonstration of how symbolism serves the majority of Israelis—members of the Jewish nation—rather than all citizens of the Israeli state.

THE MEMORY OF THE HOLOCAUST

The memory of the Holocaust has also been subject to considerable symbolic construction through legislation. The effort to ideologize the history of the Holocaust, in accordance with the *mamlakhti* ethos, is seen most profoundly in the introduction of "heroism" (part of the transformation created by Zionism, as mentioned above) into an ethos through use of the phrase "Holocaust and Heroism" in official documentation and law. This attempt to portray the Holocaust not only as a story of annihilation and destruction but also as one of heroism (symbolized, for example, in the acts of Jewish ghetto fighters who defied the Nazis) that eventually led to the creation of the state was meant to give "meaning to the death of six million Jews" (Brog 2004). Yad Vashem, the memorial authority created to commemorate the Holocaust and the heroism of Jews during this period, was established by law in 1953.[19] Of the nine memorial missions Yad Vashem is charged with, according to the law, three involve aspects of loss (of individuals, families, and communities), while six involve aspects of heroism: Jews who died in martyrdom, Jews who served in the allied forces, Jews who took part in ghetto revolts, Jews who preserved their dignity and "never ceased the efforts to save and redeem their brethren," and the "righteous among the nations" who risked their lives in order to save Jews. In 1959, Holocaust Martyrs and Heroes Remembrance Day was enacted into law for the purpose of "communing with the memory of the Holocaust that the Nazis and their collaborators brought down on the Jewish people and [with] the memory of the acts of heroism and acts of revolt in those days."[20] Interestingly, like the memorial day for fallen soldiers, this law was enacted as a result of public pressure after it had already been commemorated semi-officially following a Knesset resolution enacted in 1953 that named it Holocaust and the Ghetto Rebellion Day.[21] On this day, the state requires all houses of entertainment to close, it prohibits commercial television stations from carrying advertising, and it requires cable channels for families and children (which do not carry advertising) to broadcast a minimum of two hours of original programming reflecting, according to the Telecommunications Regulations, the "Israeli experience and Jewish heritage."

A prohibition on denying the Holocaust was enacted into law in 1986, the penalty for such action being up to five years imprisonment.[22] Preserving the memory of the Holocaust is also one of the missions of the *mamlakhti* education system.

OTHER SYMBOLIC LEGISLATION

The most important legislative acts in Israel are the enactment of Basic Laws, as each Basic Law is intended to serve in the future as a chapter of the constitution. Basic Law: Jerusalem the Capital of Israel is arguably the most symbolic of these legislative initiatives. Enacted in August 1980, the law states that "the whole united Jerusalem is the capital of Israel" and requires that the president, the Knesset, the government, and the Supreme Court be located in Jerusalem.[23]

Another interesting example of the role of symbolism in the public sphere can be found in the law forbidding the presentation in public of bread during the Jewish holiday of Passover.[24] Jewish tradition prohibits consumption and even the existence of leavened bread products during the holiday, although the national law refrains from enacting such a prohibition. Instead, it forbids the *presentation* of bread, rolls, pita bread, or any other "flour leavened" products for sale or consumption by any business, with the exception of businesses operating in towns or neighborhoods where the majority of residents, elected council members, or business owners are not Jewish, along with stores operated by kibbutzim (socialist cooperatives) that serve only their members. This is a form of legislation that deals only with the symbolism of limiting the existence of a particular element in the public sphere, not with the real existence of that element.

Legislation has also directed artistic production to an extent. Cultural policy in Israel is guided by an elaborate organizational apparatus whose center is the Culture Administration, a government arm that both solicits applications and distributes funds for the support of dozens of arts organizations (Katz and Sella 1999). A 2002 law established the Culture Administration's advisory board, the Culture and Arts Council, which existed previously with no formal legal status.[25] Within fifteen months, the Knesset amended the law, decreasing the number of members in the council from twenty-five to nineteen.[26] More significantly, the amendment decreased the share of members that should be of "stature in the fields of creativity, activity or research in culture and the arts" from 80 percent to 50 percent. No explanation was provided for this change in the memorandum appended to the draft bill or to the amendment that the chair of the council did not need to be accomplished in the field of culture and the arts.[27]

Support for media-related industries, in particular the film industry, has been expanding in recent years as support for other arts dwindles. The first attempts to support Israeli film production found expression in the Support for Israeli Film Law of 1954, which required movie theaters to show a minimum of four hours of Israeli movies, each at least ninety minutes long, every year.[28] More substantial support came with the establishment of the Foundation for the Advancement of Quality Israeli Films in 1980 by the Ministry of Education and Culture and its merging in 1989 with a similar venture supported by the Ministry of Industry and Commerce as part of a government initiative to provide funding for the arts. The 1998 Motion Picture Law provided major support for local movie industries.[29] This law designated 50 percent of the fees paid annually by commercial television and cable operators for financing of Israeli feature films, about U.S.$13 million at the time. A special council that is appointed by the minister in charge of supporting the arts determines the criteria for receiving funding under this law and distributes the funds. Although Israeli arts have benefited from longstanding government support, the Motion Picture Law was rather revolutionary in its scope, in particular in terms of the level of monetary support it generated.

Another aspect of Israeli cultural policy is the monitoring of film viewing, whose legal manifestation dates back to colonial times. The Cinematography Films Ordinance of 1927,which was subsequently incorporated into Israeli law, created a supervising council that provides licenses for screening films in movie theaters.[30] Violating the council's orders is considered a criminal offense. Until the Public Performances Ordinance was suspended in 1989, the council was charged with licensing plays as well. It is also common practice for the council to rate movies according to two major categories—"for adults only" and "for general viewing." Movie theaters are responsible to ensure that minors do not view films designated for adult viewing. In recent years, the Supreme Court has greatly reduced the scope of the council's power, although cable operators still need its formal approval to broadcast films on cable channels.

The Courts and the "Official" Interpretation of Zionism

Recently academics have focused on the role of courts in the development of national memory and identity. Maoz (2000) notes that courts have been asked to rule on questions of historical truth by parties striving for institutional confirmation of their historical narrative to facilitate the adoption of that version as the "official" historical story (605). The court's unique capacity to prevent social disintegration through binding decisions helps maintain society in its normatively determined identity. Because "law traffics in the slippery terrain of memory . . . different versions of past events are presented for authoritative judgment" (Sarat and Kearns 1999, 3). The court, explains Barak-Erez (2001), then assumes one of three roles: a judge and arbiter of historical events, a narrator of history, or a student and teacher of historical "lessons." When the court recounts history, concludes Barak-Erez, it articulates the collective memory of the society it serves. Indeed, by intervening in the interpretation of media products, the courts lend credence to some interpretations over others, utilizing the state's normative powers to maintain the state's concept of society's identity, thereby promoting the dominant interpretations of culture and maintaining dominance of interpretations that serve the status quo. Moglen (2001) hypothesizes that the need for a judicial "official version" of historical events stems from the state's inability to guarantee that this historical message will be conveyed through the mass media (616).

History shows that the Israeli courts have adopted the Zionist ethos as an ideological guideline and that Zionism and patriotism have been central elements in the narrative of the Israeli court's decisions since its inception (Levitsky 2006, 169). As early as 1972, it ruled that there is no "Israeli" nationality separate from Jewish ethnicity (*Tamarin v. State of Israel* [1970]), and in 1999, it ruled that Hebrew (whose revival and daily usage is perhaps the most symbolic of hegemonic Zionist rituals) is the "language of the Israelis" (*Adalah v. The Municipalities of Tel Aviv, Ramla, Lod and Upper-Nazareth* [1999]). These rulings were handed down even though, as the *Tamarin* decision demonstrates, the court has denied the existence of an "Israeli" identity because accepting its existence would contradict another basic mythical element of the Zionist narrative, the existence of a Jewish nationality and its embodiment in the state. Yet again, the conflict between the "nation" and the "state" was left unresolved, or in fact resolved in a manner that promotes the "nation" over the "state," the "Jewish" over the "democratic." Former chief justice Aharon Barak explained that the "nuclear" characteristics that shape the minimalist definition of Israel as a Jewish state, as spelled out in national election laws and in laws that ensure human dignity and freedom of occupation, have both a "Zionist perspective" and a "heritage perspective" and include the right of every Jew to immigrate to Israel where Jews are the majority; laws that establish Hebrew as the main official language of the state; laws that stipulate that the main holidays and symbols of the state reflect the national resurrection of the Jewish people; and laws that establish that Jewish heritage is a central component of the nation's religious and cultural heritage (*Central Election Committee v. MK Ahmed Tibi* [2002], 22). Calling a person an "anti-Zionist" is considered libelous (*Sephardi Community of Jerusalem Council v. Ya'acov Arnon* [1977]), and the "Zionistic values of the state" are the "realization of the aspirations of the Jewish people carried from generation to generation to renew its life as before, the beginning of its redemption and the implementation of the Zionist vision" (*Gaza Shore Regional Council v. The Knesset of Israel* [2005], 63).

Zionist ideology, the creation and subjugation of a symbolic order to serve a story that justifies Israel, has become, as this chapter demonstrates, a statist effort that is institutionalized in the structure of the state. The state apparatuses used a variety of strategies (purportedly within their democratic capacities) to promote this endeavor. The development of *mamlakhtiyut* allowed the Jewish nation's interests to be represented as the Israeli state's interests. Since the 1980s, Western-style neoliberalism has dominated this process, along with the Jewish credo and democratic principles of the state. These strategies included creating the *mamlakhti* educational system and streamlining its goals; institutionalizing Zionist symbols as state symbols and enforcing their presence in public ceremonies; designing national memorial days around the events that define the state in Zionist interpretations of Israeli history; and involving all branches of government—the Knesset, the government, and the courts—in supporting this endeavor. Once Israeli policymakers realized the potential of the media's involvement in this effort, they mobilized it and assigned it a central effort in this role as well.

3 Media Space and
Political Culture in Israel

Television has naturally played an important role in Israel's social and cultural history. According to Katz, Haas, and Gurevitch (1997), during the first twenty-five years of Israeli television, when only one channel existed, television became the central medium for news and information, taking on the role held by newspapers in 1970. It was a central force in promoting national unity, and the national "electronic campfire" around the nightly 9 P.M. news magazine "became a sort of civic ritual during which the society communed with itself" (5). As the most popular of modern technologies,[1] it has also played a dominant role in the transmission of culture.Televisions were present in Israeli households even before the beginning of the era of Israeli broadcasting, serving both as status symbols and a way to watch programs from neighboring countries. The initial forecasts about how popular television would become once broadcasting in Hebrew was launched were quite modest compared with the eventual outcome. A 1961 report by the United Nations Educational, Scientific and Cultural Organization (UNESCO) for the government that jump-started the Israeli television industry, predicted that 20,000 television sets would be purchased within twelve to eighteen months of the introduction of the service (Cassirer and Duckmanton 1961, 9). The Bendor Committee, appointed by Prime Minister Levi Eshkol in 1965, estimated the number of sets before the first broadcast at 30,000 and predicted that by 1972, which would be the fifth year of broadcasting, the number would rise to 300,000 (Bendor

1965, 2). But in fact, as the Central Bureau of Statistics noted in its first special report on television viewing, by the summer of 1970, two years after the first broadcast, 53 percent of all Israeli households had television sets—more than 400,000 altogether (Central Bureau of Statistics 1971). By 1991, 87 percent of all Israeli households had television sets—in other words, virtually every household with the potential to watch television. At that point, there was only one television channel in Israel and the cable industry was only beginning to take root. This may account for the fact that at that time, almost half of the households with television sets (43.5 percent) owned videocassette recorders—more than double the percentage of households that owned microwave ovens, dishwashers, or personal computers (Central Bureau of Statistics 1993).

The Israeli obsession with television, however, was not satisfied by the one-channel service and its black-and-white fare or by videocassette recorders, many of them purchased, it emerged, by people who had not an inkling about how to use many of their features (Cohen and Cohen 1989). Despite relatively high prices, a vertically integrated system, and no premium service, Israelis adopted cable television once it became an option at a record pace (Schejter and Lee 2007). Cable service was first introduced in Israel in 1991, but already by 1992, some 400,000 households had become subscribers (31 percent of all households; Weimann 1995).[2] By the summer of 1992, more than 50 percent of all households passed had subscribed to cable service (Lehman-Wilzig and Schejter 1994). By mid-1994, this figure had risen to 61 percent of all households, and in 1996 the Cable Broadcasting Council released figures claiming that 70 percent of all households had become subscribers—all within a matter of five years.[3] According to the Central Bureau of Statistics, 66.6 percent of all households subscribed to cable service in 1997. The Cable Broadcasting Council did not begin publishing official figures on penetration until 2000, when satellite service was introduced. At that time, it put the total number of households subscribing to cable and satellite service at 1,317,000, of which 1,230,000 were cable subscribers (71.6 percent of all households), almost matching the figure of 70.1 percent published by the Central Bureau of Statistics that year. More than 76 percent of Israeli households subscribed to cable and satellite service in 2000, although satellite service accounted for less than 5 percent of the total. As of 2002, both the Central Bureau of Statistics and the Cable and Satellite Broadcasting Council identified a trend of declining penetration that continued into 2003, when the number of Israeli households subscribing to cable and satellite service totaled 1,415,000, or 70.6 percent of total households, according to the Central Bureau of Statistics. In 2003, the percentage of

Israeli cable and satellite subscribers combined was lower than in 2000, when satellite service was introduced. This decline can be attributed to the economic crisis plaguing Israel as a result of the Palestinian uprising and the fact that the limited nature of the competition between cable and satellite did not lead to price reductions (Schejter and Lee 2007). This however does not detract from the fact that Israelis have been involved in an ongoing love affair with their television sets, and the government has not let this passion go unnoticed.

The Israeli Media Space

Electronic media in Israel consists of three broadcasting platforms and three governing laws: two laws regulate broadcasting and one regulates both cable and satellite. The Broadcasting Authority Law of 1965 established the Israeli Broadcasting Authority (IBA), which is charged with national broadcasting. This category includes noncommercial television funded by a license fee and radio funded by advertising and by license fees for car radios. IBA television broadcasts over two channels: Channel 1 is terrestrial and Channel 33 (which also targets neighboring states) broadcasts by satellite. Radio broadcasts consist of thematic stations such as talk, news, light music, classical music, broadcasts in Arabic, and broadcasts in immigrant languages. The Second Authority for Radio and Television Law (1990) created the Second Authority and charged it with overseeing commercial television; as of the early 2000s there were two television channels (Channel 2 and Channel 10) and a network of fourteen regional commercial radio stations.

Cable and satellite television are both governed by the Communications (Telecommunications and Broadcasting) Law, which established the Cable Broadcasting Council (CBC) in 1986. The council was expanded to oversee satellite television when it was launched in the late 1990s and was renamed the Cable and Satellite Broadcasting Council (CSBC).[4] The cable and satellite offerings include a plethora of local, locally packaged foreign channels and foreign satellite services. The local channels owned by cable and satellite operators are prohibited from carrying advertising, while the "designated channels" (independent government-licensed channels) are allowed to do so.

Israeli society has made a transition since the 1980s from a social-democratic order centered on *mamlakhtiyut* that served the state to a neoliberal nationalistic state in which old-fashioned *mamlakhtiyut* was supplanted by a new form of centralization that is dictated by wealthy individuals and corporations and is designed to benefit them and the state equally (see, e.g., Yuran 2001, 12). This transition is evident in Israel's media space as well.

Commercial television was introduced in Israel in 1993 under the auspices of the Second Authority, and throughout the 1990s, both Channel 2 (at the time the only commercial broadcaster) and cable companies (at the time the only providers of multichannel television services) were cross-owned by the nation's largest newspaper chains: *Yediot Aharonot*, Israel's most popular newspaper, with nearly 40 percent exposure daily and more than 50 percent on weekends; and *Ma'ariv*, which reaches more than 17 percent of the public on weekdays and 20 percent on weekends.[5] The Knesset, with much prodding from the ministry of justice, decided to address this media concentration, which was the outcome of a successful lobbying campaign undertaken by major newspaper owners in the late 1980s, when commercial media laws were enacted. In a major overhaul of ownership laws in 2001, the Knesset forced the newspapers to divest themselves of their commercial television and cable holdings.

Israel had only one television channel that was operated by the *mamlakhti* IBA from 1968 to 1993. The introduction of a first commercial channel in 1993, a second in 2002, and a cable system that turned digital in the early 2000s transformed the Israeli media space. Also, in 1999, an operator was licensed to launch a fully digital direct-to-home satellite service. According to official figures published by the Israel Audience Research Board (IARB) in 2007, 92 percent of Israeli households owned television sets.[6] Of these, some 90 percent subscribe to at least one of the multichannel television services. Based on this data, it would not be an exaggeration to say that the penetration of the basic service of multichannel television in Israel is virtually universal.

The commercial channels, Channel 2 and Channel 10, which are subject to the detailed regulations described in chapters 4 and 5, fill television screens with American (and some local) game, talk, and reality shows, which Liebes (2003) describes as "American dreams with Hebrew subtitles." The two digital platforms offer a wide range of channels, about twenty of which are locally packaged with programming in Hebrew or subtitles in order to attract Israeli viewers. The channel offering includes a taste of what any modern Western television system would offer: sports channels, movie channels, children's channels, soap-opera channels, lifestyle channels, and so forth. All of this is paid for by subscription fees, except for the government-sanctioned Israel Plus (in Russian) and Music 24 (both of which are discussed in detail in chapter 6), which are allowed to carry advertising. None of the other locally packaged channels are allowed to carry advertising.

The multichannel television offering consists of "must carry" channels, which include Channels 1 and 33, which are operated by the *mamlakhti* Israel Broadcasting Authority; Channels 2 and 10, which are commercial channels; an educational television channel; the Knesset channel, which broadcasts live parliamentary debates; the Russian-language Israel Plus; and the 24–hour Israeli music channel, Music 24. These channels (with the exception of the latter two) are to be offered digitally as a new digital terrestrial television service that will replace analog broadcasting, according to legislation passed in the Knesset in early 2008.[7]

The introduction of commercial cable and broadcasting took Israelis by storm. The communications revolution in Israel was not limited to the introduction of new channels or to the adoption of new technologies. It also included a dramatic transformation of viewing patterns. During the single-channel era, two-thirds of Israelis tuned in nightly to the 9 o'clock news (Katz 1996). By 1998, five years after commercial broadcasting had been launched, figures published by the IARB show that the commercial news channel's 8 o'clock news program had become more popular, although less than 40 percent of all households watched evening news broadcasts. This change was accompanied by further changes in the broadcasting fare and in the style of *the mamlakhti* broadcaster, the IBA, whose news programs increasingly began to resemble in style those of the commercial channel (Peri 2004). The switch many Israeli viewers made to the commercial news outlet followed their enthusiastic transition to the commercial channel, which started as early as 1994, the first year when commercial television broadcasted in Israel (Tokatly 2000, 201).[8]

Despite their enthusiastic response to commercial television, Israelis remained paradoxically nationalistic in their viewing patterns. At first, they found an outlet for their patriotic sentiments in the old *mamlakhti* broadcasting system. In 1998, for example, 25.7 percent of the viewers who watched the official Independence Day celebrations tuned into the *mamlakhti* channel, while only 22.6 percent watched the same programs on the commercial channel. By 2007, however, two-thirds of those who watched the broadcast of the official event watched it on Channel 2, which had come to embody the mutual interests of government and big business, the new *mamlakhtiyut* (Yuran 2002). As Katz (1996) had anticipated, the total number of viewers watching Independence Day celebrations had dropped by 2007, indicating that Israelis were abandoning the "tribal campfire" that was television and were taking less part in the civil ceremony. Thus, while commercial television has eroded the public sphere, it has also replaced it and redefined it.

Channel 2 is the most popular Israeli television channel, but since 2006, Channel 10 has been cutting into its market. Channel 2's evening news program is viewed on average by 19 percent of all Israeli households, Channel 10's news program is viewed by 9.5 percent, and Channel 1, the *mamlakhti* channel, which until 1993 was the only game in town, has been relegated to third place with an average nightly rating of 6.5 percent. By early 2008, each of the commercial channels was able to reach more than a third of the national audience at prime time, and together, on extremely competitive nights (such as when Channel 10 broadcasts the Israeli version of *Survivor*) they reach more than 40 percent of all households and nearly 60 percent of those watching television. More than a third of Israelis (and at times about half) watch television programs on channels that are provided only over cable and satellite.

A similar pattern is evident in radio. Commercial radio was introduced in Israel at the same time as commercial television. Until the mid-1990s, there were only two providers of radio services in Israel, the IBA and the Israeli military, which operates Galey Tzahal, a news and entertainment station manned by soldiers and professional journalists. In the mid-1990s, a network of regional commercial stations was launched under the auspices of the Second Authority for Radio and Television.

Since the 1990s, the Second Authority for Radio and Television auctioned fourteen regional commercial radio stations; these regional stations operate in Eilat, in the South, in Jerusalem, in the suburbs of southern Tel Aviv, in Tel Aviv (where there are two general stations and one religious station), in the suburbs north of Tel Aviv (where there are three stations), in the northern valleys, in Haifa, and in the Galilee. All of these stations sustain themselves with advertising revenue and are regulated by the Second Authority. An Arabic-language station broadcasts both in the Galilee and in the densely populated Arab-town "triangle" in the center of Israel. In spring 2007, the Second Authority announced that a new round of tenders for the same fourteen licenses, which would soon expire, would begin the following year. In addition, it authorized the establishment of a new special-interest channel that would cater to religious Mizrahi Jews, a community represented in the ruling coalition by the minister of communications. (I return to this initiative in the concluding chapter.)

A major problem plaguing the Israeli radio industry is the proliferation of unlicensed radio stations. As I describe in chapter 7, this phenomenon started in the 1970s when a lone seaman, Abe Nathan, ran a commercially supported radio station from a ship anchored in the Mediterranean Sea not far from the shores of Tel Aviv, Israel's largest city at the time. He named it The Voice of Peace and used it to broadcast a combination of Western music and peace messages. In the 1980s, a group of Jewish settlers in the occupied territories who were opposed to making peace with Palestinians in those territories launched an ideological competitor called Arutz Sheva (Channel 7). This station also broadcast from sea, although its studios were located in an Israeli settlement in the occupied territories. Arutz Sheva became the target of police raids and legal indictments, especially when plans to launch commercial radio were pushed ahead in the early 1990s by the liberal-left-wing government headed by the late Yitzhak Rabin (The Voice of Peace had by then closed down voluntarily). The right-wing government elected after Rabin's assassination by a right-wing Jewish sympathizer of the settler movement passed a law that retroactively legalized Arutz Sheva. The Supreme Court, however, rendered this law unconstitutional on the grounds that it contradicts the implied principle of equality embedded in the Basic Laws (*Oron v. Speaker of the Knesset* [1999]). Since the 1980s, Arutz Sheva has been joined by dozens of unlicensed stations, many of which are affiliated with political and religious groups whose ties to ruling coalitions have protected them (Limor and Naveh 2008). Reports that unlicensed stations were interfering with transmissions at Ben Gurion International Airport, the nation's largest and busiest airport, led to protest strikes by air traffic controllers in 2006 and 2007, but the strikes had little impact.

In 2006, TGI of the Teleseker Group conducted a study of a representative sample of 10,000 Israeli radio listeners. The study found that the IBA radio stations have lost their dominating position to Galey Tzahal. More than 45 percent of the radio audience is exposed to the Israeli army radio service, which broadcasts two stations, compared with the IBA's 43.5 percent.[9] All regional radio stations combined are listened to by more than 34 percent. (The numbers exceed 100 percent because listeners may listen to more than one station during the day.) A December 2006 study conducted for the Second Authority for Radio and Television found a similar trend: 28 percent of the population is exposed to regional radio, 33.2 percent to IBA radio's two main stations (news and Israeli music), and 37.5 percent to Galey Tzahal's two stations.[10] The most popular station, however, was still IBA's Bet station, a 24–hour news and talk service that more than 25 percent of the population listens to regularly. A total of 70.7 percent of Israelis were exposed to radio broadcasts daily in 2006.

Powerful-Effect Theory and Israeli Policymaking

One comparative study of Israeli media policymaking has observed that whether or not media are powerful, policymakers in Israel (as well as in Germany, Great Britain, and Australia) tend to see media as powerful and act accordingly (Etziony-Halevy 1987). Indications of the truth of this maxim are found in the formative documents pertaining to Israeli media, in the policies the government adopted regarding transborder news, and in court rulings, which required an assessment of the effect of the media. In this chapter, I discuss this phenomenon as it appears in two landmark reports published by foreign experts on the establishment of television in Israel, one by a UNESCO committee and another by a European Broadcasting Union (EBU) committee, and in the reports of the Bendor Committee appointed in 1965 to present recommendations establishing a television service, the Kubersky Committee appointed in 1978 to make recommendations on establishing commercial television, and the Barsela Committee appointed in 1982 to establish the rules for cable television.

In 1963, Israeli Justice Minister Dov Yossef presented a draft bill of the Broadcasting Authority Law to the Knesset. The bill was based on the October 1962 recommendations of the bipartisan Avidor Committee, which was headed by Director-General Moshe Avidor of the Ministry of Education. Justice Minister Yossef insisted that the law had nothing to do with the introduction of television broadcasting and stated that as long as the sitting Knesset was in power there would be no television broadcasting in Israel (Knesset Records, 18 June 1963, 2110). Indeed, as Caspi and Limor (1992 and 1999), Katz (1971), Katz, Haas, and Gurevitch (1997), Lehman-Wilzig and Schejter (1994), Oren (2004), and others have noted, the main reason it took until the mid-1960s for television to make its debut in Israel was the fear of the cultural impact it would have. Israel's first prime minister, David Ben Gurion, articulated this fear; it was rooted in the long-standing anxiety he and the Israeli labor movement shared about the potential of the movie industry to corrupt Israeli society (Zimmerman 2003). Nonetheless, the government invited the UNESCO and EBU committees to study the possible impact of television, and the committee experts introduced Israeli policymakers to the developmental approach to mass media, especially television. This approach sees television in terms of statist goals rather than as a commercially driven system. During one of Ben Gurion's state visits to France, French president Charles de Gaulle told him how effective addressing the public directly over television had been during the Algerian war.[11] During that visit, Ben Gurion's aides persuaded him to watch a television program about bees and the collection of honey; his personal secretary, Yitzhak Navon, reported later that he was thrilled to discover that television could also be used for educational purposes (Zimmerman 2003). The realization that television can be useful for propaganda and as an educational tool and not necessarily as a medium focused on commercial entertainment met a receptive ear among Israeli policymakers and eventually led to the creation of a television service. The establishment of a television service that would serve national and statist cultural needs was not a unique invention of Israeli policymakers. This approach to introducing media to society had its roots in policymaking in European and postcolonial nations. In Israel, this approach was proposed in the above-mentioned reports, one written by a group specializing in postcolonial policies, the other by European broadcasting experts. They covered technological as well as production aspects of the future Israeli television, but their most significant impact was in the area of content.

The UNESCO team, which consisted of Dr. H. R. Cassirer of UNESCO and T. S. Duckmanton of the Australian Broadcasting Commission, concluded that Israel should create "a publicly operated television service, financed out of non-commercial revenues, serving the entire territory of Israel with a limited number of program hours whose objective is educational and cultural" (10). It noted that "we have interpreted the term 'educational television' in its broad sense, and include in it a program range from instruction to cultural enjoyment" (ibid.).

From the perspective of the invited experts, Israel was a developing country that required a type of television service that could be mobilized to advance national goals. These goals included " the teaching of Hebrew and Israeli culture to new immigrants, their integration into the civic, economic, social and cultural life of the country, the provision of equal opportunity of education for all, irrespective of their social status or place of residence, and a proper balance between respect and appreciation for the culture of the various communities and the promotion of nationhood" (4).

The EBU team, whose members included Francis Angre, an engineer of French broadcasting authority O.R.T.F., and Bo Isaacson, a news producer of Swedish radio and television, concluded in its report that outside observers could not overlook the following basic characteristics of Israeli society when discussing the problems of organizing and planning a television service in Israel:

- a deep common spiritual-religious heritage
- a rich variety of special traditions for different groups whose differences, including linguistic, were not yet fully resolved
- a strong (though problematic) consciousness of Israel's special position and role among the nations of the world
- the felt need by the leadership and citizens alike and the internal demand for a commitment to a spiritual, political, and economic effort
- a large Arab minority in a "special situation"

The EBU team recommended that the main function of television in Israel—unlike that in the United States or Europe—should be to increase among its viewers the desire for information, an interest in cultural participation, and thoughts about (instead of escape from) reality, rather than serving as a medium for entertainment. The experts did not suggest banning light television altogether but stressed that Israeli television should contain a "certain seriousness."

In July 1965, the government decided to establish a television service under the auspices of the Israel Broadcasting Authority, which was then still a radio service. The new service would exist alongside the Instructional Television Trust already created by the Rothschild Foundation. To that end, the government appointed the Bendor Committee to study the cultural, political, and economic aspects of the decision.

The committee, comprised of representatives of all the relevant government ministries, presented its conclusions and recommendations in October 1965. The twenty-six recommendations covered the economic, technical, and cultural aspects of television. Because of the scope of this chapter, only the cultural aspects will be addressed here. The following were its recommendations (their original numbering precedes them):

1. The Broadcasting Authority should be the guarantor of the level of the programs and their *mamlakhtiyut.*
2. The power of television will be of considerable magnitude in promoting several *mamlakhti* goals, such as the ingathering of the exiles, population dispersal, the elimination of ignorance, and the teaching of Hebrew.
3. Israeli television will reduce the destructive cultural and political influence of foreign television. The less educated people are, the more inclined they are to watch television and be affected by its content. Therefore, the most vulnerable population is also the one that watches the most television.
4. Television programs should be attractive and not frugal. This is to ensure that the audience will watch them instead of turning to foreign broadcasts.

5. Television broadcasts must reach all areas of the country, especially remote areas.
6. Israeli television, especially Arabic broadcasts, will serve as a useful explanatory and information tool in neighboring countries.
7. The programs will be in one language. In certain programs in Hebrew, Arabic translation will be provided.
8. The General Television will begin by broadcasting 14 hours a week in Hebrew and about 3.5 hours in Arabic. It is preferable that broadcasts begin at the same time. In weighing quality against quantity, quality should prevail.
9. Israeli television programs will not be broadcast in the Diaspora but they will be attainable through program exchanges.
10. The programs should be as Israeli as possible to help create an industry for writing and producing television programs. . . .
17. The young television service should develop and be strengthened without outside influences. Budgetary support [beyond the license fee discussed in other recommendations] should be provided by the government rather than by advertising.

What emerges clearly from the recommendations is that the government committee focused considerable attention on cultural considerations and in fact placed them above all other considerations, including economic and technological ones. The committee described a country threatened by propaganda broadcasts from neighboring countries that reached a vast and vulnerable audience and expressed its belief that counter-propaganda could serve as an effective tool against this phenomenon. Indeed, recommendation 3 provides evidence that the committee was concerned about the possible influence of broadcasts from neighboring Arab countries on the country's Jewish Arabic-language speakers (mostly of Mizrahi origin), who were able to understand the foreign broadcasts and were considered less educated and less sophisticated and thus more vulnerable to outside influences.

As part of a mobilized media policy, the committee recommended assigning certain goals for television that went beyond the original charter of the IBA, which was formed at the same time. Not only was television to enhance certain cultural understandings, it was also to serve as a tool for advancing government policies and as a defense mechanism against foreign influences. As the creation of a television service became inevitable, government officials began seeking ways to use it to serve their own objectives.

Following the inauguration of broadcasting on Instructional Television in May 1966, the government accepted Prime Minister Levi Eshkol's proposal to postpone implementation of the Bendor Committee's recommendations. Eshkol, who was at odds with officials at the IBA, liked the idea that the only television service would be instructional television (Gil 1986). However, the reality created after the June 1967 Six-Day War, when Israel occupied vast amounts of land with a large Palestinian population, required a review of this position (Caspi and Limor 1999, 147). Throughout the period of escalating tensions that led up to the June 1967 war, many Israeli Jews were tuned into the Voice of the United Arab Republic, a radio service that broadcast false information from Cairo in Hebrew for the explicit purpose of demoralizing Jewish Israelis.[12] In response, and probably in order to up the ante, the government decided in September 1967 to launch emergency television broadcasts, using the Instructional Television installation based in Tel Aviv, which would be directed mainly at the population of the territories occupied by the Israel Defense Forces (IDF) and the Arab citizens of the State of Israel. It stated that the broadcasts would be in the format of three hours in Arabic and one in Hebrew and that the programs would be cleared by the Broadcasting Authority (Gil 1986; Oren 2004; Caspi and Limor 1999).

This propaganda-focused approach to television is also apparent in the Broadcasting Authority Law, which was enacted in 1965.[13] The law instructed the newly created *mamlakhti* radio—and the *mamlakhti* television that came under the same law in 1969—to provide broadcasts "for the advancement of understanding and peace with the neighboring countries according to the basic course set by the state." Indeed, control of transborder news and the fear of its impact is a constant staple of Israeli media policy, as I discuss further on in this chapter.

The task force created to implement the decision to establish the television service was headed by Hebrew University sociologist Elihu Katz, who later acknowledged that "in choosing me, the government could not have found a more skeptical person as far as belief in the short-term mass media effects are concerned. I did not think that television could by itself cause the Arabs to like Israelis, and I said so" (Katz 1971, 254). The first broadcast of Israeli television in May 1968, however, featured a military parade on Independence Day, set against the background of the walls of the Old City of Jerusalem, which had just been annexed to the newer western section of the city in the wake of Israel's resounding victory in the war. Very few Israelis owned television sets at the time, which makes it clear that the government's message was aimed at viewers from neighboring countries and the newly occupied territories. This conclusion is supported by the wording of the government decision to launch the broadcasts and by the content of the broadcast.

Commercial television, which was first envisioned by the Labor government in the mid-1970s, became a political reality (but not yet an actuality) following the political upheaval of 1977, in which the economically conservative Likud Party gained power for the first time in the state's history. Until then, the approach to electronic media policy reflected Zionist-socialist ideology, which sought equality and social solidarity and characterized much of policymaking in Israel in its first years (Ben Yisrael 1994). Katz, Haas, and Gurevitch (1997) note that even though the introduction of television has rendered Israel more of an individualistic society in its values and more of a "hedonistic" society in its leisure activities than before, "if one had to choose . . . whether the first 20 years of monopolistic Israeli television gave more support to the individualizing trend or to the norm of collectivism, there is a much stronger case to be made for the latter" (ibid., 18). While the launching of television was part of Israel's transition to a consumer society in a capitalist economy, the irony is that while it was broadcasting a single channel its influence in Israel strengthened collectivist values.

The political changes that led to the establishment of a second television channel that was to be financed through advertising revenues did not change the basic assumptions of Israeli lawmakers as demonstrated by the recommendations of the Kubersky Committee, which was headed by Director-General Haim Kubersky of the Ministry of Interior Affairs. The committee was jointly appointed by the minister of education and culture and the minister of communications in July 1978 to investigate the possibility of creating a second television channel in Israel. Its report served as the blueprint for the new endeavor.

The Kubersky Committee's report concluded that there were many advantages to establishing a second television channel, most of which were "cultural" in nature. Although it might not encourage abstract thought, the report said, television plays a significant role in raising the "informative knowledge" of the population. It opens up society to the world at large; since certain elements within the population do not read books or newspapers, it is their only source of information. The committee argued that television can supply more than one channel in response to public demand for news, political commentary, education, science, culture, and entertainment that would provide new content and new ways of presentation. It also pointed out that a second television channel would fulfill an important educational role by serving as an alternative to the monopolistic information supply from one television channel (Kubersky 1978, 10–12).

The committee also recommended setting up a cable television system whose function would be limited to retransmitting existing channels (ibid., 29). In addressing the cultural objectives of the commercial channel, the Kubersky Committee's report followed the guidelines created by the Broadcasting Authority Law, going so far as to copy verbatim Article 3 of the IBA law (for more, see chapter 5).

While it took three years for the government's 1965 decision to launch television to be implemented, it took twelve years from the time the Kubersky committee was appointed in 1978 until the commercial television law passed in 1990 and another three after that before broadcasting on the second channel was launched. These long delays can be attributed to fears of the effects of commercial television and the resulting controversy in the Knesset over how to design it. The fear of transborder broadcasts was apparently even more deeply ingrained, prompting the government in 1986 (under the auspices of the "launching administration" formed shortly after the first reading of the Second Authority Law in the Knesset) to establish a new government-financed "experimental" television channel. Administrators cited the need to "seize the frequencies" for fear they might be overtaken by neighboring countries, though no such attempts were ever documented (Caspi and Limor 1999, 153; Tokatly 2000, 89).

The Soroker Committee, appointed by the government in 1975, was the first to address cable television as an independent policy issue. However, its recommendations were never implemented (Caspi and Limor 1999). Cable television was mentioned again in the 1979 Kubersky Committee's report, as previously noted, but it was the 1982 report on cable television published by the Barsela Committee (Barsela 1982) that became the basis for the policy that was eventually implemented.

The Barsela Committee, headed by Deputy Attorney General Yoram Barsela, recommended taking immediate action to create regional cable franchises. The general tone of the report took into account the cultural and social impact of a barrage of television broadcasting on a country that had not yet been introduced to the concept of choice in television fare. The report, which adopted virtually the same wording as the Kubersky Committee's report in advocating the creation of commercial television, balances criticism of television and its possible effects against the potential that television could enculturate the public and fill the social need for entertainment. Unlike the Kubersky report, which advocated creating a second channel in order to provide the public with more choice, the Barsela report expressed concern that a multiplicity of programs on television will necessarily affect society in Israel. Multiplicity of programs and services via television may isolate a person in his home, and separate him, to a certain extent, from the society surrounding him. Most of the programs will be imported from foreign countries, and especially the United States. Multiplicity of foreign programming will have the effect of a foreign culture that will enter the individual's home and reside with him as part of his culture. The shallowness found in some television programs calls for special attention to this matter. (6)

The report further stated that

those questioning the future character of our society should act to preserve and nurture the uniqueness of our people, known as the People of the Book, whose thinking ability, intellect, fertile curiosity and creative thought are its main assets and need to be preserved and nurtured. . . . The medium of television—and especially the multiplicity of programs— is a factor which stands in contradiction to these characteristics or at minimum jeopardizes their existence. (37)

The report concluded that creating a cable television system required mechanisms that would allow the government to control the quantity, type, character, and quality of the programs and services it offered. What had to be protected, it noted, was not only the culture of the so-called People of the Book but the public's welfare as well, and for this reason, special attention needed to be paid to the effect of cable television on public consumption habits.

The Barsela Committee initially recommended carrying a maximum of nine television channels and several radio stations via cable. The channels would include the existing *mamlakhti* television channel, the planned commercial channel, one or two channels that would be especially created for Instructional Television, two channels for foreign programs carried by neighboring countries, a local community channel, a channel with programs, documentaries, and films directed at children, and one or two channels for films and programs initiated by the cable operator (Barsela 1982, 20–21).

The Barsela Committee report provides insight into the typical mindset of Israeli broadcasting policymakers, which was also demonstrated in the UNESCO, EBU, Bendor, and Kubersky reports. The first characteristic of this mindset is the artificial enhancement of "positive" programming, achieved in this case, as in the Kubersky report, by allowing Instructional Television to produce many of the programs. The second characteristic is the fear of propaganda broadcasts emanating from across Israel's borders. The committee recommended that retransmitted signals from neighboring Arab countries be limited to entertainment programming (e.g., Western films and soap operas) and that cable operators "black out" current affairs and news programs.

A new feature of cable television that the committee recommended was the relatively large proportion of regional channels (three of the nine) that would be locally owned and whose programming would be based on regional content. At the time the report was published, only the IBA's *mamlakhti* channel existed. The new channels were prevented from broadcasting national news so as not to impinge on the dominant position of the government-supervised news media. The decision to base a new broadcasting medium on local channels can be seen as a way of preserving the dominance of national channels in news programming.

The Barsela Committee also recommended addressing the "special needs" of the Arabic-speaking population through the creation of earmarked channels or special broadcasting hours. It warned, however, that such channels might not be the appropriate forums for raising issues deemed "controversial" (see more on this issue in chapter 8).

Concerns about the presumed effects of television were also voiced in the Knesset when the amendment to the Telecommunications Law enacting the cable service was introduced. In the first reading, on 27 March 1986, Member of Knesset (MK) Meir Sheetreet (Likud), a representative of the ruling coalition party that initiated the law, said the amendment was designed to eliminate 250 pirate cable television stations around the country. "Many of those broadcasts," he noted, "are far from offering an educational-cultural service to the population which utilizes them." The law was meant to "create order," Sheetreet said, by providing for supervision of broadcast material and promoting a service of educational, "proper entertainment" and regional programs (Knesset Records, 27 March 1986, 2356). Sheetreet's initiative drew across-the-board support in the Knesset. MK Victor Shem-Tov, then head of the opposition socialist United Workers Party (Mapam), described the existing situation as "anarchy where irresponsible people, lacking motivation to educate, enter homes and broadcast movies to children and adults with no educational direction—this the state cannot tolerate" (ibid., 2357).

Israeli courts too have acknowledged the power of television in various rulings. Paralleling the government's emphasis on film, the first acknowledgement of the power of media the courts made referred to movies rather than to television (*Film Studios v. Levi Geri* [1962]). One ruling included an explanation of why the "special moral and public responsibility of television broadcasters whose words and appearance fascinate a mass audience and whose influence on the audience's mind and taste cannot be measured" must be considered (Justice Haim Cohn in *Hachayim Book Publishers v. Israel Broadcasting Authority* [1979]). Another justice in the same ruling acknowledged that broadcasting has a "tremendous impact on a mass audience" (Justice Miriam Ben-Porat in *Hachayim Book Publishers v. Israel Broadcasting Authority* [1979]), and another justice said in another ruling that "the best medium for the implementation of freedom of expression is radio and television that perpetrate every home" (Justice Daliah Dorner in *Kidum Entrepreneurship and Publishing v. IBA* [1994]). One ruling included a statement that television is the most powerful and efficient instrument for dispersing ideas (Justice Shoshana Netanyahu in *Joseph Brand v. Minister of Communications* [1992]). In 1977, the Supreme Court recognized as reasonable the decision by the IBA to transmit in black and white programs that had been purchased abroad in color on the grounds that all programs produced locally at the time were broadcast in black and white. In arguing its case, the IBA explained to the court that locally produced programs would "pale" in comparison with the imported programs, viewers would become disenchanted, and the IBA would, therefore, be remiss in its legal *mamlakhti* duty to "reflect the life of the state" (*Yitzhak Fogel v. Israel Broadcasting Authority* [1977]).

The Public Interest Standard in Israeli Communications Law

The constant references in Israel to the media's power and the policies developed aimed at exploiting this power in order to advance certain cultural goals stem from a distorted understanding of the relationship between the development of media and the public interest. An analysis of how the public interest is addressed in Israeli law helps substantiate this claim.

As far as licensing policy in Israel is concerned, the public interest has generally served as a reason for revoking a license rather than for awarding one. Here are some examples:

- The Transportation Regulations state that a license for providing bus services can be revoked if its continuation is not in the public interest.[14]
- The Transportation Ordinance stipulates that the inspector of transportation may annul a license for operating a transportation facility due to public interest concerns.[15]
- The head of the Civil Aviation Administration can change the terms of a license if he believes the public interest calls for it.[16]

- The director of the Government Water Authority can retract a license to contaminate a water source if he finds it may harm the public interest.[17]
- The disciplinary committee of the national registry of land appraisers can delay the registration of an applicant in the national Land Appraiser registry if the public interest calls for it, as can the disciplinary committee of representative tax advisers and the disciplinary committee appointed according to the Private Investigators and Security Services Law to supervise private investigators.[18]
- A license for providing insurance services can be revoked or amended if the government-appointed inspector of the insurance industry finds that the public interest may be harmed otherwise.[19]
- The minister of infrastructure can refuse to grant a license for transmitting electricity if he believes awarding the license is not in the public interest.[20]

In none of these cases, except for the case of a license for providers of insurance services, does the public interest serve as a reason for awarding a license.

A similar approach is evident when it comes to the public's right to know and other civil rights, such as the right to a public trial and hearing. Thus, for example, the government may prohibit importing into Israel any publication it deems harmful to the public interest; a court of law may decide to hold a disciplinary hearing for a prison guard behind closed doors for the sake of the public interest; the governor of the Bank of Israel may nominate a manager, inspector, or committee to oversee the actions of a bank suspected of violating proper banking etiquette without giving the bank an opportunity to be heard for the sake of the public interest; and the Council of the Governmental Authority for Water and Sewage can deny the public the right to review any of its decisions if it believes that action to be in the public interest.[21] On occasion, though, promoting justice has superseded the public interest in judicial rulings. The justice minister, for example, may decide to conceal evidence in a trial, citing the public interest, but a court may reverse that decision if it believes that uncovering the evidence would promote justice.

Only rarely is the government or an administrator acting on its behalf required to take the public interest into consideration when awarding a license. And even in those cases, it is unclear whether the "public interest" refers to the public or to the government. The first two Israeli laws that called for taking the public interest into account when awarding a license were the Insurance Business Oversight Law and the Banking (Licensing) Law, which were legislated within a week of one another in 1981.[22] Particularly noteworthy in the context of cultural legislation is the Museums

Law of 1983, which requires the education and culture minister to consider the public interest when declaring a museum a "recognized museum," that is, a museum whose exhibits are protected from confiscation or lien and that is eligible for public support.[23] These, however, are exceptions. The increasing number of references to the public interest in the context of licensing is associated with the growing need for licenses—an outcome of the transformation of the Israeli economy from one characterized by distributive policies to one characterized by regulatory policies.

Since the 1980s, telecommunications law has also referred to the public interest mostly in the negative sense. That is to say, the public interest was a reason to revoke a license rather than to award it. Such was the case initially with the Telecommunications Law, enacted in 1982. The initial criteria for awarding a license to operators and providers of telecommunications services were the following: the government's telecommunications policy, the suitability of the applicant to provide the service, and the contribution of the license to competition in telecommunications. The public interest was mentioned only among the criteria for annulling, limiting, or postponing a license.[24] Only in 1996 was the public interest added to the list of considerations the communications minister was asked to take into account when *awarding* a license.[25] In a memorandum appended to the draft of the bill, the government explained the amendment by citing the circumstances surrounding the pending privatization of Bezeq, the state-owned telecommunications monopoly.[26] The memorandum said that telecommunications services are basic services "vital to the state's economy and security" and that therefore, the amendment was required to ensure that these services would be available at all times. Security considerations were thus equated with the "public interest."

The same conclusion emerges from the Knesset deliberations regarding the enactment of this amendment. Communications Minister Shulamit Aloni introduced the law by saying:

> As you know we initiated the privatization of Bezeq. When this was done, there was no assurance guaranteed that there would be sufficient control over essential services the government is interested in. . . . The draft proposal in front of us is here to correct this and to ensure that Bezeq services that are essential for the government will stay under supervision so that during times of emergency, or to provide for an essential need for the government, there will be a means of control, even if we sell larger parts and shares of Bezeq. (Knesset Records, 27 February 1995)

Members of the Knesset present at the time did not take issue with this statement. One noted that "today, the main mineral, the main asset a civilized and rich society has is communications, and this asset needs to be guarded. The law in front of us strengthens the state's control of this vital resource" (ibid.).

It is important to point out that even when the public interest criterion was inserted in 1996 into the Telecommunications Law, it was placed second in the list of the four criteria the minister needs to consider, after "government policy." Hence, although the introduction of the public interest criterion into telecommunications legislation may be perceived as a positive sign, it is clear that lawmakers viewed the public interest as inferior to the interest of the government.

Although the 1996 amendment to the Telecommunications Law that required the public interest to be considered when awarding licenses did filter down into other laws and regulations relevant to the telecommunications industry, its impact was barely felt in the realm of broadcasting law. The 1998 law that created the legal platform for introducing direct satellite broadcasting, for example, requires the minister to take into account the same list of considerations as when awarding licenses to telecommunications operators: government policy, public interest, applicant suitability, and contribution to competition in the industry.[27] This list was eventually copied verbatim into the Communications (Telecommunications and Broadcasting) Law when it was overhauled in 2001 to accommodate the new government policy that replaced cable franchises with cable licenses (as will be discussed in chapter 6).[28] With regard to the provision of postal services, the public interest was pushed to the bottom of the list of four criteria to be taken into account when awarding licenses.[29]

As noted, the introduction of the standard of the public interest is far less dramatic with regard to broadcasting than it was for telecommunication services. In the original 1990 Second Authority Law, the public interest is mentioned only in the context of providing a reason for nullifying, restricting, or diminishing a license or as a reason for completely disqualifying a potential contender in a tender for a television franchise.[30] The public interest is also cited as a reason for prohibiting or limiting advertising on radio and television, either in general or with regard to a particular product or service.[31] In the 1999 law, which included a provision for awarding a license for a news channel using cable and satellite infrastructures (to be discussed in further detail in chapter 4), the public interest is only to be taken into account when denying a license.[32] Not until 2005 was the public interest cited as a reason for awarding a license for the futuristic technology of digital radio, which had not yet been launched in Israel. In this legislation, the public interest finally made it to the list of considerations for awarding a broadcasting license (albeit involving a technology that was not yet available).[33] Even in this case, however, it was ranked sixth (and last) as one of "among the rest" considerations, which include the feasibility of allocating frequencies, the conditions for radio diffusion, economic considerations, the diversity of types of broadcasts, and the suitability of the license applicant.

In light of this demonstrated reluctance of Israeli policymakers to ensure that broadcasters would serve the public interest, it should come as no surprise that broadcasting institutions developed in Israel slowly and were designed to ensure maximum government controls.

4   Israeli Electronic Media
as a System of Control

Legislators' fear of the presumed powerful effect of the electronic media and their general indifference to the public interest have given rise to two formal structural systems of control of Israeli electronic media. One, described in this chapter as a system of control, ensures a government presence in the decision-making process of electronic news organizations. The second, described in chapters 5, 6, and 7, dictates the government's cultural agenda to broadcasters. The result is a closed media system with minimal requirements for transparency over which the government and corporate interests that aim to please the government exert tremendous control.

A Historical Timeline

It is possible to portray the history of media development in Israel as one in which new media were introduced gradually, as was the case in most Western nations, albeit after a delayed starting point. Indeed, it cannot be denied that there have been instances in media policy in Israel where initiatives seemed to be headed in the direction of decentralization of power and more freedom of speech. On the whole, however, centralization of formal control over electronic media outlets, especially news organizations, has been the more dominant trend. An overview of media development in Israel can be divided into five historical periods.

The first of these periods, from 1948 to 1965, was characterized by the existence of a sole government medium. This period ended with the creation of the Israel Broadcasting Authority, a *mamlakhti* broadcaster. The second stage, which lasted until 1978, was characterized by the introduction of a one-channel television service provided by the IBA and ended with the idea of creating a commercial television channel. The third period, which lasted until 1986, was a time when preparatory work for the creation of commercial television and cable television was done. It ended, surprisingly, with a law establishing cable television first. In 1990, a law establishing commercial television was passed, and the service was launched in 1993, marking the end of the fourth period. The final period, which spans to the present day, includes recent attempts to regulate the content of electronic media broadcasts even further, create new government-sanctioned channels on cable television, and introduce direct broadcast satellites.

Except for two special cases, government regulation of content broadcast by the electronic media has intensified over time. Even these two cases, which seemed to balk the trend—the creation of the Israel Broadcasting Authority in 1965 and the Second Authority for Television and Radio in 1990—were short lived. In both cases, the government kept tight reins on news broadcasting and, in both cases, the government clamped down on loopholes in the system in order to maintain its control.

1948–1965: Government Broadcasting

A short time after Israel won its independence in 1948, two radio services were created: Kol Israel (the Voice of Israel), the government's broadcasting station (which continued where the British colonial Voice of Jerusalem left off), and Galey Tzahal, an educational-entertainment station aimed at the vast military force dispersed along the country's borders. During this period, broadcasting was forbidden under the rules that were enacted during the British colonial mandate. Most notable among them was the Wireless Telegraphy Ordinance of 1937, according to which no wireless communications were allowed without a government license.[1] This ordinance refrained from stating how and under what circumstances such licenses might be awarded, especially those for broadcasting. In fact, not until the enactment of the Second Authority for Television and Radio Law of 1990 was it possible to award a broadcasting license in Israel.[2]

The first television service created in this period was the Center for Instructional Television in Tel Aviv, another government broadcaster. Following an exchange of letters in 1962 between Minister of Education

and Culture Abba Eban and Lord Rothschild of France, a limited experimental television service directed at school-age children was launched
that was limited both in scope and in content and was meant to remain
as such. Thus, in 1965, the government owned and operated all forms of
electronic media, which consisted of two radio services and the foundations of an instructional television service. But in the second half of the
1960s, two major events changed Israel's broadcasting map: the creation
of the IBA in 1965, whose purpose, according to legislation submitted
to the Knesset in 1963, was to transfer control over radio to a "public
body"; and the establishment of Israeli television under the auspices of
the newly formed public body, the IBA.

1965–1978: A Mamlakhti *Service*

The introduction of a comprehensive television service in Israel followed
the recommendations made by UNESCO and EBU experts, as described
in chapter 3. The UNESCO team concluded that as a developing nation,
Israel required a television service that could help advance national goals.
The EBU team said that the main function of television in Israel should be
to increase viewers' desire for information and spark interest in cultural
participation and thoughts about (instead of the escape from) reality.

Following Ben Gurion's resignation, the government made a decision
in principle in July 1965 to create a television service in Israel. Three more
years passed before the government, prompted by the consequences of the
June 1967 war and the occupation of vast amounts of land inhabited by
Palestinians, took the final steps necessary to implement this decision.
As television became a reality, the government began seeking ways to
use it for its own purposes. It was another eight months before broadcasts were launched and an additional six months before the government
actually transferred jurisdiction over television to the IBA (Gil 1986),
which did not happen until the second amendment to the IBA law had
been passed in the Knesset.[3] This was meant to secure the government's
control of the IBA and is the first indication of an evolving pattern: a
surge in regulatory activity every time a new medium is introduced, even
though the introduction of the new medium is meant to signal a move
in the direction of more liberal policies and less government control.

As one of the first independent authorities created in Israel, the IBA
suffered from a cumbersome structure. Its plenum had the authority to
approve the IBA's budget and programming. A subgroup of the plenum
functioned as a board that had the authority to "discuss and decide" all
issues confronting the authority. This duplication of authority was the

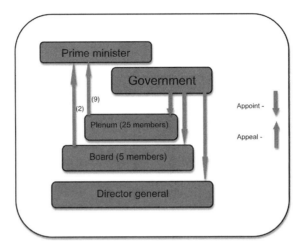

Figure 4.1: Structure of the IBA in 1965

source of much confusion for years to come and helped solidify the government's control of the *mamlakhti* broadcaster. From its inception, the IBA was closely tied to the government, much more so than the national public service broadcasters of Western Europe were. The 1965 law, for example, stated the following:

- Although the IBA's board of directors sets the annual license fee and approves its budget, the budget still needs to be ratified by the government.
- One-third of the twenty-five members of the IBA's plenum or two of the five members of its board of directors may appeal a decision made by the respective forum to the prime minister. The prime minister may then bring the issue to a vote in the government. The prime minister may also act to delay implementation of the decision until the government takes a stand on it. Since the plenum is the forum that approves the IBA's programming, this provides the government with vast influence in matters of content.
- The prime minister may demand that the board of directors submit to him or her reports on issues he deems important.
- The IBA cannot sell any property it owns (apart from "records and magnetic tapes") without government approval. It also may not pawn any of its property or rent out real estate it owns without ministerial approval.
- The government may at any time make "announcements" on the IBA's airwaves and, in times of emergency, may annul all of the IBA's powers for thirty days by unilateral decision and indefinitely

with the approval of the Knesset's Security and Foreign Affairs Committee.[4]

In 1968, following the introduction of television and after the Broadcasting Authority Law was amended, government involvement in broadcasting increased. A "minister charged with the execution of the law" replaced the prime minister as the key political executive empowered with the above-mentioned authorities. Although this change was enacted in order to solve a unique problem that arose at the time (the minister in charge was a minister without portfolio, so the law could not designate the minister by the portfolio, as is common practice), the outcome was that the job of supervising the IBA became a highly coveted one in the political power system.

According to the 1968 amendment, the director-general of the IBA (the highest executive position in the organization), who also serves as editor in chief of its news programs, was to be appointed by the government for five-year terms and the government was given the power (under specific circumstances) to fire him. Until 1968, the director-general's term in office was indefinite and the law did not provide a way of removing him from office. This attempt to subordinate the IBA director-general to the government gained further support from the government-endorsed Galili Document, named after its author, Minister without Portfolio Yisrael Galili, the minister in charge of implementing the IBA law and for whom this position was created. Dated 3 December 1968, the Galili Document clarified that the director-general is the "deciding authority"

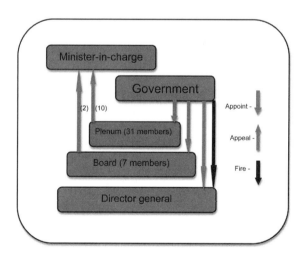

Figure 4.2: Structure of the IBA in 1968

on issues of news in subordination to "board of directors guidelines."
Even so, considering that the director-general is appointed by and can
be ousted by the government (and not the board of directors), it is not
inconceivable that ulterior motives, such as finding favor with those who
wield power over him, may color decisions made in the newsroom.

In addition, the amendment increased the IBA's plenum from twenty-
five to thirty-one government-appointed members, of whom seven serve
as the board of directors. In the original 1965 law, the board was comprised of only five members. Term limits were also set so that members
of the plenum who could have been reappointed indefinitely according to
the original law were limited to two terms in office. The right to appeal
decisions of the board was still awarded to two of the plenum members.
Now, however, two of seven could appeal instead of two of five, making
it easier for the government to wield influence in matters of content. It
likewise became easier to appeal plenum decisions. Before 1968, a third
of the plenum was needed for an appeal action. In other words, at least
nine out of twenty-five (more than one-third) were required for an appeal.
According to the 1968 amendment, only ten of the thirty-one (less than
one-third) were needed, again making it easier to revoke decisions.

The establishment of the IBA also brought about a restructuring of the
legal status of Galey Tzahal. According to Article 48 of the Broadcasting
Authority Law, the IBA was empowered with the same authority over
nonmilitary broadcasts of the IDF radio station as it had over its own
broadcasts. However, the minister of defense had exclusive authority
over military broadcasts. The minister of defense was also charged with
defining what constituted military broadcasts. Soon after the enactment
of the Broadcasting Authority Law, Prime Minister Levi Eshkol, who was
also serving as minister of defense, signed regulations that established

Table 4.1. Power Structure of Broadcasting in Israel under the Broadcasting
Authority Law in 1965 and 1968, the Year Television Was Introduced

Topic	Broadcasting Authority Law, 1965	Broadcasting Authority Law (Amendment No. 2, 1968)
Plenum members	25	31
Plenum members needed to halt decisions	9	10
Board members	5	7
Board members needed to halt decision	2	2
Number of terms per plenum/board member	Indefinite	2
Term of director-general	Indefinite	5 years
Who may fire the director-general	No one	The Cabinet

that military broadcasts include everything from news reports and commentary on security issues to reviews of the press and military literature within and outside Israel.

This definition continues to apply to this day. In a country where defense and security issues are a major component of the daily news, this effectively means that the military radio station is not meant to develop into an independent news source. It is important to note here that most Israelis consider Galey Tzahal to be a reliable news source, with little, if any, evidence to the contrary (Caspi and Limor 1999, 137–142). Even so, the station is subject to strict government controls.

During this period, then, the government maintained total control over broadcasting through its grip on the IBA. It exercised control over the IBA's budget; it had the authority to intervene in its programming, add its own messages, or eliminate broadcasts altogether; and it had exclusive jurisdiction over the IBA's property. Since 1968, it also has the authority to appoint and fire the IBA's director-general, the person in charge of news content, as well as to revoke and overturn any controversial decisions taken by the IBA, even when only a minority within the "independent" organs of the IBA are opposed to them. Although the government only once exercised its right to fire the director-general, in May 2005, it frequently wields its other powers, such as delaying approval of the IBA's budget, serving as a constant reminder to the IBA of its limited independence.[5] Needless to say, the government also had full control over all programming on both non-IBA broadcasters that existed from 1968 to 1978, Galey Tzahal and Instructional Television.

By the end of 1968, television in Israel had two outlets: a governmental instructional service and a barely independent public service that was launched as a propaganda tool and was designed for easy control. Radio included a similar dyad: the IBA channels, whose editor in chief also served as editor in chief for television, and Galey Tzahal. This two-headed service enjoyed a monopoly until the late 1980s, although the first seeds of change were sown as early as 1977.

1978–1986: Introducing Commercial Electronic Media

In May 1977, shortly after marking its 29th anniversary as an independent state, Israel experienced its first shift of political power, when the social-democrat Labor alliance lost the elections to the conservative-hawkish Likud alliance. This dramatic upheaval was the precursor to a series of policy decisions that reflected the ideologically opposed platforms of the two political blocs at the time, and the principles of social democracy, which provided many of the ideological building blocks of the state, were gradually replaced (Aharoni 1998). Most of the literature on Likud government policies between 1977 and 1984 focuses on the liberalization of Israeli currency and the resulting hyperinflation (see, for example, Plessner 1994; Wolffsohn 1987), which eventually brought about the establishment of a national unity government in 1984 and the emergency economic stabilization program of 1985. Less documented, however, is the fact that the first Likud-led government (1977–1981) sowed the seeds of a new telecommunications map for Israel. During the years of this government and its immediate successor, the second Likud government (1981–1984), the recommendations of three public committees appointed to address issues of communications policy were adopted: the Kubersky Committee of 1978, which recommended establishing commercial television in Israel; the Barsela Committee of 1982, which recommended setting up cable television; and the Herzog Committee of 1973, whose recommendation to the Labor government that it corporatize public telecommunications was adopted by the government in 1979. The first two media-oriented initiatives got off to a slow start because of fears (shared by socialists and liberals alike) that the government might lose control of the information flow guaranteed by a single television channel designed by the "old" social-democratic regime, which ensured maximum government control over the flow of information. The new coalition, however, was committed to a free market ideology, and one of the first issues on its agenda was creating more choice in broadcasting. To this end, the Kubersky Committee, whose report was discussed in chapter 3, was appointed to create a blueprint for a new channel to be financed through advertising. The committee was also to decide whether the new channel would be created within the IBA or independently of it and what type of channel it should be. It ended up recommending that an independent channel be created with similar cultural obligations to those of the publicly funded channel. Even though this was only a modest revolution, as content would continue to be highly regulated, it was another fifteen years before commercial broadcasts were launched in November 1993.

In the meantime, a cable television system was being created, the outcome of a separate policy process. Although the Kubersky Committee had already referred to the possibility of establishing cable television in Israel, the plan offered in 1982 by the Barsela Committee, which was also appointed by a Likud government, served as the blueprint for the new service (Barsela 1982). Based on the Barsela Committee's recommendations, the government initiated the fourth amendment to the Telecommunications Law in 1986, which created the Cable Broadcasting Council, which consisted of eleven members.[6] This council was subject to even tighter government controls than the IBA. Five members represented the government, two represented local government, and the remaining four represented what the minister of communications (the appointing minister) deemed "consumer interests" and "educational bodies."

This government-controlled council was initially given a very broad mandate. First, it was to award franchises to government operators. Next, it was to create policy concerning the type of programs; the topics of programs; and content, level, scope, and schedule of programming these operators provided. In addition, it was asked to determine policy concerning local broadcasts and original programs, supervise the franchising process, and advise the minister of communication on technical issues.

Furthermore, the law clarified that cable operators were not to broadcast any self-produced national news programs and were obligated to retransmit all over-the-air national channels.[7] In this way, government control of the flow of news was maintained even in the new multichannel environment, since over-the-air broadcasting was limited to the IBA and the yet-to-be-established commercial entity.

The Telecommunications Regulations (Broadcasts by a Franchisee), published in 1987, were a much more specific document than the 1986 Telecommunications Law (amendment no. 4) and defined, in meticulous detail, the content obligations of cable operators.[8] These rules were somewhat amended in 1997, 1998, and 2002 (following the 2001 overhaul of the Telecommunications Law).[9] The basic idea of specific content regulation by a council of government representatives, however, has not changed. On the contrary, the new regulations are even more specific and cover topics never before covered in broadcasting regulations, as I discuss in chapter 6.

The intense regulation of content on cable television and the repeated delays in inaugurating the commercial channel were accompanied by constant attacks on the independence of the IBA. A case in point was a Knesset resolution passed in December 1979. After a series of confrontations between the newly appointed director-general of the IBA, who was acting on behalf of the new government formed in 1977, and IBA journalists, the 1979 resolution determined once again that the director-general is also the editor in chief of IBA broadcasts. This resolution underscores the fact that final decisions at the IBA are in the hands of an official who only the government can appoint and only the government can fire.

During this period, the High Court of Justice was asked in two instances to prevent the IBA from censoring unpopular (in the government's eyes) forms of speech. In 1981, the court overturned a decision that prohibited interviews with supporters of the Palestinian Liberation Organization in the territories occupied in the 1967 war (*Zichroni v. Board of the Broadcasting Authority* [1981]), and in 1985, it overturned a decision that banned interviews with the racist MK Meir Kahane (*MK Rabbi Meir Kahane v. Board of the Broadcasting Authority* [1985]).

1986–1993: Introducing Commercial Television

During the 1980s, various attempts to pass the law envisioned by the Kubersky Committee that would have inaugurated a commercial terrestrial television channel failed. In the process, at least two drafts of a new law were presented to the Knesset.[10] The law, which was finally enacted in 1990, was amended five times before broadcasting was launched in November 1993. Among other obstacles, a tender issued by the government for potential franchise owners drew no bidders.[11] While it is beyond the scope of this study to explain the competing pressures on the government and the Knesset regarding the issue of creating a second channel and its future character, the outcome demonstrates that the eventual decision taken on the matter was motivated not by the desire to offer the Israeli public greater choice in media fare but by the desire to maintain control over broadcasting content.

There is no question that the Second Authority for Television and Radio Law of 1990 was far more liberal than the IBA law in that it did not provide the government with as many ways to influence broadcasting. Most important, all broadcasts under this law were to be (and eventu-

Table 4.2. Comparison of Broadcasting Law in Israel, 1965 and 1990

	Broadcasting Authority	Second Authority for Radio and Television
Plenum members	31	No plenum
Plenum members needed to halt decisions	10	No procedure exists
Number of members	7 board members	15 council members
Board members needed to halt decisions	2	No procedure exists
Nomination of director-general	The government at its discretion	Nominated by government, approved by council
Reappointment of director-general	The government at its discretion[a]	Discretion of council[b]
Term of director-general	5 years	5 years
Who may fire the director-general	The government	The council

[a] This has not occurred in forty-three years.
[b] This has occurred once.

ally were) financed exclusively by commercial franchise holders and the government had no impact on their budgets.

The Second Authority for Television and Radio Law created a fifteen-member council to supervise broadcasting on the commercial channel. Unlike the IBA law, the Second Authority Law did not give the government the exclusive right to appoint the director-general of the Second Authority (a task it shared with the council) or give the government any say in the firing of the director-general (a matter left in the hands of the council). Nor did it provide for any procedure to appeal decisions about programming to the government, as was the case at the IBA. Similarly, the law did not provide the government with a role in the budget approval process of the Second Authority or provide it with any claims to its property. Unlike the IBA law, the new law did not provide the government with the right to broadcast "announcements" on the air, save for times of national emergency. Still, some elements of governmental control were maintained in the new law, as follows:

- The government was given the power to appoint the council and approve the appointment of the director-general of the Second Authority.
- Political parties were allotted free time prior to elections, equal to the time allotment the IBA is required to provide.
- The government was given the right to broadcast announcements during times of "national emergency" and expropriate the frequencies used by the Second Authority, with the approval of the Knesset, for an unlimited amount of time.
- The minister in charge of the Second Authority had the authority to demand that the council create guidelines to solve specific problems that might arise over time.
- The government maintained control of the salaries of employees at the Second Authority and the size of its workforce.
- Broadcasting was divided among three franchises, each awarded two days of broadcasting while rotating on Saturdays. This minimized the leveraging power of individual franchisees in the event that face-offs with the government surfaced in the future.
- More significant, news programs were to be handled exclusively by a News Corporation created by law, in which each franchise holder held 20 percent of the shares and the government-appointed Second Authority Council held 40 percent. The candidate for director of this corporation had to earn 75 percent of the vote of the News Corporation's board to be appointed. This made it impossible to appoint a director not supported by at least half of the Second Authority's representatives (who were appointed by the government) in the news corporation's board.

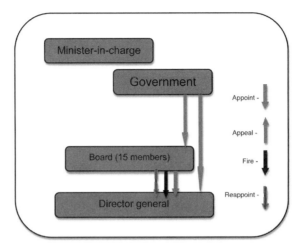

Figure 4.3: Structure of the Second Authority in 1990

- One-seventh of broadcasting time was to be allotted on the commercial channel to Instructional Television, the government broadcaster
  that was already broadcasting daily at the time, from 8:00 A.M. to
  5:30 P.M. on the IBA's channel.

The establishment of commercial radio in Israel has its roots in the
1990 Second Authority Law and was not based on the Kubersky report.
The law called for a regional system of commercial radio broadcasters
to be set up whose main characteristic would be their regional nature.

The law also required the regional radio stations to carry the national
news broadcasts of the existing broadcasters (that is, the IBA, Galey Tzahal, or the News Corporation) and prohibited them from broadcasting
any news on their own beyond local news, except under special circumstances that required the Second Authority's approval.

Still, despite many proclamations and initiatives aimed at creating
commercial and "independent" terrestrial broadcasting between 1978
and 1993, little was done to advance this endeavor.

1993–2009: *Establishing Broadcasters and Closing Loopholes*

Many perceived the inauguration of commercial television at the end
of 1993 as a sign of a new openness on the Israeli media scene. In fact,
though, it represents the beginning of the final stage of the government's

clampdown on broadcasting. The structure that emerged created three fiscal monopolies: terrestrial-*mamlakhti* broadcasting, terrestrial-commercial broadcasting, and cablecasting, each of which relied almost exclusively on one source of income. The IBA (terrestrial-*mamlakhti* broadcasting) is funded by revenues from license fees and is prohibited from broadcasting advertising on television; the commercial channel (terrestrial-commercial broadcasting) is funded entirely through advertising; and cable television is funded through subscription fees and is prohibited from selling advertising over the channels it owns and operates. Any attempt to bypass these funding restrictions, in particular by selling advertising on *mamlakhti* or on cable television, requires special government approval. This gives the government yet another weapon it can use to exert power over broadcasters. During the 1993–2007 period, the government exerted control over broadcasting through these financing restrictions and through regulations that affected content. Cable television franchise holders could not broadcast national news; the News Corporation's appointment of the director-general could be vetoed by the government; and the position of editor in chief of *mamlakhti* broadcasting required government approval. This list of restrictions would grow in the coming years.

In 1997, the Knesset passed an amendment to the Telecommunications Law that clarified government and government-appointed CBC's control over the use of one-sixth of the cable infrastructure.[12] The government, the Knesset, and the CBC agreed that two of the new channels on the cable infrastructure should be news channels. In 1999, another law included a provision for a 24-hour cable/satellite news channel.[13] All of these news channels (none of which were ever created) were to be licensed by the government-appointed Cable and Satellite Broadcasting Council through competitive tenders; this system gave the government the ability to determine who news broadcasters would be. This stage of regulation was preceded by an amendment to the Telecommunication Law in January 1998 that legalized direct broadcast satellites. Here, too, the government's power to award licenses was maintained and even strengthened, as direct broadcast satellite (DBS) licenses were to be awarded by the minister of communications and not by the CSBC.[14]

Like cable operators, direct broadcast satellite operators were prohibited from producing or broadcasting news. The only news programs DBS license holders were allowed to provide were national news programs (those produced by the IBA, Galey Tzahal, and the Second Authority News Corporation, for example), local news channels approved for broadcasting on the cable system, or foreign newscasts approved by the

CSBC. Although the goal was "opening the sky" and creating choice, once more, the new regime created more restrictions and ensured the continued subjugation of news providers to the government or the bodies it appoints directly and controls.

And indeed, this is what happened. On 10 January 2002, the CSBC rejected a request to approve a channel of general and economic news, to be provided only in text, on the emerging digital platforms of cable and satellite. It explained that

> limiting the ability of different organizations to broadcast news over cable and satellite emanates from the assumption that broadcast news has a central effect on the public and social agenda in Israel. [Therefore] it is advisable to decentralize the control of newscasts as well as set limits on the appropriateness of news production and its quality. In addition, the requested broadcasts have a potential for wide influence and implication, emanating from their transmission over the medium of television, which is accessible to different groups in Israeli society and to a wide circumference within it. This is especially relevant in the State of Israel, which is characterized by high sensitivity to news in general and in particular.
>
> News is to be defined as: new information, updated information, information broadcasts in proximity to the actual happening, and it necessarily influences the public. The requested broadcasts are of the type of issues that influence the public agenda and are noticeable in the nature and effect, even in the way they are edited in the printed press, from other areas of knowledge.[15]

Further moves to block the flow of information across national borders, which began with the launching of broadcasting and before the commercial channel was launched, were made during the second Palestinian uprising that began in September 2000 and as preparations were under way for the American-British invasion of Iraq in 2003. At first, the government was concerned with how the violent events of the Palestinian uprising were being portrayed on foreign news channels transmitted abroad and retransmitted locally on cable and satellite. In August 2002, the Cable and Satellite Broadcasting Council allowed the three cable operators operating at that time[16] to drop the American Cable News Network (CNN) from their menus, provided they replaced it with the American Fox News Channel so as not to reduce the number of foreign channels offered to consumers.[17] The CSBC refused to publish the minutes of the debate leading up to this decision and was especially adamant about not making public details of the debate surrounding the "anti-Israeli" slant CNN was supposedly broadcasting (Balint 2002a). This left the public to speculate about whether the content of CNN broadcasts had prompted the decision. In April 2003, history repeated itself when the CSBC allowed the cable operators to remove BBC World from their offering.[18] A press release cited a commercial dispute between the BBC and the cable operators rather than the content of the broadcasts as the reason for this decision (Balint 2003a). Whether commercial justifications were the reason behind the decision of this ad hoc coalition of operators and regulators remains in question. What is certain is that the government believed that CNN and BBC World broadcasts were "anti-Israeli." This was demonstrated clearly in July 2003 when the government announced its decision to boycott the BBC, citing the broadcasters' "anti-Israeli approach" to coverage of the conflict (Sade 2003b) and its portrayal of Palestinian leader Yasser Arafat as a hero (Sade 2003a).

Neither CNN nor the BBC were indifferent to the outcry of official Israel. A senior CNN official visited Israel in June 2002 and "admitted mistakes," after which CNN began broadcasting special programs that portrayed Israeli victims of Palestinian violence (Ettinger 2002). The BBC appointed a senior official to examine its editorial policies regarding the Middle East conflict (Sade 2004). Both CNN (Balint 2002b) and BBC World (Balint 2003b) eventually were restored to the Israeli cable offering. But CNN was finally removed from the cable offering in 2007, this time, apparently, due to a dispute over finances with the cable operator.[19] However, it remained on the satellite menu.

After being subjected to Iraqi missile attacks during the American-led invasion in 1991 and amid speculation in 2003 that Iraq had since obtained the capability to attack Israel with weapons of mass destruction, the Israeli military sought ways to control the flow of information in case of future Iraqi attacks. In January 1991, only a handful of Israelis subscribed to the newly launched cable television service (Lehman-Wilzig and Schejter 1994). The IBA was the only television broadcaster of news because the commercial channel was still in its "establishment" stage; it was being run by the government and was not broadcasting any news (Tokatly 2000, 258). The only "pluralism" offered to Israelis were the competing public radio services, IBA and Galey Tzahal, whose broadcasts the government had no difficulty unifying in its effort to maintain full control over content during this time of national emergency (ibid., 262).

By 2003, however, cable and satellite reached 78 percent of households and the cable offering consisted of dozens of foreign channels, at least four of which (BBC World, CNN, Fox News, and Sky News) were international news channels. The military devised a plan that in the event of an Iraqi missile attack, all broadcasting would cease on both radio and television, including the foreign networks, to be replaced by a five-minute video prepared by the military press office followed by fifteen minutes of instructions and explanations as the army deemed fit. The Supreme Court struck down these extreme measures in the *Kirsch* case (*Michael Kirsch v. Chief of Staff of the Israeli Defense Forces* [2003]), but only by a vote of 2 to 1. The majority of justices, Daliah Dorner and Eliezer Rivlin, said that blocking foreign channels during a time of emergency was extreme, unreasonable, and unjustifiable under the Israeli constitutional framework. The government's paternalistic assumption that it knows better than its citizens what information they need is at best far fetched, said Dorner, adding that when it acts under such assumptions, it should do so with more humility. Hence, government policies aimed at controlling the free flow of news at times of national emergency have to date been put on hold, having been described as unjustifiable within existing values.

During this period, a second commercial channel, legally named The Third Channel and popularly known as Channel 10, was introduced.[20] As was the case with Channel 2, Channel 10 was required to maintain a separate news apparatus and to refrain from broadcasting news by itself. The 2000 law that launched Channel 10 also defined "news" as both "news programs and news magazines," not leaving much room for any other interpretation than that all programs dealing with time-sensitive issues could only be broadcast through the news corporations.[21] This was the first time Israeli law had defined news in this broad way.

Because the Channel 10 News Corporation was subject to the same structural requirements as its Channel 2 predecessor, a problem had arisen by the time Channel 10 started broadcasting in 2002. According to Article 67 of the 1990 law, the chair of the news corporation was to be the director-general of the Second Authority, who was to be directly appointed by the government. Once two news corporations were competing with each other, it no longer made sense to have the most senior regulator chair only one News Corporation (or both at the same time). As a result, the law was amended in 2003 with new guidelines about the structure of the boards of both news corporations.[22] According to the new guidelines, each board would consist of a minimum of five members, two of whom would be appointed by the regulatory council for three-year periods and one of whom would serve as chair. The 2003 amendment provides an example of some of the tactics the government used to maintain its control over electronic news outlets, reminiscent of its restructuring of IBA in 1968. Although preventing the director-general of the Second Authority from chairing the board weakens the government's grasp of the news

Table 4.3. Government Control of News Outlets in Israel, 2008

Platform	National News Provider[a]	Form of Control
Government television	Israel Educational Television	Unit in the Ministry of Education
Government radio	IDF[b] Radio	A military unit; IBA[c] supervises "non-military" broadcasts[d]
Public broadcasting[e]	Israel Broadcasting Authority	Government appoints council; appoints and can fire director-general
Commercial television	Two news corporations	Government appoints council, whose members' votes are needed to appoint director-general
Commercial radio	Only over-the-air broadcasts of "others"	"Others" category includes only IDF radio, IBA, and NC[f]
Cable television	Only retransmission of signals of government-selected news providers or "others"	"Others" category includes only IETV[g], IBA, and NC
Satellite television	Only retransmission of signals of government-selected news providers or "others"	"Others" category includes only IETV, IBA, and NC

[a] Local news can be carried independently by commercial radio and by cable TV operators.
[b] Israel Defense Forces.
[c] Israel Broadcast Authority.
[d] "Non-military" broadcasts are broadly defined.
[e] Includes radio and television.
[f] News Corporation.
[g] Israel Educational Television.

corporation, the amended legislation has reduced the number of board members from ten to five, leaving the government with 40 percent of the seats on the board. The amendment did not change the policy that the director-general be appointed or reappointed with the approval of 80 percent of board members. These provisions give each government representative far more power than before in overseeing each of the news corporations, Channel 2's News Corporation and the News Corporation of the Third Channel (a.k.a. News 10).[23]

With the inauguration of Channel 10 and the restructuring of commercial broadcasting, holders of commercial franchises found themselves at the mercy of the government. The implications for the healthy functioning of a free press are quite obvious. Between 2000 and 2007, the Second Authority law was amended at least twelve times. At least six of these amendments dealt in one way or another with extending the franchise periods or with lifting other franchise requirements, in particular with regard to Channel 10. Because of the Israeli political culture, which enables broadcasters and lawmakers to rub shoulders frequently, the transition from government broadcasting to a regulatory regime has not in any way reduced the dependence of broadcasters on the government, resulting in an inevitable quid pro quo relationship. The inherent dangers of this sort of relationship, which requires broadcasters to pander to the government, are obvious.

5   *Broadcasting*

Both developing and developed countries impose cultural obligations on broadcasters. Katz and Wedell (1977) have observed that the goals of introducing electronic media in developing countries include promoting national integration—that is, creating a sense of belonging to the new nation-state (171)—and cultural continuity and change (191). Shaughnessy and Fuente Cobo (1990) have compiled a list of what they refer to as the "cultural obligations of broadcasters" in all European countries, Machet and Robillard (1998) have identified the cultural obligations of broadcasters in Europe and Canada, Blumler (1992) has compiled a series of studies demonstrating how policymakers in Western Europe use broadcasting in order to defend "vulnerable" social values, and Jamias (1993) has reviewed the cultural obligations of the mass media in Asia.

Israel, therefore, is not unusual in this respect. What makes the cultural obligations I describe in this and the next two chapters unique is the form they assume and the cultural preferences they promote. They illustrate the contradiction between Israel's democratic credo and its policies in practice.

The Broadcasting Authority in its Monopoly Years

From the beginnings of broadcasting in Israel, policymakers have been preoccupied with the question of what type of cultural obligations to impose on the media. The initial draft of the Broadcasting Authority Law, which the government published in February 1963, stipulated that the IBA would maintain the Israeli Broadcasting Service as a *mamlakhti* service.

The Knesset's preference for the term *"mamlakhti"* over the term "public" that was more common in Europe at the time was not accidental. A number of Knesset members referred to it during the debate that preceded the vote on the law's final version. Most notable was MK Shmuel Mikunis of the Israeli Communist Party (Maki), who proposed to change the determination of the new service from *"mamlakhti"* to *"mamlakhti*-public," since a *mamlakhti* service "resembles a government service" (Knesset Records, 8 March 1965, 1455). His amendment was not approved.

The following tasks were delegated to the IBA in Article 3 of the draft:

1. To broadcast programs in the fields of policy, society, education, culture, science, arts, and entertainment, in order
   a. to reflect the life of the State, its creation, achievements, and struggle;
   b. to propagate means of good citizenship;
   c. to deepen the knowledge of Jewish heritage and its ways;
   d. to expand the knowledge of listeners and their education;
   e. to reflect the life of the nation in the Diaspora, its fate, and its struggle;
2. to promote Hebrew and Israeli creativity;
3. to provide decent broadcasts in the Arabic language for the needs of the Arabic-speaking population and for the advancement of understanding and peace with the neighboring states, according to the basic course set by the State;
4. to maintain broadcasting to the Diaspora;
5. to broadcast abroad programs that are of interest to the State.[1]

The Knesset approved the final version of the law with the following alterations:

1. To broadcast education, entertainment and information programs in the fields of policy, society, economics, culture, science, and the arts, in order
   a. To reflect the life of the State, its creation, achievements, and struggle;
   b. To propagate good citizenship;
   c. To strengthen the connection with the Jewish heritage and its values, and to deepen the knowledge of;
   d. To reflect the lives and cultural assets of all tribes of the nation from the different countries;
   e. To expand education and to distribute knowledge;
   f. To reflect the life of the Jews in the Diaspora;
   g. To enhance the aims of *mamlakhti* education as described in the Mamlakhti Education Law of 1953;

2. To promote Hebrew and Israeli creativity;
3. To provide broadcasts in the Arabic language for the needs of the Arabic-speaking population and for the advancement of understanding and peace with the neighboring states, according to the basic course set by the State;
4. To maintain broadcasting to the Jews of the Diaspora;
5. To broadcast abroad.[2]

A comparison of the two versions demonstrates that the Knesset recognized the need to create a more independent service that was less paternalistic, more Jewish, more "activist Zionist," and more *mamlakhti* than had been originally intended by the government. Table 5.1 highlights these changes.

Table 5.1. Israeli Broadcasting Authority Aims: Draft and Law

---

1963 Draft

1(a) To reflect the life, creation, achievements, and struggle of the State
 (b) To propagate ~~means of~~ good citizenship
 (c) To deepen the ~~knowledge of Jewish heritage and its ways~~
 (d) To expand the knowledge and education ~~of listeners~~
 (e) To reflect the life, ~~fate, and struggle~~ of the ~~nation~~ in the Diaspora
 (2) To promote Hebrew and Israeli creativity
 (3) To provide ~~decent~~ broadcasts in the Arabic language for the needs of the Arab-speaking population and for the advancement of understanding and peace with the neighboring states according to the basic course set by the state
 (4) To maintain broadcasting to the Diaspora
 (5) To broadcast abroad ~~programs that are of interest to the State~~

1965 Law

1(a) To reflect the life, creation, achievements, and struggle of the State
 (b) To propagate good citizenship
 (c) To strengthen the <u>connection with</u> Jewish heritage and its <u>values</u> and to deepen its knowledge
 (e) To expand education and to <u>distribute</u> knowledge
 (f) To reflect the life of the <u>Jews</u> in the Diaspora
 (2) To promote Hebrew and Israeli creativity
 (3) To provide broadcasts in the Arabic language for the needs of the Arab-speaking population and for the advancement of understanding and peace with the neighboring states according to the basic course set by the State
 (4) To maintain broadcasting to <u>the Jews of</u> the Diaspora
 (5) To broadcast abroad
 (d) <u>To reflect the lives and cultural assets of all the tribes of the nation from different countries</u>
 (g) <u>To enhance the aims of *mamlakhti* education as described in the Mamlakhti Education Law of 1953</u>

Notes: Strikeout indicates text that is not present in the 1965 law; underlining indicates text that was not present in the 1963 draft legislation.

The following changes should be noted:

- The two content obligations added by the Knesset take a more inclusive view of the Jewish majority by adding that broadcasting would serve the *mamlakhti* educational system and by adding the words "cultural assets of all the tribes of the nation."[3]
- The reference to the "education" of listeners was replaced with the less loaded term "knowledge."
- Deleting the language "that are of interest to the State" reflects an attempt to exempt the transborder broadcasting from the mission of propaganda.
- Deleting "decent" from the description of Arabic-language broadcasting and using the language "cultural assets of all the tribes of the nation" to refer to the Jewish population can be interpreted as efforts to create a less paternalistic service.
- Adding "to strengthen the connection with the Jewish heritage" to "deepening the knowledge of" demonstrates a greater commitment to the Jewish religion.
- Deleting the language "fate and struggle" minimized the draft legislation's description of life in the Diaspora. In addition, the final law replaced the term "nation" with the term "Jews." It also added "Jews" to describe the target audience of broadcasts abroad. While they may seem semantic, these linguistic changes are evidence of a new approach to Diaspora Jewry that distances them as a group that was part of the nation and minimizes their historical role but at the same time distinguishes them as a separate audience from that described by the more general term "broadcast abroad."

Both versions make a strong distinction between the purpose of broadcasting for the Jewish population and the purpose of broadcasting for the Arab population. While broadcasting content for the Jewish population was to include the values of Judaism and the life of the Jewish people, the purpose of broadcasting to the Arab population was to serve its "needs." The law provided no detailed description about what those "needs" might be and no reference to cultural needs. Indeed, following a cumbersome description of the "Jewish" objectives that are to be sought through broadcasting, such as Jewish heritage and Jewish "cultural assets," the law provides no specifics about the "needs" of the Arab population.[4]

The Knesset reaffirmed the aims of IBA broadcasting in a resolution approved on 17 December 1979:

Television broadcasts, according to the Broadcasting Authority Law, must reflect the life of the State, its struggle, creation, and achievements; propagate good citizenship; strengthen the connection with Jewish heritage and its values, and deepen knowledge of; expand education, distribute knowledge, reflect the lives of Jews in the Diaspora; promote the aims of *mamlakhti* education as described in the Mamlakhti Education Law of 1953; and promote Hebrew, Israeli, and Jewish creativity.[5]

This resolution was initiated by a mainly right-wing coalition that included the nationalist Likud, the National Religious Party, the ultra-orthodox Agudat Israel, and the liberal Democratic Movement. It was a retreat from the path taken by the Knesset in 1965. Two years after the first transfer of political power to the right, the Knesset chose to make Israel's Jewish population the focus of the cultural obligations of the IBA, effectively ignoring the non-Jewish population. In its reference to creativity, the Knesset for the first (and only) time introduced the adjective "Jewish" in addition to the adjectives "Hebrew" and "Israeli." Article 3, therefore, was used to create that impression that the law was designed to ensure that the electronic media serve the interests of the demographic groups who had assumed political power in 1977.

VICKI SHIRAN V. ISRAEL BROADCASTING AUTHORITY

Article 3 was challenged in court in the *Shiran* case of 1981. In the early 1980s, the IBA began production of a nineteen-episode documentary series called *Pillar of Fire* that portrayed the history of Zionism. A group of Mizrahi intellectuals petitioned the high court to demand that the series not be broadcast, since it did not provide an accurate account of the contribution of Jews from Asia, Africa, and the Balkans to the Zionist endeavor and the establishment of the State of Israel and devoted a disproportionate amount of footage to the history of Zionism in Europe (*Vicki Shiran v. Israel Broadcasting Authority* [1981]). After reviewing eleven scripts for the series and meeting with its creators, the petitioners argued that the program ignored indisputable historical facts that are proof of the contribution of Jews of Mizrahi origin to the Zionist enterprise, among them the arrival of Jews from Asia, Africa, and the Balkans to Palestine at the end of the nineteenth and beginning of the twentieth century, the massive illegal immigration from these regions during the pre-state years, and the large number of Jews from these regions who had immigrated to Israel since its founding. It should be noted that while the series focused only on the period leading up to the founding of the state, the petitioners argued that the relatively large proportion of Mizrahi Jews who immigrated to Israel after the establishment of the state was an important part of the history of Zionism as well and therefore deserved mention in the program.

The Supreme Court rejected the petition. Rather patronizingly, the justices complimented the plaintiffs' attorney (a law professor, himself of Mizrahi origin) on his presentation, noting that its "good taste" had compensated for the extreme and unreasonable demands put forth in the affidavits and appendixes to the petition (*Vicki Shiran v. Israel Broadcasting Authority* [1981], 376). Although the plaintiffs based their demands on the IBA's legal obligation to "reflect the lives and cultural assets of all the tribes of the nation from the different countries," the court said that this argument was not valid, since it is prohibited from ruling in ideological disputes over national heritage. Indeed, the court said there is no need for proportional ethnic representation in the historical narrative and that anything that might have transpired in the history of the Jewish people anywhere in the world becomes part of the entire nation's experience, rendering the question of ethnic affiliation irrelevant. This traditional view that "all Jews are responsible for one another," argued the court, is no less valid than the plaintiffs' view—a view that the court did not elaborate on but can be understood to mean that the plantiffs' ancestors (Jews of Mizrahi origin), as well, deserve recognition for their contribution to the Zionist endeavor (385). The court was not required to elaborate any further after it declared that it was upholding the IBA's right to freedom of expression. Still, it went on to provide its own romantic interpretation of Zionism. Justice Meir Shamgar declared that "it would be clichéd to repeat" that Zionism was "a wondrous phenomenon, apparently with no historic equivalent" (although the justice did not mention where he had made such a statement in the past). He continued to wax poetic about Zionism, describing it as a movement

> whose essence is the maintenance of loyalty and the daily love, lasting for thousands of years, between a nation and its land, when the majority of the nation is separated and far away from the land. There is room to argue, that in a [television] series such as this one, it be noted that the origins of this movement are rooted in the rivers of Babylon thousands of years ago, when the dream of returning to Zion was first woven, and that its tangible expression has taken the form of the return of individuals and groups for generations. . . . Had the series taken such an approach, the petition would have been obsolete. However, its creators chose a narrow description based on the persecution of Jews in Europe in the late 19th and early 20th centuries. (ibid.)

Justice Miriam Ben-Porat, who expressed outrage that the petitioners, as "Jews from the East," should in any way feel slighted, then joined Shamgar. Jews are Jews, she argued, regardless of their place of origin, and "Jews from the East" are part of the same people as "Jews from the

West"—a people who should be guarded from a damaging split from which "the scent of distancing hearts emanates" (388). Ben-Porat expressed skepticism about the claim made by the petitioners that the television series might damage the image of Mizrahi Jews in their own eyes as well as in the eyes of others, as if Mizrahi Jews were "an independent body, carrying itself, and the rest of the nation is, presumably, 'others.'"

In 1998, the IBA broadcast a sequel to *Pillar of Fire* that documented the first fifty years of the state. A petition filed with the Supreme Court this time claimed that the series was both historically inaccurate and, even more, "not loyal to the state." The court did not bother to address the issue of historical truth and rejected the petition outright (*Elias Yaakov v. IBA* [1998]).

Introduction of Commercial Broadcasting: The Second Authority

The Second Authority for Television and Radio Law was passed in the Knesset in 1990 after fifteen years of political infighting instigated by the political upheaval of 1977. Two things were clear from the outset: that this would be a commercial service, since the government had said it would not participate in financing a second television channel, and that a key decision to be made was whether the new channel would operate under the auspices of the IBA or independently.

Although a new and more liberal approach seemed to be taking hold, the Kubersky Committee, whose views of "powerful effect" I described in chapter 3, was headed by an official closely associated with the National Religious Party—the only party to survive the political change by replacing its historic alliance with the left-leaning Labor Party with a new alliance with the Likud, whose members embraced a neoliberal economic ideology. This becomes relevant when examining the differences between the Broadcasting Authority Law, the Kubersky report, and the eventual Second Authority Law of 1990. The committee's findings were highly influenced by the concept of Independent Television as it appeared in the United Kingdom at the time. The first draft of the commercial television law was even entitled "The Independent Broadcasting Authority Law."

The Kubersky report concluded that the time was ripe for a second channel in Israel and that this commercial enterprise should be established independently of the IBA. However, the committee believed the new television channel should follow the same cultural guidelines as the IBA and should be structured in such a way as to minimize financial hardships that had the potential to affect the print media and movie theaters.

When the Knesset was legislating the Second Authority Law of 1990, it chose to create a new list of cultural obligations. Article 5 of the law states that

> a. The roles of the Authority will be to maintain the broadcasts and supervise them, and this in the fields of learning, education, entertainment, and information on the subjects of policy, society, economics, culture, science, art and sports.
> b. In fulfilling its obligations the Authority will act in order to
>   1. Promote Hebrew and Israeli creativity;
>   2. Propagate good citizenship and strengthen the values of democracy and humanism;
>   3. Give expression to Jewish heritage and its values and to the values of Zionism;
>   4. Give expression to the culture of the nations, the human work of art, and the values of civilization over the generations;
>   5. Broadcast in Arabic for the needs of the Arabic-speaking population and for the advancement of understanding and peace with the neighboring states, according to the basic course set by the State;
>   6. Give expression to the cultural diversity of Israeli society and the different points of view in society;
>   7. Broadcast reliable, fair, and balanced information;
>   8. Maintain broadcasting aimed at providing education to the public at large and to specific populations;
>   9. Maintain broadcasting in foreign languages for new immigrants and tourists;
>   10. Prevent forbidden broadcasts according to this law.

The fact that different roles were assigned to the IBA and to the Second Authority may be explained by the passage of time or by the fact that commercial broadcasting was seen as inherently different from *mamlakhti* broadcasting or, most probably, by a combination of the two. A comparison of the texts of the two laws shows that the policymakers of 1990 were more open to and more aware of the "outside world" but still wanted to maintain clear divisions between Jews and "Arabs." This trend also emerges in the changes inserted in 2000 to the Mamlakhti Education Law, as noted in chapter 2. Table 5.2 illustrates these differences.

In the 1990 law, the order of cultural obligations was rearranged (although this has been corrected in the table). Instead of starting with the "life of the State" and the other obligations regarding broadcast content, the list starts with the requirement that broadcasters promote local production. This can be attributed to a shift in the role policymakers assigned to television—from that of a mobilized medium in the service

Table 5.2. Comparison of Goals of the Israeli Broadcasting Authority and the Second Authority

Broadcasting Authority (1965)

(2) To promote Hebrew and Israeli creativity

(b) To propagate good citizenship

(c)(c) To strengthen the ~~knowledge heritage and its ways, of~~ connection with Jewish heritage and its <u>values</u> and to deepen its knowledge

(a) ~~To reflect the life, creation, achievements, and struggle of the State~~

(3) To provide broadcasts in the Arabic language for the needs of the Arabic-speaking population and for the advancement of understanding and peace with neighboring states according to the basic course set by the State

(d) To ~~reflect the lives~~ and cultural assets of all the tribes of the nation from different countries and different points of view in society

(Article 4) The Authority will make certain that in the broadcasts an appropriate expression will be given to different ideas and points of view existing in the public and that balanced information will be broadcast

(e) To ~~expand~~ education and distribute knowledge

(g) ~~To enhance the aims of *mamlakhti* education as described in the Mamlakhti Education Law of 1953~~

(f) ~~To reflect the life of the Jews in the Diaspora~~

(5) ~~To maintain broadcasting to the Jews of the Diaspora~~

(6) ~~To broadcast abroad~~

Second Authority (1990)

(1) To promote Hebrew and Israeli creativity

(2) To propagate good citizenship <u>and strengthen the values of democracy and humanism</u>

(3) ~~to and to deepen the knowledge of~~ to give expression to Jewish heritage and values <u>and the values of Zionism</u>

(4) <u>To give expression to the culture of the nations, the human work of art, and the values of civilization over the generations</u>

(5) To provide broadcasts in the Arabic language for the needs of the Arabic-speaking population and for the advancement of understanding and peace with neighboring states according to the basic course set by the State

(6) To <u>give expression</u> to the cultural <u>diversity of Israeli Society</u>

(7) To broadcast reliable, fair, and balanced information

(8) To maintain broadcasting aimed at <u>providing</u> education to the public at large and to specific populations
~~To enhance the aims of *mamlakhti* education as described in the Mamlakhti Education Law of 1953~~

(9) <u>To maintain broadcasting in foreign languages for new immigrants and tourists</u>

(10) <u>To prevent forbidden broadcasts according to this law</u>

Note: Underlining indicates text that was not present in the draft legislation.

of government to a cultural medium in the service of human creativity and art. In other words, the underlying theory of mass media presented here is cultural rather than the "effects" approach the government articulated in the 1960s. More proof of this change can be found in language differences. In 1965, the IBA was instructed to "reflect" aspects of society, whereas in 1990, the commercial channel was asked to "give expression" to them. Broadcasting, as perceived in the 1990 law, is not only a way of documenting reality, it is also a forum for cultural expression and creativity. The long list of social and cultural goals in the 1990 law, however, minimizes the significance of this change.

Unlike *mamlakhti* television, which was seen as a mouthpiece for the state, policymakers in 1990 viewed commercial television as a proper industry. The 1990 Second Authority Law also shows more openness to the world than the Broadcasting Authority Law. Here again, it can be argued that this change in approach reflects the role of the specific medium—commercial versus public. Taking a more historical perspective, however, it appears that the siege mentality that influenced policy in 1965 had given way to a more cosmopolitan approach by 1990, one more open to the world and to foreign influences that reflected the changes in Israeli society during this period.

These changes are also evident in various textual changes made in the Second Authority Law, such as the transition from the desire to reflect the "life of the state" to give expression to "the culture of nations" and a shift from promoting values of Judaism to promoting the more secular values of Zionism. The values of democracy and humanism were added to those of good citizenship, providing a more Western-oriented slant. Even more noteworthy are the two changes in the law's reference to "the nation." First, the heritage of different demographic groups in Israeli society, according to the 1990 law, was to be "expressed" rather than reflected, as in the 1965 law. Second, the reference in the Second Authority Law to "Israeli society" instead seems to imply that lawmakers had a larger role in mind for the non-Jewish members of society. Indeed, when the IBA law was voted on in 1965, MK Moshe Unna, who presented the legislation, explained the addition of the "tribes of the nation" as a reference only to the diversity of the Jewish nation (Knesset Records, 8 March 1965, 1450). This provides further proof that the textual changes in the law between 1965 and 1990 not only reflected different approaches to the various media but, even more important, reflected changes in the value systems of the lawmakers. Still, the paternalistic and narrow reference in the 1990 law to the "Arabic-speaking population" is a verbatim repetition of the reference made to this group in the Broadcasting Authority Law. While there may have been lawmakers in 1990 that recognized the need to provide expression over the airwaves to non-Jews, the majority still referred to this demographic group in the archaic terms used in 1965—as a linguistic minority who had the potential to become an enemy from within.

One vital difference between the two laws concerns Diaspora Jewry. The Broadcasting Authority Law included a requirement that the IBA broadcast to Diaspora Jews and reflect their culture in local broadcasting; these requirements were omitted from the Second Authority Law. Indeed, it would seem natural to require a *mamlakhti* broadcaster to broadcast to Jews in other countries but unjustified to require commercial broadcasters to broadcast noncommercial programs, especially in the service of the state. The omission of the requirement that broadcasters depict life in the Diaspora in the Second Authority Law illustrated another cultural change affecting Israeli society: foreign influences were beginning to be considered desirable, whereas the portrayal of Jewish life in foreign countries was beginning to lose relevance for Jews in Israel.

The Second Authority Law was enacted with a general "forbidden broadcasts" clause, Article 46, of which subsection (a)(2) states that "a franchisee will not broadcast programs, which contain . . . (2) incitement to racism, discrimination, or actual damage to a person or a group of people, on the basis of their belonging to a religion, race, nationality, gender, ethnic group, lifestyle, or origin." This and the other provisions of Article 46, which include a ban on broadcasts that are illegal and a ban on partisan or election campaign materials, apply, according to Article 86(1), to the content of advertising as well. In 1994, the Second Authority published regulations regarding both programming and advertising.[6] The programming regulations created by the Second Authority Council, which were designed to regulate the daily functioning of the television station that began broadcasting in November 1993, were more specific about defining forbidden broadcasts than the Second Authority Law. Among the prohibitions regarding advertising, the Second Authority banned broadcasting of advertisements on Memorial Day, Memory of the Holocaust and the Heroism Day, and Tisha B'Av.

What was initially unique about commercial (as opposed to public) broadcasting policy in Israel was the quota system imposed to ensure a minimum share of local Israeli production in the broadcasts. Sections 59 and 60 of the 1990 law read:

> 59. At least one-third of total television broadcasts shall be of local production; but the Authority will act in order to enlarge the share of

television broadcasts of local production, including within the initial franchise period.

60. At least one-half of broadcasts allotted to local productions, according to sections 55 and 59, will be of purchased local production and [will be] according to the rules of the council.

The quota system, which first appeared in the Kubersky Committee's report, is common practice in European nations and appears prominently in the European Union's broadcasting treaty, known as the Television without Frontiers Directive. Initially, the Israeli rules, like their European counterparts, defined "production" very vaguely. The cultural defense mechanism this quota system was meant to create did not attempt to improve the quality of programming; it only tried to maintain a certain quantity of programming. While it may seem, then, that Sections 59 and 60 were inserted to serve the broadcasting industry financially rather than culturally or linguistically, this was clearly not the intent of the Kubersky Committee report, which stated that "the broadcasts should contain a proper ratio of Israeli and Jewish original works of art. The Authority will, periodically, enact rules on this" (Kubersky 1979, 40).

The lawmakers chose to fix this rate themselves rather than leaving it to the Second Authority. They eliminated the words "Jewish" and "Israeli," leaving just the word "local," which refers to the place of production rather than the content of broadcasts, and replaced the phrase "work of art" (which can also be translated as "creativity") with the less-demanding term "production." However, content intervention seemed more evident in the following requirement of commercial broadcasters in Article 55 of the Second Authority Law. Indeed, this is a uniquely Israeli requirement.

> 55. (a) The council will grant Instructional Television, without a bid, a franchise for television broadcasts for the first franchising term [of six years], as is defined in article 34(b). Such a franchise will be given for a broadcasting unit in the scope of one-seventh of the total broadcasting units, for instructional-educational subjects only, and in hours in which the population for whom they are directed watch . . .
>
> (c) At least one-half of the total of Instructional Television broadcasts will consist of local production as defined in article 58.

Caspi and Limor (1992, 123) describe in detail how this provision evolved as a purely political compromise between the ministers of education and communication at the time the law was drafted in the mid-1980s. However, the idea of allotting time for broadcasts of Instructional Television and the Open University had already been conceived of in the Kubersky Committee report.[7] This provision, which provides the government, through the education ministry, with broadcast time in a commercial enterprise, again suggests that lawmakers might not have internalized the fact that the new venture was of a different character than the IBA. Indeed, this provision became a bone of contention between Instructional Television, the franchise holders, and the Second Authority, eventually leading Instructional Television to petition the Supreme Court and argue that the one-seventh of broadcasting time it was awarded was not a "formal seventh" (a technical term that can be quantified in total hours) but rather a "fundamental seventh" (a value statement that one-seventh of all programming at all times should be of an educational nature). Thus, they claimed, they were entitled to broadcast during prime time in order to reach a broad audience and be able to fund Instructional Television operations through the greater income that would be achieved by selling advertising for prime-time hours (*Israeli Instructional Television v. The Second Authority* [1999]).

The court was not convinced by Instructional Television's claim that its target audience included adults as well as children and pointed out that there are differences between a government broadcaster and a commercial one. It ruled that the Second Authority's decision to limit instructional broadcasts to the afternoon hours was reasonable.

The law was only an authorizing platform for the Second Authority it established. The Second Authority Council created detailed rules to regulate the daily functioning of the television station, which began broadcasting in November 1993. The rules were particularly cumbersome with regard to establishing quotas for local productions and defining forbidden broadcasts.

In 1992, the council broadened the mandate of the commercial broadcaster beyond the wording of Article 5 of the law to include the following provision:

"[The franchisee] will give expression in its broadcasts to the varied cultural texture of Israel, to the interests of all the citizens of Israel in all the areas of the country and all the patterns of settlement, to the variety of lifestyles, standards of living, education, occupation, culture and religious beliefs of the citizens of Israel."[8]

The way to achieve these ambitious goals, according to the regulations, was to maintain quotas of a variety of genres of programs. Regulation 10(a) stated that approximately one-third of the broadcasts should include programs in each of the following general categories: information, sports, and current affairs; drama; and entertainment. What is striking is that little emphasis was put on broadcasting news. By making sports part of the information and current affairs genre rather than part of the entertainment genre, where it rightfully belongs, the franchises were gently dissuaded from providing the public with what would be considered hard news. Putting current affairs together with the information genre seemed to make soft news as legitimate as hard news, and soft news competed with hard news for the same time slot.

IBA in the 1990s: Local Production Quotas, Diversity, and the National Myth

In 1996, the IBA law was amended as part of an overhaul of media laws, and for the first time, a requirement that the IBA broadcast a quota of locally produced programs and programs produced by independent producers was enacted.[9] The law required the IBA to allot a minimum of 40 percent of its broadcasting time for "local productions," defined as television programs produced for broadcasting in Israel and whose production team consists mostly of Israelis. In addition, the IBA was required to spend at least 30 percent of its production budget each year on purchasing "production services" from providers outside the IBA. In this vein, the Knesset passed the Law for Support of Songs in the Hebrew Language in 1998, which requires that at least half the songs broadcast on the IBA radio stations each month be "songs in the Hebrew language," defined as songs for which the majority of the words are in Hebrew.[10]

Interestingly (or paradoxically), in 1996, the Knesset passed two laws aimed at strengthening two Jewish languages of the Diaspora threatened by extinction: Yiddish, spoken by Jews of Ashkenazi descent, and Ladino, spoken by Jews of Sephardic descent (but not necessarily by all Mizrahi Jews). The National Authority for Ladino Culture and the National Authority for Yiddish Culture were founded on the same day.[11] Representatives of the IBA were to serve on the boards of each of these new authorities. The need to involve the IBA in these two institutions says a lot about the cultural preferences of policymakers in the 1990s regarding public service (or rather *mamlakhti*) broadcasting.[12] But while involving the IBA in the preservation of these distinct languages illustrates an acceptance of the diversity of the Jewish community and of the role of the Diaspora in national culture, it would be difficult to argue that this openness to the Diaspora experience was a guiding motto of Israeli policymakers, as the requirements for local production and Hebrew-language songs attest. The Hannah Senesz case provides further proof that these requirements were intended to serve the dominant and hegemonic national culture.

SENESZ V. BROADCASTING AUTHORITY

Several days before she was caught, tortured, and executed by Nazi forces in Hungary, Hannah Senesz, a 23-year-old Jewish paratrooper deployed from pre-state Israel to gather intelligence information behind enemy lines in her former homeland, wrote a poem that paid tribute to a metaphorical match that lit a flame in the hearts of those who died "in dignity." It was later found among her belongings and together with other poems she had written as well as her personal diary led to her coronation as one of the prominent icons of the Zionist narrative. Her story contained many of the key elements of this narrative: courage, defiance, determination, sacrifice, and commitment to Jews in the Diaspora. Senesz was a source of vindication for her fellow Zionists, who were accused of indifference to the plight of Diaspora Jewry during the Holocaust. Her decision to leave the Zionist homeland in order to help save her Hungarian brethren provided evidence that not all Zionists were so indifferent about Diaspora Jews. In her personal act of self-sacrifice, Senesz came to symbolize both the "sabra-esque" Israeli heroine and the Jewish heroine (Baumel 1996). Further proof of her iconic stature can be seen in the decision to transport her remains from Hungary for reburial in the national military cemetery on Mt. Herzl in Jerusalem in what was the first official high-level military funeral held in the newly established State of Israel in 1949 (Baumel 2002).

The story of Senesz meshes well, therefore, with the *mamlakhti* interpretation of the meaning of the Holocaust in the Zionist experience. Yet her story and her legacy are at the center of a controversy over a docudrama produced in Israel in the mid-1990s. The fact that it was dragged into the debate on the role of broadcasting as a purveyor of the national culture makes it a good case for demonstrating the theme of this study.

In 1994, the IBA aired a three-part docudrama that purportedly depicted the events surrounding the criminal libel trial of Malchiel Grunwald in the 1950s, better known as the Kasztner trial. Grunwald, a little-known publisher of an even-lesser-known newspaper, claimed that Rudolph Kasztner, a former leader of Hungarian Jewry and in the 1950s a high-ranking member of the ruling Mapai Party, had collaborated with the Nazis in occupied Hungary in the 1940s in order to save himself as well as his friends and relatives. Under immense political pressure from Mapai ministers, the attorney general filed criminal libel charges against Grunwald. The trial challenged the established interpretation of certain events surrounding the Holocaust by pointing an accusing finger at Rudolph Kasztner (Lahav 1997) and addressed the role played by Jews who were able to save their own lives and those of their next of kin by purportedly cooperating with the Nazis during World War II. Indeed, the outcome of this trial—Grunwald's acquittal—was so traumatic that it led to the resignation of Prime Minister Moshe Sharett (Hecht 1961/1967; Weitz 1996) and motivated Attorney General Gideon Hausner, the chief prosecutor in the trial of Nazi war criminal Adolph Eichmann, several years later, to "create a narrative of heroic memory" (Douglass 2001, 156) in the design of his arguments and questioning of the witnesses.

One scene of the television docudrama *The Kasztner Trial* suggested that Senesz may have broken down under torture and betrayed two of her fellow paratroopers. As the libel trial at the center of the drama unfolds, Kasztner, a tragic figure in both the real trial (in which he served only as a witness) and the docudrama, grows increasingly desperate. When Katerina Senesz, Hannah's mother, takes the witness stand in the televised drama and testifies that Kasztner did not assist her daughter while she was being held captive by the Nazis before her execution, Kasztner interjects and accuses Senesz of breaking down during her interrogation and betraying her fellow paratroopers, a scene that never took place in real life. The Kasztner trial's reincarnation on television forty years later not only opened old wounds but aggravated them by suggesting that the mythic Senesz may have been a traitor or, at minimum, far less heroic than had been assumed by her countrymen.

Not only Senesz's family but the entire Israeli establishment fought the attempt to rewrite Senesz's role in the Zionist narrative; Yad Vashem, the national Holocaust memorial authority, decided to join as a petitioner in the suit against the IBA. The Israeli Supreme Court conformed with this effort. *The Kasztner Trial* was a docudrama, or, as the author writes in the introduction to the script, "a fictitious drama inspired by events that actually took place" (Lerner 1995). However, the author also noted that "the depiction of these events obviously necessitates many diversions from the real events. . . . The script provides an interpretation of highly controversial events, and clearly, many readers and viewers will choose to see in it an intervention in the chronicles of history" (11). In their petition, Hannah Senesz's brother, Giora Senesz; his sons; the deputy chairman of Yad Vashem; and others demanded that this extremely short scene be deleted from the program (*Senesz v. Broadcasting Authority* [1999]).

The court's 2 to 1 decision to allow the docudrama to be broadcast in its entirety was delivered a few days after the petition was filed and on the day the program was aired, but the opinion of the court was not made public until nearly five years later. The majority opinion, written by Chief Justice Aharon Barak with the support of Justice Eliahu Matza, maintained that preserving the dominant interpretation of Zionism was a matter of public interest. Barak noted in the opinion that the controversial scene damaged both Senesz's reputation and "the myth that surrounds it" (section 12 of *Senesz v. Broadcasting Authority* [1999]). He agreed that the public interest, which deserves constitutional safeguards, is not a predefined and constant term and that it reflects society's credo and expresses its interests from the collective viewpoint. These interests include propagating cultural values, art, and language; preserving language as a national tool for expression and as a cultural value; being attuned to the public's desire to promote social tolerance; preserving historical continuity; respecting national values; and preserving historical truths. Barak acknowledged that the controversial scene was untrue and had damaged the "myth of Hannah Senesz" (a phrase repeated in sections 4, 12, 18, 22, and 27 of the verdict) and hurt the public's feelings, thereby betraying the public interest. He noted, however, that when the values of freedom of speech and creativity conflict with the public interest, the former supersede the latter. The circumstances under which the court may intervene in editorial decisions taken by the IBA, Barak noted, had already been established in the *Pillar of Fire* case, namely, in extreme circumstances that include clear and present danger to the public safety or unambiguous illegality of content. When what is at issue, on the other hand, are hurt feelings, wrote Barak, the degree of pain should be so great that it "shakes the foundations of mutual tolerance in a democratic society," and since that would not be true in this case, the program should be broadcast as planned.

In the dissenting minority opinion, Justice Mishael Cheshin argued that it was not the IBA's right to freedom of speech that was being challenged but that of the creator of the program. He noted in his opinion that docudrama has a powerful effect on its audiences, going on to explain that a docudrama mixes fact and fiction, thereby misleading the audience about accepted historical truths. Because the creator of this docudrama distorted historical facts, Cheshin argued, his right to freedom of expression was limited, especially when it was weighed against the indisputable right of Senesz to maintain her good name. Two individual rights were in dispute, argued Cheshin: the author's right to free speech and Senesz's right to protect her good name. Since the author was not telling the historical truth, her right superseded his. It emerged that despite their dissenting opinions, Cheshin and Barak were in agreement about the myth and its significance. Cheshin even quoted from Senesz's poetry and described her in superlatives derived from the prevailing narrative about her life and death. Their only disagreement was over whether upholding the myth was in the public's interest or in the interest of the mythologized person.

Thus, while Israel in the 1990s seemed to be embracing a more deregulatory neoliberal approach to commercial broadcasting, both the Knesset and the Supreme Court seemed to agree that the *mamlakhti* broadcaster should remain the cultural torchbearer and that the cultural message it conveys should have a traditional Zionist slant. The 2000s ushered in a new frenzy of activity in cultural obligations and regulation, this time aimed at commercial broadcasters as well.

The 2000s: Reaffirming the Commitment to Local Production

The early 2000s saw the launching of Channel 10, a commercial channel designed much like Channel 2 that was given identical cultural obligations.[13] The launching of the channel was introduced as part of the omnibus bill that serves as the annual add-on to the national budget.[14] As a result, policymakers explained in the accompanying memorandum that the main objective of the new channel was to achieve an economic goal, which was to expand the choice of over-the-air television while lowering the price of advertising on television. However, the introduction of this new channel provided regulators and legislators with an opportunity for cultural soul-searching.

The issue of the content and cultural obligations of commercial broadcasters came up in the debate that emerged in the Knesset Finance Committee (which was charged with preparing the law since it was being discussed as part of the omnibus bill) because the bill seemed to propose that the license would be awarded to the highest bidder while content obligations would play a minor role. The committee chairman, MK Eli Goldschmidt, expressed the following concern to the finance ministry representative who was present at the debate: "There is a will in the committee to prevent Americanization of the channels. We know that in the United States as well the standard of programming is terrible. How do you as a regulator ensure this, not as a censor, not as a commissar?" (Knesset Finance Committee Records, 24 January 2000, 23). He proposed inserting into the law the general terms of the tender to give more weight to the content requirements than to monetary considerations (27).

In response to the chairman's request, the government introduced in the next meeting a detailed list of program types—genres—that would be required of the new franchise and included them in an appendix to the legislation that would be approved by the Knesset. The communication minister's adviser said that there was no precedent in Israeli media law for the "exact quotas" fixed by law (Knesset Finance Committee Records,

3 February 2000, 4). In addition, in order to win the support of the Knesset members, the new law raised the share of original (local) productions required of the new channel to 40 percent of its total programming and included among the criteria that the Second Authority needed to consider in the tender process both the number of original productions offered and the number of programs dedicated to content produced in "the periphery." The same "goals of the state" identified in the expert and committee reports of the early 1960s, which included both the resurrection of the Hebrew language and the dispersion of the population, had found their way into commercial television regulation of the 2000s!

The law enacting Channel 10 included a very detailed list of program requirements imposed on commercial television broadcasters. According to the law, commercial broadcasters must broadcast between 7 p.m. and 12 A.M. on all weekdays, providing a minimum of 74 hours of "elite genre" programs on Channel 2 and 111 hours on Channel 10. An "elite genre" program was defined as one of the following three:

1. "documentary program"—a program that documents social, political, or cultural phenomena; natural phenomena; or scientific discoveries that is not a program on current affairs
2. "drama program"—a program containing a comic, dramatic, melodramatic, tragic, or other plot belonging to one of the following groups:
    - single drama—a single-episode drama or a drama that is part of a miniseries that includes both indoor and outdoor footage usually and is at least fifty minutes long
    - docudrama—a drama portraying real characters or events that strives to reconstruct those characters or events, remaining as loyal as possible to evidence and documents portraying them
    - drama series—a drama consisting of a few episodes, each at least twenty-four minutes long
    - made-for-television film—a program reminiscent of an individual drama, but usually, at least 80 minutes long and with a script requiring outdoor footage
3. "special program"—a program of a special format and special value whose quality, acting, and directing the Second Authority deems to be of exceptional quality, including the following types:
    - a program of high-quality skits at least fifteen minutes long
    - a program with an original and innovative format at least fifteen minutes long;
    - a single drama, docudrama, or drama series, all at least thirty minutes long

In addition, the appendix to the law stipulates that franchise holders in both Channel 2 and Channel 10 should dedicate a minimum of 5 percent of their total weekly broadcasting time to a variety of programs in Arabic or Russian or translated into Arabic or Russian. This provision was said to be a response to requests raised during the debate in the Knesset Finance Committee to fulfill the cultural needs of the speakers of both these languages. In fact, however, the committee relaxed the existing requirements imposed on commercial broadcasters, at least in the case of Arabic.

After these amendments were inserted into the law, and once Channel 10 was launched and a new tender for Channel 2 was issued, the Second Authority rewrote its content regulations in 2002, amending the original 1992 regulations.[15] The section devoted to the "character of the broadcasts" (Section 8 in the 1992 regulations; Section 6 in the 2002 regulations) deserves the most attention, as it illustrates how Israeli regulators viewed commercial broadcasting after the amendments to the law.

Table 5.3 shows that Israeli regulators are no less intent today than they were forty years ago on exploiting broadcasting for ideological purposes. Not only do these cumbersome regulations show that policymakers perceived commercial broadcasting under public supervision to be a form of public broadcasting, but they also reveal some of their ideological biases, as these examples demonstrate:

- In subsection 1, the Second Authority adds the words "through its total spread of programs" to the requirement to reach a maximum number of viewers. As will be further demonstrated in the rules regarding radio and cable television, this provision calls for using what is perceived to be public broadcasting to create cultural ghettos, albeit tacitly and unofficially. While one of the goals for commercial broadcasting was to reach the largest audience possible in the old regulations, the new regulations sought to maximize the size of the audience not by creating one program that would appeal to all audiences but rather by creating different programs that would appeal to different audiences.
- The Second Authority added a new goal in 2002: "expressing . . . the core of Israeli essence, the Israeli-Jewish discourse." This addition can be interpreted in two ways: either that the core of Israeli essence is the Israeli-Jewish discourse or that the core of Israeli essence and Jewish-Israeli discourse are separate goals. "Jewish-Israeli discourse" is listed ahead of other elements that can be seen as part of the "core of Israeli essence," including "Israel's diverse cultural texture" and the diverse "religious beliefs" of Israeli citizens. Whatever the case may be, these regulations created a new tier of communications,

Table 5.3. Broadcast Obligations of Franchise Holders in Israel in the Second Authority for Television and Radio Regulations (Television Programs Broadcast by a Franchise Holder), 1992 and 2002

Second Authority Regulations 1992
(1) will broadcast programs of a wide as possible variety of types and topics and for a varied target audience, considering the viewing habits of the various target audiences while attempting to reach a maximum number of viewers
(2) will broadcast programs in different areas including the areas of learning, education, entertainment, culture, art and folklore and information on issues of policy, society, economics, culture, science, art, sports, folklore, religion, history and so on
(3) will give expression in its broadcasts to the varied cultural fabric of Israel, to the interests of all the citizens of Israel in all the areas of the country and all the patterns of settlement and to the variety of lifestyles, standards of living, education, occupation, culture, and religious beliefs of the citizens of Israel and will express the goals of the Authority outlined in section 5(b) of the Law and the policy of the Authority as prescribed from time to time
(4) will give expression in its broadcasts to the interest areas of defined groups within the population, such as pensioners, the handicapped, children, adults and exceptional people
(5) will ensure that its broadcasts fit their target audience, without lessening its commitment to ensure their quality

Second Authority Regulations 2002
(1) will broadcast programs of a wide as possible variety of types and topics and for a varied target audience, considering the viewing <u>and leisure</u> habits of the various target audiences while attempting to reach <u>through its total spread of</u> <u>programs to a maximum number of viewers, without lessening its commitment to ensure their quality</u>
(2) will broadcast programs in different areas including the areas of learning, education, entertainment, culture, art and folklore and information on issues of policy, society, economics, culture, science, art, sports, folklore, religion, history and so on
(3) will give expression in its broadcasts to <u>the core of Israeli essence, the Israeli-Jewish discourse,</u> the varied cultural fabric of Israel in all the areas of the country and all the patterns of settlement, <u>to the unique issues of the different areas of the country, including programs broadcast from these areas,</u> to the variety of lifestyles, standards of living, education, occupation, culture, and religious beliefs of the citizens of Israel
(4) will give <u>adequate</u> expression in its broadcasts to <u>Jews and Arabs, immigrants and old-timers, will attend a variety of audiences, tastes and ethnicities, and will engage in</u> the interest areas of defined groups within the population, such as pensioners, the handicapped, children, adults and exceptional people
(5) <u>will work to integrate in its broadcasts the best forces of cultural creativity in Israel, in productions that include innovativeness and originality aside with the best of the television and motion picture tradition</u>
(6) will express the goals of the Authority outlined in section 5(b) of the Law, and the policy of the Authority as prescribed from time to time

Note: Underlined text indicates language that was not present in the 1992 regulations.

that of discourse, although they limited this discourse to Israeli Jews. This follows the 1990 law, which transformed television from a form of one-way broadcasting to a means of "providing expression." This reference to "discourse" also comes up in subsection 4, which refers to "giving expression," the list here including "Arabs and Jews" as well as "immigrants and old-timers." From this it is clear that the reference to "Israeli-Jewish" in the previous section is neither co-incidental nor accidental and is meant to limit "discourse" to that particular group. Although others have an opportunity to be exposed to media, they do not have an opportunity to engage in discourse.

- Subsection 4 further demonstrates the Second Authority's "ghet-toized" view of Israeli society in its juxtaposition of "Arabs and Jews" and "immigrants and old-timers" as parallel dyads that are inherently different, underscoring the belief of policymakers that broadcasting should maintain this stereotypical dissonance by expressing it rather than by overcoming it through discourse.
- Subsection 4 further refers to other groups in society viewed as "inferior." They include pensioners, the handicapped, children, adults, and the "exceptional." These groups are referred to in the context of "interests" the broadcasts should serve. They are not listed in the paragraph stating who should have the right to "express" themselves. Only "Jews and Arabs" and "immigrants and newcomers" had that right. The terms "adults" and "exceptional people" need to be understood here in their cultural context. The words "exceptional people" refer to the exceptionally different rather than to the exceptionally talented (as they are likely to be understood in the English language). As for the adults," their inclusion in this section can either be seen as neutral, juxtaposed against "children," or as a euphemism for old people. Since all the other groups in this list—"handicapped," "pensioners," "children," and "exceptional"—are stereotypically weaker elements of the population, the latter meaning of "old people" was probably the intent.
- Subsection 5 simply reiterates the main characteristic of the regulation of culture as it refers to both broadcasting and cablecasting: the promotion and support of local production in defense of the national culture.

These attempts by policymakers to turn content obligations into law and to tighten up regulations met some practical obstacles when they were implemented. When Channel 10 failed to meet its regulatory obligations, the Knesset responded with two measures. On the one hand, it passed an amendment to the Second Authority Law stipulating that if the Channel 10 licensee was able to meet its legal obligations between 1 November 2003, and 27 January 2004, it would be as if it had met its obligations for the previous two years.[16] At the same time, the Knesset enacted a new appendix to the law, only this time, instead of requiring minimum hours of programming, it required the franchisees to commit funding to purchase and produce programs and to commit a specific sum to the production of "elite genre" programs. The amount of funding was calculated as a percentage of the net income of each channel or as a minimum sum, whichever was the higher of the two.

This is further evidence that legislators were not about to let themselves get swept away with the new neoliberal trend of deregulation, at least as far as supervision of content was involved. Indeed, subsequent legislation allowed Channel 10 to delay meeting its obligations for another few years.[17] But the detailed definitions of what represents the "elite" genre, as opposed to what does not, have become an integral part of the Israeli legal code.

The IBA was further weakened in the early 2000s in the context of growing political instability. Between the assassination of Prime Minister Yitzhak Rabin on 4 November 1995 and March 2006, general elections were called five times. Just as many committees and task forces were appointed to reform the IBA. In the 1990s, two major committees, the Livni Committee, headed by former director-general of the IBA Yitzhak Livni, and the Zuckerman Committee, headed by former director of IBA television Arnon Zuckerman, were appointed to present recommendations for restructuring the IBA. The Livni Committee was appointed by the Rabin government and the Zuckerman Committee by the government headed by Benjamin Netanyahu. In 1999, Prime Minister Ehud Barak appointed a one-person task force, retired general Raphael Vardi, to propose solutions for the problems afflicting the public broadcaster, and in 2000, the minister of culture, science, and sports, who was serving under Barak, appointed the Beresheet Committee, headed by Professor Haim Beresheet of Sapir College, to do the same.[18] The recommendations of the Dinur Committee, headed by Director-General Ra'anan Dinur of the Ministry of Industry, Trade and Employment and appointed by Prime Minister Ariel Sharon's government in 2003 to recommend needed reforms in the IBA, were the only ones among this long list of committees that were accepted by the government, which adopted them "in principle" in October 2005.[19] But no real steps have been taken to suggest that they will ever be implemented, and in July 2007, the IBA itself announced that it was adopting another plan for restructuring that had been recommended by a consulting firm it had hired. Most of the recommendations of the Dinur Committee were designed to loosen the government's hold on the IBA by stripping it of its authority to appoint the broadcaster's different functionaries, although the report did recommend that the government and the Knesset maintain control over the IBA's budget. Even so, the Dinur Committee's recommendations illustrate a new thinking among Israel's policymakers about the eventual role they foresaw for Israeli media. In the final version of the report, the committee wrote that public broadcasting is an essential element of democracy because it "provides expression to the centrality of the individual and as part of the public, and to the relationships between a person with himself and with his fellow person" (Dinur 2005, 7). Although the report illustrates the traditional patronizing attitude toward Israel's Palestinian minority and a chauvinistic approach to society, as will be discussed in chapter 8, it also expresses a shift in focus in Israeli values from the collective to the individual. In 2007, the Knesset passed a new IBA bill based on the Dinur Committee's recommendations in first reading and the IBA itself started a restructuring effort based on its own assessment of its needs.

6 Cable and Satellite

While the regulation of the cultural obligations of broadcasting focuses on direct content obligations, the regulation of the cultural obligations of cable television can be further achieved by innovative structural design of the cable service. As Turow (1992, 28) and Napoli (2001, 15) explain, the impact of technical and structural regulations on content can be as important as specific content regulations. In the case of regulating the Israeli cable industry, the development of policy and the transition it has made took place on both the content-specific and structural levels. Policymakers used a bi-level approach and made many changes in policy over a relatively short period of time. Multichannel television regulation went through four different structural phases, each of which had a different cultural emphasis, until its current format emerged. This complex development took place in a short time; cable television was not introduced until the third stage of development of Israeli electronic media, in the mid-1980s. It may very well be that the resounding success of cable television in Israel, which had not been anticipated, and the paradigm to which policymakers subscribed, which focused on the powerful effects of television on Israeli culture, led them to design this service so that it would serve a cultural agenda. During the mid-1980s and the early 2000s, however, their own cultural agenda kept changing.

This chapter analyzes the historical and political roots of the cultural policies behind cable television regulation in Israel based on the blueprint provided by the Barsela Committee (see chapter 3). It shows that Israeli policymakers used cable television as a tool to promote their view of Israeli society and that they redesigned this policy repeatedly to accommodate changes in the political landscape and the way it reflected changes in Israeli society. Unlike the case of broadcasting, where we can attribute changes in the cultural preferences of lawmakers and policymakers to the introduction of new media outlets, in the case of cable television—at least until the appearance of direct broadcast satellite, the fourth and last stage—policy changes did not stem from technological change but from shifts in the cultural (and political) balance of power in the country. Still, the forces that influenced changes in broadcasting policies in the 1980s are evident in Israeli cable policies in the early 2000s, illustrating that the cultural understandings and power structure in Israeli society were similar in both time periods.

Four Stages of Cable Television Policy

Three stages of cable television policy can be identified during the period that spans a little more than the ten years after cable television was introduced and before the fourth stage of policy began, which started with the launching of direct broadcast satellite: the national unity stage, followed by the market-driven stage (which included a minimal "cultural" element that served the hegemonic sense of national unity), and finally, the multicultural stage. The introduction of direct multichannel satellite television did not change the basic cultural policy because the government continued to focus on devising the proper formula to generate competition. In this final stage, during which direct broadcast satellite was introduced, the government maintained "multicultural" policies with a new emphasis on local production and further attempts to sideline the Palestinian minority. Throughout its evolution, cable television policy in Israel has placed considerable emphasis on the effect of mass media, as illustrated explicitly and implicitly in policy documents, drafts, laws, and regulations. The government had repeatedly cited the effect of cable television on Israeli society as a rationale for its policies. It may be argued, then, that cable television policy in Israel, just like the nation's broadcast television policy, is a form of social regulation.

The First Stage: Preserving National Unity

Historically, "national unity," the Ben Gurionist–Mapai Party ideal expressed through *mamlakhtiyut,* was a goal associated with big-party politics that was shared with the rival Beginist Likud Party. Cable television policy was initially designed to homogenize Israeli culture, as were policies in the fields of education, culture, and broadcasting. This typical approach in Israel's formative years was evident even in the initial policies concerning commercial media. Before cable television was established, it was considered to be merely a technological means for offering the public slightly more choice. As such, it was thought best to adopt an enhanced regional model, one that required future franchise holders to provide local communities with programs and production facilities, as was common in the United States when cable television was first regulated in the late 1960s and early 1970s (Parsons 2008). The initial recommendations of the Barsela Committee were taken into account in the first version of the Telecommunications Law relating to cable, which emphasized the regional role of cable television and prohibited cable television operators from broadcasting national programs.[1]

The 1986 Telecommunications Law created the Cable Broadcasting Council (CBC), whose role was to create and supervise the implementation of cable policies.[2] The CBC divided the country into thirty-one service areas and began awarding franchises in 1988. Cable television service began operating one year later. The service areas were awarded in pairs so the CBC could require franchise holders to provide cable television in less lucrative areas and thereby ensure cable service to the entire population. In practice, some adjoining areas were awarded to the same operator. For example, the two areas that were originally carved out of Tel Aviv were awarded to the same operator, as were the two areas that were originally carved out of Jerusalem. Eventually, all the areas were awarded to a total of five operators. The franchises were awarded for an initial period of twelve years, and in effect, the law did not create distinctions between operators and programmers, nor did it create effective barriers against cross-ownership and cartelization, despite the recommendation of the Barsela Committee that it do so.

Regulating the content of cable television is far more complicated than regulating the content of broadcast channels because of the quantity of material involved. The Barsela Committee recognized this difficulty and initially suggested that no more than nine channels should be carried via cable, demonstrating considerations that have by now become common among Israeli broadcasting policymakers: the fear that propaganda broadcasts will emanate from across Israel's borders and the desire to influence cultural programming.

The relatively large proportion of regional channels in this limited offering that were based on regional content or ownership (three of nine channels) introduced a notion of "localism" that was unknown in the Israeli media landscape before the emergence of local print weeklies in the 1980s. The idea here was not to serve or preserve "localism" (a major feature of media policy in the United States, for example) but rather to ensure the economic viability of the new media by basing them in local markets and allowing them to tap into the market for local advertising, which had not yet been fully exploited, thereby helping cable operators meet the costs of deploying infrastructure. Still, the decision to base a new service on "local" channels can also be seen as a way of preserving the dominance of the existing national channels, in this case the IBA's Channel 1, which was the only broadcast service in existence at the time. (The prohibition on broadcasting national news on cable channels, which has survived to this day, is discussed in chapter 4.)

The report of the Barsela Committee was so thorough it seems almost prophetic today. It recommended imposing a list of cultural obligations on franchise operators, under the assumption that they would not bother to produce programs on their own but would prefer to purchase them abroad (which is what eventually happened in the first stage). To limit the importation of programs, the committee recommended that the operators be required to:

- Provide communities with the hardware needed to create local productions
- Broadcast and produce local and community programs
- Give special attention to the needs of the Arabic-speaking population by creating designated channels or allotting specific broadcasting hours. (The committee warned, however, that these might not be the appropriate forums for raising issues considered "controversial," as will be further discussed in chapter 8.)
- Create a special fund for financing local programs
- Prohibit programs that might offend good taste or the principle of fairness, incite criminal activities, act in an offensive manner, emphasize violence and sex, include political or election propaganda, or encourage gambling
- Limit the number of foreign films broadcast

Thus, the same patronizing attitude evident in terrestrial broadcasting policies—toward the Israeli population in general and the Palestinian minority in particular—surfaced again in the 1980s with the introduction of cable television.

The CBC fulfilled the task of social regulation more vigorously than was required by law. Content regulation became the focus of its activities, and since 1987, it has drafted and redrafted a series of detailed regulations on content, some appearing in the format of rules published in the official register, known as *Rashumot*, and others published over the Internet when it became available. These regulations initially targeted the programming cartel created by the five local franchise operators and their refusal to create "tiered" groups of channels, as is common in Western countries. While it allowed the cartel to exist, the CBC demanded that franchise operators provide subscribers with a "super basic" service that would include five themed channels: family, movies, sports, children, and "culture."

The 1986 law limited the content obligations of the franchise operators to

- Broadcasting news and current affairs programs that concern only the franchise area
- Broadcasting a variety of movies and programs in the fields of entertainment, music, art, education, culture, and sports, while giving adequate expression to the topics and needs of the area
- Retransmitting all legal over-the-air radio and television broadcasts (the "must carry" provision)
- Refraining from selling advertising on their own channels during the first five years of the franchise
- Refraining from broadcasting films that had not been approved by the Film Censorship Board
- Refraining from broadcasting materials considered an abomination based on criminal law
- Refraining from broadcasting racist or nationalistic incitement
- Refraining from broadcasting political propaganda
- Providing the state with the right to determine the use of one-sixth of the total cable system capacity

The CBC defined the services offered by cable franchise operators in great detail. Indeed, the cultural obligations imposed on franchise owners were more numerous than those imposed on any of the broadcast media at the time. The regulations stipulated that a franchise operator had to provide a family channel, a children's channel, a sports channel, and a movie channel.[3] Each of these channels had to broadcast a minimum number of hours per week: 44 on the family channel, 21.5 on the children's channel, and 16 (not including live broadcasts) on the sports channel. In addition, operators had to broadcast at least ten first-run feature films on the movie channel.

However, the first stage of cable regulation went beyond setting quotas and broadcasting requirements. The regulations went as far as to define what "Israel's holidays" are and how they should be celebrated. These definitions have survived the eventual rewriting of the policies in subsequent years. According to the regulations, holidays include the two-day Jewish New Year, the Jewish Day of Atonement (Yom Kippur), the first and eighth days of the Feast of Tabernacles (Succoth), the first and seventh days of Passover (Pesach), the Feast of Pentecost (Shavuot), and Independence Day, as defined by the Independence Day Law of 1949. No other legislation has defined national holidays as broadly since the state's first week of independence.[4]

Franchise operators are not allowed to broadcast their own channels on the Day of Atonement and in the first version of cable regulations were required to broadcast the following on each of the other holidays:

- Thirty percent of all broadcasts on the family channel had to be first-run, locally produced, and self-made "holiday programs."
- The movie channel had to air at least one local production.
- Forty percent of all broadcasts on the children's channel had to be first-run, locally produced, and self-made "holiday programs."

These requirements were relaxed in 1996 to include a minimum of two hours of first-run original programming on each holiday and official memorial day.

The regulations included special rules regarding "memorial days," which were defined as the Holocaust and Heroism Memorial Day, the Memorial Day for Israel's Fallen Soldiers, Tisha B'Av (the ninth day of the Hebrew month of Av, which traditionally marks the destruction of the First and Second temples in Jerusalem in 586 B.C.E. and 70 A.D., respectively), and any other memorial day that the state might declare.[5] The regulations stipulated that on memorial days, broadcasts should reflect the special nature of the day and that the family channel could not broadcast "light-hearted" programs. In addition, franchise holders were required to broadcast first-run, locally produced, and self-made programs that would account for 50 percent of the day's broadcasts. Like the requirements for holidays, the requirements for memorial days were eased in 1996 to mandate only two hours of original programs on each memorial day.

Aside from the local production quota, the original regulations required that cable operators broadcast quotas of certain program genres. These were created to fulfill the legal obligation of "broadcasting a variety of movies and programs in the fields of entertainment, music, art, education, culture and sports, while providing proper expression to the topics and needs of the franchise area." They included drama-melodrama, documentary-docudrama, comedy-satire, thriller, horror, western, science fiction and fantasy, teleplays, musical, adventure, soap opera, TV entertainment, classical music, opera concert, pop music/jazz/rock, animation, and sport/sport event summaries. Franchise operators had to include all these genres in their broadcasts.

These regulations clearly illustrate how the cultural obligations of cable television operators, just like those of terrestrial broadcasters, were formulated to serve the Jewish segment of society only, in particular the Ashkenazi elite. Indeed, the definition of holidays is determined solely within the context of the Jewish calendar. No special rules are made for channels aimed at non-Jews, if and when such channels ever materialize, and the definition of memorial days and the ban on broadcasting on certain days are rooted exclusively in Jewish and Israeli cultural and national considerations. The list of musical genres that could be broadcast on television over cable includes classical music, opera, jazz, rock, and pop music but no Mediterranean or Middle Eastern genres. Interestingly, even though the change in the political power structure has generated changes to serve the rising Mizrahi elites in Israeli society, the list of genres listed has never changed.

LOCAL PRODUCTION IN THE EARLY STAGE OF CABLECASTING

Local production received brief mention in the Barsela Committee's recommendations, which were generally less oriented toward content and more focused on the economic and legal facets of the new industry. The committee recommended that "a license holder be obligated to broadcast original productions of Israeli character" (Barsela 1982, 17). In addition, the committee recommended that a fund for original broadcasts be created that would be financed through a tax of U.S.$1 on each subscriber.

The 1986 law did not make any specific demands of this nature. Instead, it stated that the proceeds from royalties paid by licensees would finance activities created by the Telecommunications Law. Regulations enacted in 1991 stipulated that each franchise holder spend a minimum of U.S.$120,000 per franchise each year beginning in the third period of cablecasting (each period consists of four years of cablecasting within the twelve-year license).[6] In addition, each franchise operator was required to provide local productions they do not have a stake in (see Table 6.1).

At least the same sum of money was to be invested in programs produced by the operators on the following topics: education and society, music, art and culture, religion and heritage, local sports, hobbies, volunteer work and immigrant absorption, consumerism, employment, leisure activities, senior citizens, environmental issues, municipal services, and housing. Each of these types of programs was to be broadcast at least once a month with the total amount of air time allotted to such programming reaching 60 hours per quarter by the third four-year period of broadcasting. It is virtually impossible to ascertain, however, to what extent franchise

Table 6.1. Local Production Programming Quotas in Israel as Required in Telecommunications Regulations (Broadcasts by a Franchise Holder) 1991

Genre	Number of Programs/Year in Three License Periods[a]			Length (minutes)
	First	Second	Third	
Feature Films	12	14	18	90
Drama	2	3	4	30–90
Documentary	5	6	7	30–90
Magazine/Host/Game	26	26	48	30
Song/Entertainment	6	12	12	30
Judaism/Heritage	12	24	24	30
Theater/Ballet/Concert/Dance	3	3	4	30–90
Children/Youth	12	24	24	30
Student Film	10	10	10	30

[a] Each period is four years long.

operators fulfilled these obligations. Communications Minister Shulamit Aloni, responding on 14 February 1994 to questions in the Knesset, admitted that the CBC had been ineffective in the previous two years. She said she hoped that franchise operators "would keep their promise" and noted that they had "started preparing original programs and things will expand" (Knesset Records, 14 February 1994). The first stage of cable policy was a mix of social regulatory policies in which regulators strove to create a nationally unified culture by controlling genres and promoting local productions and local languages. This policy fitted well with previous media policies that affected public and commercial media.

The Second Stage: A Market-Driven National Broadcaster

The rise of neoliberalism in Israel in the 1990s led to the second stage of development of Israel's cable system, which was driven by aggressive corporate players. Somewhat ironically, the Israeli public owes the demise of the first stage of social regulatory policy initiated by the government to the antitrust violations of franchise operators. The cooperation scheme developed by cable franchises in order to deliver a unified program menu created a national programming structure, which contradicted the original regional structure envisioned by the 1986 law. The state, however, continued to maintain a strong presence in the area of content in the second stage as well.

When the service was launched in 1989, four of the five cable television franchise operators teamed up to create Israel Cable Programming

Ltd. (ICP). This conglomerate was established to purchase all the programming and "package" all the cable channels that the operators were to produce to fulfill the CBC's regulations. In addition to local channels, franchises carried a wide selection of about thirty-five foreign satellite services. The antitrust battles that ensued between the CBC, the antitrust commissioner, and the cable companies as a result of the founding of ICP ushered in the second stage of cable television policy in the first half of the 1990s.

In 1989, responding to complaints that ICP's role in the video programming market amounted to a form of cartelization, the antitrust commissioner accused cable operators of establishing an illegal cartel. The commissioner proposed a compromise that would allow the cartel to exist for three more years, after which a permanent settlement would be reached that could lead to the breakup of the cartel. In the meantime, the ICP was to invest an agreed-upon amount of money in promoting local production and producing a "cultural" channel at its own expense. The idea behind this proposal was to enable the cable industry to continue to enter Israeli homes and at the same time force it to fulfill some of its cultural obligations. In other words, the decision exploited the cartel-like structure of the industry in order to enhance "cultural" understandings. Yet paradoxically, instead of the CBC directing this initiative, it was the antitrust commissioner who assumed the role of planner of cultural policy in Israel.

This development underlines one of the major challenges of communications policymaking worldwide: how to create a balance between economic considerations and social considerations when designing a media system. Israel was not exempt from this virtually inherent conflict as it made the transition from limited government broadcasting to a multichannel environment in which economic considerations played a key role. The fact that the antitrust commissioner became a key player in the design of the media market, however, does not detract from the social regulatory nature of his decisions. In fact, it could be said that his involvement demonstrates even further how deeply engrained the hegemonic interpretation of Israeli culture is; it has become an integral consideration of economic regulation.

The antitrust court rejected the compromise the antitrust commissioner offered and declared ICP an illegal cartel, ordering that it be immediately liquidated on the grounds that limited ownership was a danger to democracy. The court also said that the cable industry was legally designed as a regional television service and that therefore there was no legal ground for a settlement that allowed it to operate nationally (*I. C. S. Israel Cable Systems, Ltd. v. The Antitrust Commissioner* [1994]). Before the court had an opportunity to complete its deliberations over a new compromise (*Idan Cable Corporation v. Antitrust Commissioner* [1995]), the Knesset passed an amendment to the Telecommunications Law; this was initiated by the government and legalized the cartel. This decision signaled the government's formal acceptance of the second stage of the policy: the establishment of a national cartel of service providers and programmers.

However, requirements regarding local production and production by cable operators became entangled with efforts to authorize the cartel. Knesset members who supported the legalization of the cartel saw the local production requirement as the "payment" the industry made for being allowed to cartelize. The changes in the law rendered the detailed first-stage regulations obsolete. In the ten-year deal eventually reached between legislators and franchise holders, a minimum of 10 percent of the time on each of the joint channels run by regional franchises would be devoted to locally produced programs. However, the meaning of the word "local" had changed. It no longer meant "regional," as in previous legislation. Now it meant "Israeli" (as opposed to "foreign"). This understanding became the law in 1996.[7]

The Encouragement of Original Israeli Production in Television Broadcasting Law of 1996 is little more than a fee in the form of Israeli-produced programs that the cable operators finance. This system allowed the cable companies to continue what the antitrust court and antitrust commissioner had deemed an unfair practice. The law imposed quotas not only on the cable programmers but also on the IBA.[8] The regulations enacted as a result of this legislation required franchise holders to invest specific amounts in local production and eliminated the minimum time requirement for broadcasting these programs.

Thus, Israeli regulators imported one of the most common social regulatory media policies: minimum quotas on local production. As MK Dedi Zucker noted when introducing the law on 16 November 1994: "It seems to me that what is good for most democratic European countries is good for a state like Israel, which is the only state where the Hebrew language is spoken, and the management of public televisions should not be left to the whims of the market alone" (Knesset Records, 16 November 1994).

As they created the new legal cartel, regulators abandoned their original design of the cable industry that foresaw regionally based channels in favor of a national unified system. The government presented details of the new system to the Knesset during the second reading of a proposed amendment to the Telecommunications Law on 1 May 1996 as a clarification of the meaning of the original Telecommunications Law and not as a dramatic change in the cultural role of cable television that entailed its transformation from a small limited regional cablecaster to a large multichannel national entity. This may have been a good strategy for the government, since shortly thereafter it introduced the third stage in the evolution of Israeli cable television policy—the "ethnic" or "multicultural" stage.

Third Stage: The Multicultural Model

In 1996, following a change in Israel's electoral system, big-party dominance gave way to more fragmented political representation.[9] A new law allowed Israelis to cast separate votes for the prime minister and the Knesset. This gave voters an opportunity to vote for a leader of a large party for prime minister and for a party for the Knesset that best represented their group orientation. Dramatic changes in the structure of the Knesset ensued. Even though an average of slightly more than twelve parties had been elected to each 120–member Knesset between 1949 and 2006, in general, until 1969, the largest party was significantly larger than the second-largest party, and since 1973, the two major parties had been comparable in size. As of 1996, many small parties turned into medium-sized parties that were gaining in political power, and the major parties had to reckon with them. While in the 1980s the major parties—Labor and Likud—each had more than forty members in the Knesset, since 1996, many smaller factions have grown to consist of more than ten members each and parties that represent special interests have together been able to garner more than 40 percent of the vote. The representation of the religious parties increased from 14 (of 120) seats in 1992 to 23 seats in 1996. A Russian immigrant party won 7 seats in 1996 (compared with none in the previous elections). Of the 23 religious seats, 11 were awarded to a religious party whose members were mainly Mizrahi Jews (compared with 6 in the 1992 elections). By comparison, in 1981, the two largest parties won 48 and 47 seats and none of the other eight parties won more than 6 seats. In 1984, while the two largest parties won 44 and 41 seats, none of the other thirteen parties garnered more than 5 seats each.

In the new regime, more small parties were needed to form a ruling coalition, and the payoffs required were soon reflected in the policies regarding cable television. The policies that evolved became a mirror image of the very fragmented state of Israeli society, especially among its numerous ethnic groups. Serving these small groups became a top priority of the policy, as they were suddenly able to wield a disproportionate

amount of power in the political system. At this time, the last phase of
the pre-competition policy was launched. In order to protect the new
political structure and maintain its power with a completely different
focus, under the guise of advancing multiculturalism, the new policy in
fact ended up promoting segregation of cultural groups and creating cultural ghettos in television programming. Cable television became a tool
in the hands of specific audiences who gained political power in those
years and were interested in maintaining their separate group identity.
At the same time, the new policy preserved the divisions between Palestinian Israelis and Jewish Israelis; the parties representing Palestinian
Israelis did not gain more members, and regardless of which large party
was in power, they did not become members of the ruling coalition.

The new policy created nationally sanctioned special-interest channels on the portion of the cable system allotted for state use by the Telecommunications Law. This portion had previously been used only for a
national home shopping network. The 15th amendment to the Telecommunications Law, adopted in 1997, created a new entity—designated
channels. One-sixth of the capacity of the cable network was awarded to
the state, which was authorized to decide how to use it. The state first
exercised this right when it put out to tender the home shopping channel in 1995. This move, still part of the national broadcaster (second)
stage, was unopposed and virtually unnoticed, as the shopping channel
reflected the common acceptance of the rise of consumerism and did not
seem to threaten any of the existing players.

But in 1996, when the CBC proposed creating an Arabic-language
service on the state's share of the cable network capacity that would be
financed through advertising, commercial television broadcasters claimed
that the government had no authority to undertake such an endeavor.
The Knesset responded by passing an amendment to the law that gave
the government this authority. However, the amendment, which was
enacted by the subsequent Knesset elected in 1996, represented a new
fragmented political reality and the return of the right-wing Likud to
power. It allowed the government to create special-interest channels on
its share of the system.[10] As Communications Minister Limor Livnat
explained when introducing the law for its first reading: "We are talking here only about special-interest channels, we are not talking about
another general channel to broadcast for the entire public" (Knesset Records, 4 November 1996).

The law defined designated channels as channels aimed at a certain
linguistic, cultural, or traditional audience or centered on a particular

topic. The law was therefore designed to create specialized channels for certain minority groups. In order to maintain each channel's distinct nature, the law specified that language-based channels must carry most of their programs and all of their advertising in the language on which the channel is based. This was to ensure that only the particular minority whose members speak the language would watch the channel, thereby calming the fears of commercial channel franchisees that new general-interest commercial channels would be created through the back door.[11] While the commercial incentive for segmentation is clear, market forces pushed lawmakers into creating a system that serves the controlling forces in the market, in this case the commercial channel's monopoly on Hebrew television advertising.

A few months after the amendment was enacted, a new policy report was published by the Peled Committee (headed by Yossi Peled, a retired general and the former chair of the Second Authority), which Benjamin Netanyahu's neoliberal government appointed to recommend ways to further liberalize the broadcasting market. The Peled Committee report recommended massive deregulation of the market in the long term, but in the meantime, it proposed creating an interim period when market forces would gradually be allowed to take control while the government advanced its cultural balkanization plan. The committee recommended operating five thematic channels that the government would tender:

- A channel in Arabic
- A channel for Russian and Amhari (Ethiopian) speakers
- A channel for programming about Jewish tradition
- An Israeli music channel that would include Mediterranean music
- A news and information channel (Nissan 1997)

Not surprisingly, these were based on the same models for special-interest channels the minister of communications had presented in the first reading of the amendment, which preceded the Peled Committee report by about six months. Nor is it surprising that three of the thematic channels proposed in the recommendations catered to groups that found themselves in positions of power in the new government coalition: religious Jews, Jewish immigrants from the former Soviet Union (with lip service being paid to immigrants from Ethiopia), and "Mediterranean" Jews.[12] As the minister noted in introducing the law: "We could broaden the broadcasting scene and transmit dedicated broadcasts to that public we think deserves to have dedicated broadcasts" (Knesset Records, 4 November 1996). It turned out that the decision to award a channel to the

Palestinian minority, which was not represented in the new ruling coalition, was also nothing more than lip service, as will be further discussed
in chapter 8.

Under the new political system, minority groups quickly learned
that maintaining their cultural uniqueness would enhance their political power. The Peled Committee recommended adopting a model based
on serving special interests instead of one based on meeting national
unity goals. It recommended doing away with the unified cable system
and introducing "tiering," a technology that further segments viewing
patterns using economic or cultural categories. In addition, the report
recommended abolishing regional commercial radio in favor of national
stations based on themes and special interests. The idea to create thematic special-interest radio channels was not new. In 1996, the Second
Authority had awarded two specialized regional franchises: one in Arabic
in the northern Galilee region and one for religious Jews in B'nei Berak,
an ultra-orthodox city.

Fourth Stage: Culture through Local Production Industries

Very few of the ideas that emerged in the multicultural stage ever ma-
terialized. Only two designated channels were eventually created, one
Russian-language channel and one Israeli music channel, apparently
because the elaborate channel scheme had no economic backbone to
rely on. Promoting competition in the offering of multichannel services,
however, seemed to policymakers to be an economically viable idea, and
as another offspring of the Peled Committee recommendations, direct
broadcast satellite (DBS) service was introduced. This digital platform
created a new cultural playing field.

Indeed, from a legalistic and bureaucratic point of view, the DBS and
cable platforms were subject to different rules. The satellite amendment
was approved in a hasty process in 1998, reminiscent of the hasty passage of the cable law in 1986.[13] The outcome was further concentration
of power in the hands of the minister of communications, as the new
law gave the minister—and not the CBC—the authority to award DBS
licenses and set their terms. The CBC, renamed under the new law the
Cable and Satellite Broadcasting Council (CSBC), was allowed to impose
on satellite operators the same regulations it imposes on cable operators.
The CSBC could only make nonbinding recommendations to the minister
about regulations that pertain specifically to satellite operators. In 2001,
in wake of the Internet revolution, the Knesset undertook another major

overhaul of the Telecommunications Law, setting the stage for the final consolidation of the remaining three cable operators into one entity and the emergence of a cable-satellite duopoly.[14] At the same time, the amendment (known as Amendment No. 25) gave the CSBC tremendous powers: it required operators to obtain CSBC approval for their content offering, and it required any entrepreneur interested in launching a channel on any of the platforms to first acquire a license from the CSBC. More than anything else, the creation of the cable-satellite duopoly meant that the vision of a limited channel offering had become obsolete. Both cable and satellite operators began developing digital platforms that offered dozens of channels, mostly foreign; some of these were repackaged for Israeli audiences (dubbed and translated into Hebrew), while others remained in their original format.

In wake of all this restructuring of the industry, the CSBC took upon itself a new cultural mission. The focus of the CSBC's energies shifted from structural regulation to content regulation, in particular as it concerned original programming.

The biggest threat to competition between the unified cable operator and the satellite operator was the purchasing power of the ICP cartel. As a result, on 23 March 2000, the CSBC forced ICP to sell the satellite operator its national bouquet of channels (series,[15] movies, sports, children, and arts and science) in order to create market conditions that were more fair, at least as far as locally packaged materials were concerned.[16] The must-sell provision, however, exempted locally produced programs in order to encourage both platforms to invest in the local market and compete for local talent.[17] The CSBC required cable operators to invest a minimum of U.S.$25 million each year in local production. It required the satellite operator to invest U.S.$7.5 million in local production in 2000 and U.S.$10 million the next year because it was considered a fledgling industry. In 2003, the CSBC fixed the satellite operator's investment at 8 percent of its annual income from subscriptions, so long as that amount did not fall beneath the original investment requirements.

At the first stage of implementation, the council created specific rules regarding the share operators were required to invest in each of the channels. The CSBC's micromanagement of the investments of the operators continued and was changed over the years in numerous decisions and regulations. In fact, the CSBC started making investments the condition for approving other channels the operators wanted to introduce. Hence, in January 2001, the CSBC required the translated National Geographic channel to invest U.S.$1.6 million each year in local production as a condition for carrying the channel over cable with a Hebrew translation. Of this investment, U.S.$1 million would be earmarked for a minimum of ten hour-long documentaries and the rest for at least 30 half-hour programs not taped in studios. In August 2002, the council agreed to consider allowing the National Geographic channel to broadcast a game show that was "based only on knowledge and not on luck" as part of the "lower genre" requirement that was eligible for funding from the balance of $0.6 million of the annual investment. It granted its approval for one year only.

In November 2002, however, the CSBC changed the rules and lifted the investment requirements in individual channels, instead imposing new investment requirements based on types of programming in a system that was reminiscent of the "genre" system the Knesset created for the broadcasting industry.[18] Here, too, the level of micromanagement was very high. For example, a 2002 decision defined a "complex drama" as 48 minutes long, while a subsequent decision in February 2006 defined it as 45 minutes long.[19]

When Amendment No. 25 to the Telecommunications Law passed in 2001, it allowed for a gradual consolidation of what by now were three cable operators, and it changed the terms of their operation from a limited-time franchise to an unlimited-time license. Ensuring funding for original programming over cable became a condition for this transition. In an April 2002 decision about a request for an indefinite license from Matav, one of the cable companies, the council said it attributed "extreme importance" to guarding Israeli creativity and nurturing the independent programming and production industry. The council informed Matav that if it wanted to be awarded the indefinite license, it would have to invest approximately U.S.$2.4 million in ICP immediately. It imposed a similar condition on Tevel, another cable company, in May 2002.

In March 2003, the CSBC spelled out its policy regarding programming for children in the new multichannel environment: "Children's channels have an educational and cultural effect of the first order on infants, children and youth in Israel; therefore it is vital that they include programs that express Israeli culture and essence."[20] The council said it would work to meet the need for Israeli content on all children's channels, taking into account the character, exposure levels, and target audiences of the channels. The council's policies forced operators of both cable and direct broadcast satellite companies to invest in original programming on all the children's channels they carried, even imported ones, such as Fox Kids.

The CSBC did not limit its self-prescribed role of monitor of enculturation to promoting local productions. Following the tradition established in the 1980s regarding national holidays and memorial days, in July 2001, the council approved a request by operators that broadcasting of ceremonies be considered original local productions.[21] Technically, a ceremony would fall under this definition if the majority of the crew involved in its production were Israeli residents and if the ceremony met the "character of the channel in which it was broadcast" and was recognized as a "non-elite" genre. Fulfilling its self-prescribed role of instituting public ritual, the CSBC announced a new policy in May 2002 regarding "broadcasting of events of great public importance" that stated that events the council designated as having great public significance should be broadcast over channels available to all subscribers as part of the basic cable tier.[22] An event of great public importance had to meet at least two of the following four criteria:

- Interest in the event and its circumstances and its outcome among the Israeli public is great, and in the case of sporting events, greater than the average audience that usually follows such events
- The event has cultural significance because it helps create national identity and a sense of belonging
- A national team or other representative of the state is taking part in the event or is part of a competition or central international event
- The event, or events of its kind, have been broadcast in the past over national channels and received a high rating

The council agreed that in cases when several events take place at the same time as part of one event (such as the Olympics), some of them may be broadcast over premium channels that are only available to subscribers willing to pay an extra fee. The list of the events appended to the decision included the following:

- The World Cup: opening game, semifinals, final, and any game in which the Israeli national team participates
- The European Football Championship: opening game, semifinals, final, and any game in which the Israeli national team participates
- All official international games of the Israeli men's football and basketball teams, including the qualifying rounds of the World Cup and European Championship
- Semifinal and final games in which Israeli teams take part in the European Champions League, the UEFA cup, the Euroleague (men's club basketball), the Roncatti cup (women's club basketball), the Koracz Cup (men's club basketball), the Saporta Cup (men's club basketball), and the EuroCup (men's national team basketball)[23]
- Semifinal and final game of the Israeli football and men's basketball cup and the final game of the women's basketball cup
- Semifinal and final game of a tennis grand slam tournament in which an Israeli tennis player is taking part
- The summer Olympics

Amid this frenzy of work on content regulation, the CSBC did not abandon its original mission of promoting cable television as a provider of regional content. In September 2000, the council decided to adopt the recommendations of a public committee, the Nof Committee (headed by Akiva Nof, former MK of the Likud), to earmark Channel 9 on both cable and satellite as a national channel dedicated to regional programming, thus attempting to breathe new life into the forgotten idea that multichannel television should serve as a regional medium and support regional content.[24] This decision was short lived: When the Russian channel Israel Plus was launched in 2002, it was awarded the lucrative position of Channel 9.

In April 2001, the council began drawing up regulations for introducing a tiered service to replace the remnants of the "super basic" package created under the ICP arrangement of the early 1990s.[25] In the basic cable tier, the council included the following channels:

- IBA broadcasts (Channel 1 and satellite Channel 33)
- Educational Television (a made-for-cable/satellite channel produced by the government entity referred to in previous legislation (and in chapters 3, 4, and 5) as Instructional Television, which became Channel 23)
- Over-the-air commercial Channels 2 and 10 (the latter of which was not yet created)
- The "designated channels"
- The home shopping network
- The community channels
- An electronic program guide

The council presented similar recommendations about the satellite platform in August 2002.[26] By then, two more channels had been added: the Knesset channel, which was established temporarily by law as an IBA broadcast in 1997 and was made into a permanent independent channel as of 2003; and the IBA's Middle East channel, a propaganda channel that targeted neighboring states.[27] Hence, the policy had gone full circle since the recommendations of the Barsela Committee, which focused on a limited offering of educational and regulated broadcast channels, entertainment, news, local programming, and propaganda. Notwithstanding the technological developments and social changes the country underwent over the years, the basic cable package was to provide to Israeli citizens the sum of all the trends and changes of the years: national regulated services, educational television, and some propaganda in Arabic (all remnants of the cable television policy's initial stages). The only new element in the basic service was the provision for "cultural ghettos" that could be added later as such groups emerged. The requirement that cable services carry the home shopping network can also be interpreted as a nod to Israel's growing consumer culture, a far cry from Ben-Gurionist socialism and confirmation of his fear that television would contribute to increased consumerism and the Americanization of Israeli culture. This final point is borne out in the January 2007 groundbreaking license amendment for the designated Israeli and Mediterranean Music channel.[28] According to this amendment, for one year, the channel is entitled to devote 10 percent of broadcasting time to "foreign music," defined as "music that is not Israeli music"; after a year, the council can reconsider its policy. Whether this is merely a window in the cultural ghetto or whether it represents the Americanization of Israeli culture and the political establishment's acceptance of that process is yet to be determined.

7   *Transborder Broadcasting*

Transborder broadcasting may weaken control of electronic media in meticulously planned systems that are rooted in strong ideological convictions by introducing unplanned messages (Thomas 1999). Israel is a case in point, as the traditional motives influencing Israeli media policy—a fear of external propaganda and a desire for social uniformity—are very relevant to the issue of transborder broadcasts. Israeli law and policymakers have identified three arenas in which transborder broadcasting may interfere with national planning. Two—news and culture—are specifically based on content, and control of these arenas has been described throughout this book. The third arena, which is based on the market, is advertising. Regulating advertising includes regulating elements of content and ultimately serves the same goals as mere content regulation, as many commercial media sources are owned by transnational corporations whose economic prowess and cultural agenda converge and threaten both local corporations and local culture (Schiller 1993). Attempts by Israeli and foreign entrepreneurs to circumvent the cultural obligations of commercial, cable, and satellite broadcasters licensed in Israel by providing commercial services from across the border have sparked numerous legal battles.

The First Confrontation: The Story of the Odellia

Even though commercial television did not become an option under Israeli law until 1990, Israeli lawmakers and regulators were forced to confront the issue of transborder advertising over television as far back as the early 1980s, when private entrepreneurs put together plans to broadcast commercial television to Israeli audiences from the Mediterranean Sea. The idea was that broadcasting from the sea would circumvent the monopoly Channel 1 enjoyed and the ban imposed on television advertising.

The owners of a ship named *Odellia* planned to launch a commercial television channel from the sea in 1981. At the time, a radio service that was broadcasting from a ship sailing the Mediterranean was selling advertising time in Israel; it was operated by peace activist Abe Nathan. The government apparently saw no threat in the "peace" message of the lone seaman, who was very popular among Israelis after serving as a volunteer pilot in the 1948 War of Independence and attempting to fly to Egypt to "talk peace" with its rulers in the mid-1960s. The government responded to the threat of the *Odellia* by initiating an amendment to the Wireless Telegraphy Ordinance that prohibited television broadcasting from the seas.[1] The minister of communications explained that the law was initiated because of a "particular ship" that was planning to launch commercial television broadcasts aimed at Israel (Knesset Records 22 November 1981). The new law made it illegal to assist such broadcasts by selling advertising time in Israel on their behalf. To determine whether such broadcasts were in fact "directed at Israel," the law set basic tests: that the programs "use the Hebrew language" or that the station broadcast "advertisements for products or services marketed in Israel."[2] This was a stricter standard than the one the proposed bill would have established; the standard set by the government in the proposed law in order to determine whether the broadcasts targeted Israeli audiences was that the whole broadcast be carried in Hebrew. The practice of outlawing broadcasts from ships was not an Israeli invention; it already existed with the European Agreement for the Prevention of Broadcasts Transmitted from Stations outside National Territories of 1965.[3]

There is no evidence in the Knesset records that any direct or indirect commercial effect of the *Odellia*'s reliance on advertising income on the media outlets that existed at the time was discussed, leaving the Knesset actions open to interpretation about whether the fear of the *Odellia* was based on the content of its programs or on its presumed economic impact. The *Odellia* case was the first attempt by television broadcasters not originating in a neighboring Arab country to target Israeli television audiences and for purposes other than propaganda. The prompt action taken by Israeli legislators to end the foreign broadcasts and maintain the IBA's monopoly on broadcasting was both impressive and successful. But what motivated them? Although the broadcasts from the *Odellia* were an isolated incident, a review of the rules and regulations regarding cable and satellite television that evolved over the following decades sheds light on this issue.

The Development of Policy Regarding Retransmission of Foreign Broadcasts: The Planning Stage

Although discussions about cable television began in Israel back in the mid-1970s, the issue of transfrontier broadcasts via cable was addressed only implicitly at first. In 1979, the Kubersky report supported the introduction of cable television in Israel but said it should only carry existing broadcast channels rather than serve as a platform for creating new channels, which would necessarily include foreign broadcasts (Kubersky 1979, 29). In 1982, the Barsela report recommended creating regional cable franchises immediately; the committee recognized the cultural and social impact of a barrage of television programming on a country not yet familiar with the concept of choice in television fare, especially with the effects of foreign television, and it used dramatic terminology to describe it (Barsela 1982, 38, 43). In describing the possible negative effects of television, the report expressed concern about the potential effect of retransmitting foreign channels on the cable system, noting that the "multiplicity of foreign programming will have the effect of a foreign culture that will enter the individual's home and reside with him as part of his culture" (6). It recommended allowing a limited number of channels (20–21).

Although the Telecommunications Law adopted most of these recommendations, it disregarded the recommendations limiting the number of television channels. Most notably, it disregarded the recommendation regarding foreign satellite channels. In fact, the law noted that franchise holders could rebroadcast foreign channels, including satellite channels, with no restrictions. No documentation has been found to explain this change in position.

Seven years later, when Communications Minister Shulamit Aloni was petitioned to use her ministerial powers and allow advertising on cable channels the operators own,[4] she said in an affidavit to the Supreme Court that she had adopted the recommendations of a committee appointed to study the issue that had found that advertising on foreign channels retransmitted into Israel was the status quo, was allowed, and should be continued.[5] A previous committee appointed by one of Aloni's predecessors, Raphael Pinhasi, had reached a similar conclusion (Ish-Horowitz 1992). When asked to address the issue of advertising on foreign channels, the deputy attorney general ruled on 13 July 1995 that the law does not prohibit advertising on retransmitted satellite channels.[6]

The "Open Skies" Policy and the Case of METV

The Peled Committee proposed a new policy based on the principle of "open skies" in the mid-1990s that made transfrontier broadcasting inevitable (Nissan 1997). The Israeli government adopted the recommendations of the report in 1997 and seemed to be ready to embark on a policy of openness regarding the televised retransmission of transfrontier channels.[7] Yet the 1998 legislation that supposedly implemented the Peled Committee's recommendations not only ushered in "cultural engineering" by balkanizing the broadcasting map along ethnic lines, as described in chapter 6, it also ended up closing the skies and constructing new barriers to the free flow of transborder information.

Cross-frontier financing of channels through advertising is an established practice in Europe (Weddel and Lange 1991). As of January 2004, 218 channels in Europe originated in one country and targeted others, 162 of which targeted specific countries (European Audiovisual Observatory 2004). Finding financing for such channels is not easy. In the tumultuous Middle East, even the transnational Al Jazeera Arab network that originates in Qatar and is received by 30 to 50 million viewers needed government subsidies to finance operations (Weisman 2005). The Israeli government sought to restrict broadcasts that originate in other countries and plan to rely on income from advertising aimed at Israeli audiences. An amendment to the Telecommunications Law, which was enacted in 1998, forbade Israelis or persons residing in Israel from launching a satellite service aimed at Israel, both from within Israel and from outside its borders, without a license.[8] It deviated, however, from the definition given to such broadcasts in the *Odellia* case and defined broadcasts as "targeting Israeli audiences" if they met at least one of the following three criteria: (1) they broadcast a majority of their programming in Hebrew; (2) they regularly broadcast programs in Hebrew during prime time; (3) they regularly broadcast advertising for products that are predominantly aimed at the Israeli market.

A series of Israeli legal cases involving Middle East Television (METV) in 1999 (*Tel'Ad Jerusalem Studios, Ltd. v. The Minister of Communications* [1999]; *M. E. Television Services Ltd. v. The Minister of Communications* [1999]; and *Netanel Gal-Er v. the Minister of Communications* [1999]) were the first to deal with transfrontier broadcasting after the enactment of the 1998 law. These cases were not directly related to the new law because they involved the retransmission of a station owned by a Christian American corporation that had been broadcasting from Southern Lebanon since 1982 (Badran and Badran 1991; Boyd 1991, 1993) and from Cyprus since 2000, while the law referred to signals that were owned by Israelis or were broadcast from Israel.[9] The METV signal was transmitted from terrestrial stations, and it was in fact one of the first five foreign stations whose retransmission was permitted as a "foreign broadcast" under the telecommunications regulations introduced in 1987.[10]

Back in the early 1990s, METV's broadcasts drew the attention of Israeli regulators because of their evangelical message. The Supreme Court established that these broadcasts were transmitted to the cable operators via a microwave link and thus were not transmitted "over the air," which was a requirement for the permission cable operators needed to retransmit the broadcasts. This enabled the Court to make a ruling that responded to public demands that the Christian broadcasts be removed from the cable system (*Yisrael Ben David v. Minister of Communications* [1995]). However, when transmission was launched on the Amos satellite, the cable operators reintroduced them as part of their offering, since retransmitting satellite signals was allowed. In the summer of 1998, the Channel 2 franchisees campaigned to remove METV from the cable channel offering, arguing that the foreign-owned station threatened their commercial interests by targeting Israeli audiences with advertising. They filed a petition with the Supreme Court urging the CSBC to remove the channel (*Tel'Ad Jerusalem Studios v. Minister of Communications* [1999]). The petition prompted the CSBC to create a new category of channels called "satellite channels aimed at Israel," popularly known at the time as "converted" channels (Knesset Economics Committee Records, 20 March 2001).[11] The council adopted the criteria created by the 1998 law that prohibited launches of satellite channels that targeted Israeli audiences and extended the criteria to channels not necessarily owned by Israelis or not necessarily broadcasted from Israel. METV filed a petition with the High Court of Justice (*M. E. Television Services v. Minister of Communications* [1999]),[12] which eventually led to a compromise agreement allowing METV to continue being transmitted.[13] At the same time, the CSBC set up a regulatory regime targeting all "converted" channels and published a first draft of these regulations that would have allowed channels to be created in the new category subject to two major restrictions: (1) they could not carry advertising for products marketed predominantly in Israel, advertising in Hebrew, or home shopping in Hebrew; and (2) they had to invest a minimum of $1.5 million in local Israeli programming, which would have constituted at least 10 percent of their programming fare.

The new policy made foreign channels participants in the government's controlled programming offer, since foreign channels were to create local programming in order to dilute the "non-Israeli" fare in their broadcasts. This created a basic contradiction. On the one hand, the channels were prohibited from advertising in Hebrew, while on the other, they were required to broadcast original programs in Hebrew that were to be produced in Israel. This new policy, however, was never enacted.

The Aftermath of the METV Case and the Enactment of Amendment 15

Amendment No. 15 to the Telecommunications Law, which was adopted in 1997, created a new category of channels—designated channels—that were to be carried on one-sixth of the cable network's available channels, originally designated for use at the government's discretion. "Designated channels" were defined as channels that targeted a unique linguistic, cultural, ethnic, or other "special interest" community. To ensure that language-based channels did not threaten the established general-interest channels, the 1997 law specified that these channels had to carry most of their programs and all advertising in the language of the channel. This policy stemmed from pressures from the franchise holders of the commercial broadcast channel, Channel 2, to pass laws that would maintain their dominance, if not their monopoly, of the Hebrew advertising market. As described in chapter 6, the government identified the following as special interests: a channel in Arabic; a channel for Russian and Amharic[14] speakers; a channel focused on the Jewish tradition; a channel focused on Israeli and Mediterranean music; and a channel focused on news and information.

While tenders have been published for all these channels, only two have been created: an Israeli music channel and a Russian-language channel. The latter channel was intended to compete with the Russian-language transfrontier package offered by Israeli cable and satellite operators and minimize their uncontrolled impact on viewers (Caspi et al. 2002). Presumably aware of the fact that ethnic media use leads to stronger ethnic identification over time (Jeffries 2000), the government must have also realized that uncontrolled ethnic media can help sustain existing ethnic identification and work against the government's vision of cultural uniformity.

Like its broadcast predecessors, the Russian-language channel broadcasting from within Israel was given very specific cultural obligations. These are listed in an appendix to its license; they include providing an "adequate representation to the way of life in Israel, to the Israeli character of life." Notably, they call for 150 weekly minutes of programming dedicated to issues on the general public agenda in Israel and 135 minutes of programming dedicated to issues on the agenda of the Russian-speaking population in Israel. In addition, the license requires 260 minutes of "enrichment programs that may help in the absorption of Russian-speaking immigrants in the Israeli experience." The channel is allowed to buy its news programs only from a body licensed to broadcast news in Israel—in other words, one that has a government license or is under government supervision.

According to two new sets of regulations created in 2002 following the METV cases, a cable or satellite operator cannot retransmit a satellite channel without the CSBC's approval. In addition, two key concepts— "own broadcasts" and "broadcasts targeting mostly the Israeli public or a part thereof"—were redefined.[15] "Own broadcasts," which were defined in the original 1987 regulations as "broadcasts whose source is the studio of the franchise holder, whether self-produced or purchased," were now defined as "including broadcasts that are not broadcast in the franchise holder's own channels, that are intended mostly for the Israeli public or a part thereof." In other words, the council defined "own broadcasts" to include broadcasts that did not fit this category by its own admission, explaining that even though they are not "own broadcasts" in the literal sense, they fit this category in the legal sense. Indeed, such paradoxical definitions exist elsewhere in Israeli law, the most renowned example being the Fishing Ordinance 1937 (1937 Palestine Gazette, 137), Article 1 of which defines "fish" as "all marine creatures whether they are fish or whether they are not fish." Bending words to the extent that they lose their meaning altogether, however, is a rare practice.

New criteria were therefore required to identify "broadcasts aimed at the Israeli public," including one that established that even if at least half of the broadcasts are *not* in Hebrew, the council can still rule that they are targeting Israeli audiences or a part thereof, clearly an admission that a large minority in Israel speaks other languages. On the other hand, the council said that a channel viewed by at least 8 million households outside Israel that complies only with the standard that it broadcasts advertising in Hebrew can be considered as "not being aimed at Israel." This rule was broadly understood to permit the retransmission of the U.S.-based music channel MTV, which was broadcasting advertising in Hebrew.

These new rules established a new standard of absurdity in the Israeli government's ongoing efforts to "close the skies" to combat the barrage of digital content made possible by the introduction of cable and satellite. On the one hand, the government-licensed Russian-language channel was not allowed to broadcast advertising in Hebrew in order to prevent competition with the commercial Channel 2. On the other hand, the channel was awarded a de facto monopoly on advertising in Russian in Israel. Thus the cultural ghetto was upgraded to an economic ghetto. Another aspect of this arrangement is the government's differentiation between the channels based on their presumed cultural impact: While the regulations restrict the public's access to a foreign-based Russian-language channel in order to avoid dilution of the cultural "absorption package" aimed at new immigrants that is offered to them through a government-licensed channel with detailed "cultural obligations," they do allow American culture aimed at Hebrew-speaking Israeli youth to continue to permeate the airwaves by allowing retransmission of the MTV channel and including Western music on an "Israeli music channel," as detailed in chapter 6.

The Media Most Case

These regulations and their constitutionality were challenged in the Supreme Court by Media Most Ltd., the Israeli representative of an American-based Russian language channel called RTVi that was retransmitted by Israeli cable and satellite operators and was financed exclusively through advertising (*Media Most v. Cable and Satellite Council* [2004]). The decision in this case, written by Justice Esther Hayut, clearly supported the government's goal of minimizing the impact of transborder channels. Hayut asserted that "the broadcasting channels of the electronic media are a limited resource, and thus, the legislator is required to regulate their usage and not leave them wide open for the forces of the market" (9). She then acknowledged that the initial ban on advertising, as defined, did not apply to retransmitted transborder channels, only to the cable operators' "own" broadcasts. However, she conceded that changing times might necessitate new definitions. Although the ban on advertising on cable channels was originally enacted to protect the financial viability of newspapers, its purpose today is to protect commercial television channels. Hayut argued that the term "own" should be interpreted to mean "all" channels transmitted by a cable or satellite operator, whether they own them or not. This change in the definition is justified, she asserted, since technological change makes possible the creation of versions of channels that target the Israeli population and threaten local channels in a manner that was not possible before. The court concluded that preserving the viability of Israeli commercial channels is a reasonable government policy and that the change in interpretation of the meaning of the term "own channels" is reasonable as well. On this basis, it rejected the petition and allowed the Russian-based channel to be banned.

This chapter demonstrated how the Israeli government's regulation of transfrontier broadcasting emerged out of a desire to mold and protect an Israeli culture from foreign influences by trying to limit the exposure of its citizens to foreign television signals. However, such regulations have not been able to move ahead with the times, despite technological changes that have made them ineffective. Policy measures that were adopted over the years outlawed terrestrial television broadcasting from ships, the retransmission of satellite signals that had been "converted" to meet local commercial needs, and transmissions from "converted" channels that threatened the government's plan to absorb immigrant groups. (The regulations also blocked satellite signals for political reasons, as discussed in chapter 3.) The government's mobilization of the legislative, executive, and judicial branches to support this effort leaves little room for doubt about its motivations, as it left no legal stone unturned and reverted to extreme interpretations of law in order to maintain this closure.

In this book's discussion of the ways of muting Israeli democracy, this chapter stands out. It identifies very specifically the types of messages Israeli policymakers fear and the measures they will take to ensure that such messages do not become part of the Israeli public sphere. The next chapter discusses two other aspects of the government's relationship with satellite broadcasting—its selection of which signals can be transmitted and the launching of satellite broadcasts with the goal of influencing citizens in neighboring countries.

8 The Palestinian Minority

This chapter demonstrates how Israeli society has effectively denied the collective cultural rights of its Palestinian minority, especially the right of this minority to express its identity through the mass media and be an equal participant in the process of building a national culture. Media law denies Palestinian Israelis the right to express themselves collectively as a cultural minority by branding them a linguistic minority and it portrays them as the "enemy within," expressing a widely held view among Israelis in general and policymakers in particular. These policies rule out the participation of Palestinian Israelis in the development of mainstream Israeli culture.

Israel's Palestinian Minority

The relationship between the Jewish majority and Palestinian minority in Israel must be examined in its historical context. Resolution 181 of the United Nations General Assembly, enacted on 29 November 1947, established Israel as a "Jewish State" that was to reside next to an "Arab State" in the former British colony of Palestine.[1] The Israeli Declaration of Independence adopted this same construct, but it promised equal civil rights to the Arab minority that would end up living within its borders. As a result of the war that erupted soon thereafter, Israel's initial borders were redrawn and most Palestinian Arabs originally living within its borders were displaced. Many Palestinian Arab families were separated, and many of the refugees ended up living in areas originally carved out for the Arab state that was never formed. This territory was instead occupied until 1967 by Egypt and Jordan and after 1967 by Israel. In 1992, the Israeli constitutional framework defined Israel as a "Jewish-Democratic" state. As early as 1951 it created the right to repatriation for all Jews, regardless of their place of birth, but Israel denied a similar right to indigenous displaced Arabs.

The characterization of the state as "Jewish-Democratic" is in line with United Nations resolutions. The Israeli parliamentary democracy awards all citizens an equal right to vote regardless of their ethnicity as an indication of their "Israeliness" and of its self-description as "democratic." Yet Israeli courts have traditionally subscribed to the Zionist maxim that Israeli nationality cannot be separate from Jewish ethnicity (*Tamarin v. State of Israel* [1972]). It is indisputable that the Arab citizens of Israel, many of whom have since assumed a Palestinian identity and align themselves with the yet-to-be-formed Arab state, are economically and socially removed from positions of power in Israeli society and are systematically discriminated against (Hasson and Karayanni 2006; Cook 2006). This has led observers to classify Israel as an ethnic democracy (Smooha 1990, 391; 1997, 205) or as a flawed "Ethnic Constitutional Order" (Peleg 2007, 47). Palestinians living in Israel, who constitute approximately 18 percent of the country's population, are most commonly referred to as "Arab Israelis," a description that dates back to the time of the creation of the State of Israel (Bishara 1993, 203).

Rubinstein and Medina (2005) argue in their definitive description of the Israeli constitutional system that Arab Israelis enjoy a de facto cultural autonomy, as they administer their religious matters independently and study in Arabic in public schools located in towns where they constitute a majority (423–424).[2] But they fail to note that the curriculum in these schools is dictated by the Israeli Ministry of Education and that the Palestinian educational system in Israel receives inferior allocations in terms of physical facilities, teacher training, and curriculum development (Golan-Agnon 2006). Hence, the supposed autonomy enjoyed by this minority, which lives mostly in towns that are exclusively Palestinian, is, in fact, a mechanism for further discrimination. Rubinstein and Medina contend, however, that because of the existence of these autonomous spheres, it would be "imprecise" to say that Palestinian Israelis have a limited citizenship simply because they cannot claim their cultural identity as a collective. Smooha (1990, 405) concurs that Palestinian Israelis function well as a cultural minority but believes that the Jewish majority tolerates this situation only because the separate minority status of the Palestinians serves its interests. The main problem, he observes, is that Palestinian Israelis are denied the status of a national minority, a status Rouhana (1997, 125) argues is central to their identity. The outcome is that lacking both the power to determine their minority status in Israeli society and the ability to identify with the emerging independent Palestinian state, they cannot develop normally as a collective (Ghanem 2001, 8), although it should be noted that Palestinians, among themselves, have developed competing narratives pertaining to their identity (Nassar 2002). Officially, however, at least since 1993, Israel has been negotiating directly with non-Israeli Palestinians about how to fulfill their national aspirations alongside the State of Israel, effectively accepting the existence of a Palestinian nationality.[3]

The Israeli Supreme Court contributes to the less-than-equal status of Palestinian Israelis. It has refused to recognize Palestinian Israelis as members of a discrete and identifiable "nation." In 1999, Adalah, the Legal Center for the Rights of the Arab Minority in Israel, filed a petition with the High Court against the municipalities of Tel Aviv, Ramla, Lod, and Upper Nazareth requesting that street signs in these municipalities include Arabic as well as Hebrew. The majority—Justices Aharon Barak and Daliah Dorner—stipulated that these municipalities were indeed obligated to add Arabic to street signs in all of the towns' streets, including neighborhoods where no Palestinians lived (*Adalah v. The Municipalities of Tel Aviv, Ramla, Lod and Upper-Nazareth* [1999]). As Levitsky (2006) describes, Chief Justice Barak pressured Justice Dorner to remove from her opinion the word *parhesia*, a Greek word that refers to the classic determination of free speech as a natural right, in order to ensure that the right awarded to the Palestinian minority in this case would be an individual and not a collective right (300). Barak wrote in his verdict that Hebrew is the "language of the Israelis" and is the "power that brings us together as children of one country" and is, therefore, not the property of a specific group within society, the way French is the language of all the French people or English the language of all the English people. Barak maintained that Hebrew does not function the way that these languages do by serving as a fundamental pillar of these nations' sovereignty. If all the citizens of the State of Israel were to study Hebrew, contended Barak, their equal rights as citizens would be guaranteed. He argued that London, Paris, and New York do not have street signs that reflect the linguistic diversity of the residents of those cities. The chief justice did, however, acknowledge that the Arabic language is "distinct" because it is the language of Israel's largest minority and a core element of its culture. In his explanation for why their request for street signs in Arabic should be denied, Justice Mishael Cheshin said that the petitioners were attempting through this request to establish a legal precedent, namely, a new type of "right," a "collective right" of the Israeli Arab minority to maintain and nurture its national identity and distinctive culture. This type of right should be pursued through political, rather than legal, channels, argued Cheshin. Cheshin's predicament notwithstanding, cultural laws in general, and media laws in particular, are little more than political statements whose enactment through legal channels legitimizes them. Indeed, as this book demonstrates, the law is more often than not a tool that promotes cultural-political understandings serving those who have gained power over the legislative process through political means. Arrangements that apply to broadcasting to and for the Palestinian minority who live within Israel's borders have been a dominant feature of the Israeli system since the 1960s and further proof of this maxim.

The 1960s: Creation of IBA and Launching of a Television Service

Section 3 of the 1965 Broadcasting Authority Law states that "maintaining broadcasts in the Arabic language for the needs of the Arabic-speaking population and broadcasts to advance understanding and peace with neighboring states according to the basic aspirations of the state" is one of the IBA's goals. Another goal of the *mamlakhti* broadcaster, namely "to reflect the life and the cultural assets of all the tribes of the nation [who arrived] from different countries of origin" was added to the original draft and was subsequently explained in the Knesset as applying only to the Jewish people (Knesset Records, 8 March 1965, 1450).

Israeli media policymakers recognized the need to provide special broadcasts for the Palestinian–Israeli population from the outset:

- In 1961, the UNESCO task force said that creating a television service would help achieve the national goal of striking a reasonable balance between respecting different ethnic cultures and promoting a unique national identity.
- In 1965, the report of the European Broadcasting Union team stressed that any decision to establish a television service in Israel could not ignore the existence of a large Arab minority in the country and recommended launching a simultaneous bilingual service that would allow all viewers to watch the same programs in the language of their choice.
- The Bendor Committee, which was appointed to examine how to implement the government decision of July 1965 to establish a national television service, following these two reports of international experts by expressing concern about the Arabic-speaking Jewish population of the state (which it described as the most susceptible to television's presumed effect), noting that these citizens

owned television sets and watched "uninterrupted" broadcasts from neighboring countries. It recommended that the national television service provide fourteen hours each week of broadcasting in Hebrew and three-and-a-half hours each week of broadcasting in Arabic to "explain" Israel's positions in neighboring countries.[4]

- Television broadcasts were launched in 1968 following a September 1967 decision that called for "emergency broadcasts" aimed primarily at audiences in the occupied territories and at "Arab Israelis." These broadcasts were to include three hours of Arabic programming and one hour of Hebrew programming each day as a way to dilute the impact of propaganda broadcasts from neighboring Arab countries on Jewish and Palestinian citizens and to promote understanding between the two populations.

The 1970s: Preparing for the Launch of Commercial Television

The Kubersky Committee, which recommended creating a commercially funded television channel that would be separate from the IBA, copied verbatim the words the Broadcasting Authority Law used to define the goals of the IBA regarding commercial television. The committee did not feel that providing more broadcasting to Palestinian Israelis (at the time, the IBA was providing only ninety minutes of daily programming in Arabic on its sole channel) was a prime objective of the commercial channel, although its report noted that establishing a second channel might reduce the number of television programs from neighboring countries viewed in Israel and, to a certain extent, might also fill the "political-security related" need to enhance Israel's propaganda presence in the region (Kubersky 1979, 27).

Although Article 3 of the IBA law (which articulated the IBA's goals) was never amended, in 1979 the Knesset adopted a resolution that stipulated that, according to that law, an objective of television broadcasts should be to promote Hebrew as well as "Israeli and Jewish" creativity (Knesset Records, 17 December 1979, 970). This reference to "Jewish creativity," it should be noted, does not appear in the IBA law. The IBA's goals regarding Israel's Arabic-speaking population were not mentioned in the resolution.

The 1980s: Planning and Launching Cable Television

The Barsela Committee, which drafted the blueprint for cable policy in Israel in 1982, was of the opinion that Palestinian Israelis deserved special attention as a "large public with a separate linguistic and cultural affinity" (Barsela 1982, 76). It did not make specific recommendations on the matter but urged the government to consider "special channels or special hours for programming aimed at the Arabic-speaking population in Israel." This programming required "special supervision" to ensure that such programming did not "slip into discussion of controversial issues for which this medium was not meant" (77).

While the committee's recommendations were arguably at the heart of the amendment introduced into the Telecommunications Law of 1986, which launched the cable service, its specific recommendation regarding the needs of the Palestinian Israeli population was disregarded. On the whole, the law paid little attention to content; it restricted operators from broadcasting anything but local current affairs and programs that served the unique needs of each franchise area. The majority of programming, as envisioned by the 1986 law, was to be comprised of rebroadcasts from Israeli terrestrial and foreign satellite channels. However, the first set of regulations governing the cable industry, which were enacted in 1987, included a minimum requirement for broadcasts in Arabic. The regulations stipulated that in a franchise area in which the mother tongue of at least one-quarter of the potential subscribers was Arabic, a weekly minimum of four fifteen-minute newscasts and one full-length feature film should be broadcast.

The 1990s: Launching Commercial Terrestrial Broadcasting

Article 5 of the Second Authority for Radio and Television Law, enacted in 1990, repeats verbatim the Broadcasting Authority Law's requirement that Arabic-language programs be broadcast to serve the Israeli Arabic-speaking population and to promote peace and understanding with neighboring countries. This is the only section of the Broadcasting Authority Law that appears verbatim in both the Kubersky report and the Second Authority Law. The Second Authority law was more "liberal" than the Broadcasting Authority Law; one of the cultural obligations it imposes on commercial broadcasters is providing "adequate expression of the cultural diversity of Israeli society" (Article 5[b][6]). This implied a broader acceptance of the diversity of Israeli society beyond its Jewish constituency (which the Broadcasting Authority Law had focused on). The Second Authority was also empowered to require commercial broadcasters to broadcast programs (Article 61) as well as news in Arabic (Article 63[c]). The original regulations, which were enacted in 1992, required broadcasters to allot no less than 2.5 percent of their total programming time and in any case no less than thirty minutes a week to programs in Arabic.[5] Half of this quota was to be filled with original local productions. The law did not mention news, however. In 1997, the quota was raised to 8 percent of total weekly broadcasting time and thirty minutes for original programming.[6] In 1999, the quota was raised again, this time to 18 percent, reflecting the share of Palestinian Israelis in the country's total population.[7]

RESPONDING TO THE "NEW MIDDLE EAST"

While the IBA's public and propaganda missions were rooted in the hostile Middle East environment of the 1960s, the Gordian knot that tied the IBA's propaganda missions to its public service missions reemerged in government decisions taken in the early 1990s, a time when the first official reconciliation talks between Israel and Palestinians were being held and Israel was enjoying improved relations with other Middle Eastern Arab countries. In 1993, at the government's behest and financing, the IBA launched a satellite channel (commonly known as Channel 33) that was charged with broadcasting in Arabic to neighboring countries. As part of its effort to woo viewers who preferred the newly launched commercial channel, Channel 2, the IBA began to reduce its Channel 1 terrestrial broadcasts in Arabic (Asheri 1996).

ATTEMPTS TO REFORM THE IBA

During the 1990s, the government appointed numerous committees to present recommendations on how to restructure the IBA in the age of commercial and cable broadcasting, as detailed in chapter 5. Although none of the recommendations of these committees was ever implemented—they provide valuable insight into the mindset of Israeli policymakers and illustrate what they, or at least the advisers they appointed, found to be wrong with existing policy. In 1993, the Livni Committee recommended that the law be rephrased so that it would stipulate that "in maintaining the broadcasts, the authority will focus on creating a unique Israeli culture by expressing and documenting the life, cultural assets and heritage of all the citizens of Israel" (Livni 1993, 3).[8] It recommended that the IBA maintain broadcasts in Arabic to "reflect the heritage and way of life of Arabic-speaking Israeli citizens" (12). It also recommended that these broadcasts comply with the rules that apply to broadcasting in Hebrew and refrain from serving as a propaganda service aimed at Israeli Palestinians. The committee explained that broadcasts in Arabic are necessary to provide a means of expression for the Arabic-speaking population (18). In 1997, the Zuckerman Committee's recommendations reiterated that the obligations of the IBA include maintaining broadcasting in Arabic for "Israeli-Arabs" and promoting understanding and peace with the Palestinian people and with neighboring countries (40).[9] It proposed that a model be adopted that distinguished between the IBA's internal mission of broadcasting to the Israeli public (which it felt should continue to be funded directly by the public through a license fee) and the broadcasts outside Israel it would carry out at the request of the government (which it felt should be funded through the national budget) (11). The committee recommended eliminating the IBA's Channel 33, which targeted the Palestinian Authority and neighboring states, since the IBA's regular broadcasts could be received in these areas and thus there was no need for a dedicated propaganda broadcast (86–87). The committee noted that the IBA's radio broadcasts in Arabic fulfill two tasks—broadcasting to Palestinian Israelis and broadcasting to neighboring Arab countries (25)—and proposed that the latter be funded separately from local broadcasts (86). The committee did not see a need to separate the propaganda content of these broadcasts from their public service content.

THE DESIGNATED CHANNELS

When the minister of communications and the CBC appointed by Yitzhak Rabin's Labor government began contemplating setting up an Arabic-language channel in 1995, a petition to the Supreme Court filed by commercial broadcasters initially blocked them. The petitioners feared that the new channel would serve as a platform for a competitor and wanted to guarantee that its mandate would be limited to broadcasting in Arabic. The government agreed to define the channel and its goals through legislation before taking any further steps to promote the plan. Amendment 15 of the Telecommunications Law established the designated channel platforms, channels that were to be identified and licensed as such if they limited their content to a designated topic, an identifiable audience, or a unique language, culture, or heritage. The Knesset decided that the communications minister and the council would share the authority to award licenses to such channels. It created special terms for raising funds through advertising on designated channels in order to allay the fears of commercial terrestrial broadcasters:

- A minimum of 20 percent of the programs on these designated channels was to be locally produced.
- All of the programs and advertisements on channels designated by language were to be made accessible to speakers of the language.
- Half of the programs on channels designated by language were to be dubbed or broadcast in that language, including at least half of the programs broadcast during prime time.

While the Knesset was debating the law in 1996, the conservative Likud government elected after the assassination of Rabin appointed the Peled Committee to present recommendations on further deregulation of the broadcasting industry. Although this committee's recommendations focused on deregulation (Nissan 1997), they provided "professional" retroactive support for the government's decision to promote the designated channel plan. In August 1997, the government decided to adopt the Peled Committee's recommendations (even though the law had already passed a few months earlier) and established the Broadcasting Regulation Administration (BRA) to oversee implementation. Even though the idea for a channel in Arabic that would serve Palestinian Israelis was the catalyst and precursor of the process that led to the creation of the designated channels and the Knesset's Economics Committee listed an Arabic-language channel first among the designated channels in its July 1998 decision on designated channels, the BRA placed the Arabic channel at the bottom of its list, which was published in December of that year.[10]

At the same time, a 1997 amendment to the cable regulations lowered the threshold that would initiate Arabic-language broadcasting. Under the amendment, the requirement would begin when at least 20 percent of the population in a franchise area was Arabic-speaking rather than the original 25 percent. In addition, the amendment provided the cable council with discretion to replace the required newscasts and feature films with other programs that targeted Arabic-speaking subscribers.

The 2000s: The Designated Channel in Arabic: Special Legislation

A draft amendment to the Telecommunications Law that was meant to redraw and somewhat liberalize the regulatory landscape of the cable industry was presented to the Knesset in 1999. It included a provision that authorized the minister of communications to allow a designated channel to be broadcast as an unencrypted satellite channel. As the amendment went through the legislative process, this provision was renamed the "designated channel in Arabic provision." Its final version as it appears in Amendment No. 25 to the law stipulated that in order to give the public maximum access to the designated channel in Arabic, it should be allowed to broadcast over an unencrypted satellite signal.[11] It also said that within two years of launching, the channel would pass from the jurisdiction of the CSBC to that of the Second Authority. When this transpired, it would be regulated as a commercial terrestrial channel, even though technologically it would remain a satellite broadcast.

The Knesset Economics Committee devoted lengthy discussions to this provision, mainly because of objections raised by members who represented nationalistic and religious right-wing parties. While initially it appeared that their objections were simply procedural, it eventually emerged that they were ideological. Representing the nationalist Herut faction, Knesset Member Michael Kleiner said he objected to the proposed channel because the only "Arab channel" that should exist is a government-owned channel, namely the IBA's Channel 1 (Knesset Economics Committee Records, 18 July 2001). Kleiner described the proposed privately owned channel as an enemy channel with an official stamp of approval and argued that since it would have to broadcast "what they want to hear" in order to survive economically, it was destined to serve the enemies of the state. His position was endorsed by Knesset Member Yigal Bibi of the National Religious Party, who described the proposed channel as a "lifetime license to broadcast propaganda" without proper supervision. Kleiner later raised similar concerns on the Knesset floor (Knesset Records, 25 July 2001). The first tender for a designated channel in Arabic was not published until January 2003, after tenders had been published and licenses had been awarded for designated news, music, and Russian-language channels. The Arabic channel has still not been established and a license for its establishment has not yet been awarded, after the winners (and only competitors) in the 2003 tender retracted their bid. By 2005, the CSBC had scrapped the minimum Arabic-language programming requirements in densely Arabic-speaking cable franchises as well and replaced them with a general obligation to broadcast in Arabic that had been introduced in previous regulations.

THE NEW COMMERCIAL CHANNEL

It is not only extreme right wing and religious parties who have been known to refer to Palestinian Israelis as "them" and to broadcasting in Arabic as "their broadcasts." When amendments were inserted into the Second Authority Law in 2000 to establish Channel 10, the move was justified in the explanatory memorandum appended to the draft of the bill only by the need to increase the range of commercial television programs available to viewers and lower the price of advertising. Nothing was said about increasing the range of programming in Arabic. This lack of regard for the media needs of the Palestinian minority was reflected in an exchange that took place in the Knesset Finance Committee when it was debating the method of distributing the proposed channel. The committee chairman, MK Eli Goldschmidt, asked how each of the technological means of broadcasting the channel—terrestrial, cable, or satellite—would affect viewership. In response to his question "What proportion of the population does not have cable and in your assessment will not have DBS either?" the director-general of the communications ministry answered:

> About 70 percent of households subscribe to cable. DBS is another 10 percent. The remaining 20 percent include ultra-religious, who will not subscribe, and Arabs—who have dishes for receiving broadcasting in Arabic and don't care what we broadcast (Knesset Finance Committee Records, 3 February 2000, 7)

Providing special broadcasting to serve the needs of the Palestinian-Israeli constituency did not appear to be a goal of the policy. In the detailed appendix to the law, in which the Knesset fixed program quotas, the term "local programming" was redefined to include programming in Arabic and in Russian, so long as the majority of those involved in production were Israeli citizens. The appendix set the minimum time allotted to programming in both Arabic and Russian, including programs with subtitles, at 5 percent of total programming time. When a representative of the Knesset Finance Committee presented the law on the Knesset floor, he explained that this provision was meant to "protect the Arabic language" (Knesset Records, 28 March 2000), even though at the time Second Authority regulations required that Arabic programs be allotted 18 percent of broadcasting time. Helping Russian immigrants who understood only Russian feel that they were "partners in the content of a television channel in the State of Israel" was the reason cited for the provision requiring a similar quota (5 percent) of programs in Russian.

More alarming than that, the communication ministry's assumption (and the eventual legislative outcome) was wrong: The Palestinian Israeli minority does indeed "care what we broadcast." As Jamal (2006) demonstrates in his comprehensive study of media consumption among Palestinian Israelis, Channel 2 ranks second among televised news sources for this segment of the population and Channel 1 fourth, while the IBA's Arabic-language radio service ranks first, the Second Authority's Arabic-language station Al Shams second, and IBA's Hebrew-language news station third. The reason Palestinian Israelis drift to Arabic-language channels of foreign origin is because there is no Israeli Arabic-language channel (Cohen and Tukachinsky 2007).

In wake of the new legislation, new regulations were enacted in 2002 that redefined "the character" of commercial broadcasts. While the original regulations made no reference to minorities, the new regulations urged franchise holders to express "the core of Israeli existence" in their broadcasts; this was defined as "the Jewish-Israeli discourse" as well as "the culture and religious beliefs of the residents of Israel" and of "Jews and Arabs, immigrants and old-timers . . . a variety of audiences." The new regulations reversed the upward trend of previous years regarding the amount of broadcasting and lowered the minimum quota of Arabic-language broadcasting to 5 percent to match the quota that appeared in the appendix to the law. The regulations maintained the minimum of thirty minutes a week of original programming and imposed similar requirements on Arabic programming. In addition, for the first time, Russian-language programming was included in the law and received the same "treatment" as Arabic-language programming.

In 2003, the Knesset intervened again in the content of commercial broadcasts by adding a second appendix to the law that stipulates how much commercial television broadcasters are required to invest in the production of genres of programs they are legally obligated to broadcast. Regarding programming in Arabic and Russian, however, this second appendix merely repeated the first appendix's requirement that 5 percent of broadcasting time be allotted to programming in these languages. The Knesset record does not explain why the minimum quota for distinct language broadcasts was not fixed in monetary terms as well. However, this is an important distinction. The monetary minimum was instated to ensure a minimum quality for the programs. Refraining from requiring a monetary minimum for the language-quota programs clearly indicates that the regulators did not care about their quality. The minimum investment also encourages producers to compete for this niche, which also contributes to the quality of the programs. Competition did not apply to the language programs.

In September 2004, the Second Authority published a new tender for a ten-year license commencing in November 2005 for two franchise holders for Channel 2. While the requirements for the tender were stipulated in the law, the Second Authority formulated its own set of conditions for fulfilling the requirements. These included producing and broadcasting "preferred programs," which the Second Authority defined as "programs of knowledge and culture, heritage and Jewish culture." A requirement for a minimum number of programs in Arabic dealing with issues relevant to "Israeli-Arab society" was also included, although it is not clear whether this was meant to be part of the "preferred programs" quota that was fixed at 5 percent of the total value of the offer. What is clear is that franchise holders are not required to offer Arabic-language programs or programs produced and created by Palestinian Israelis in the most important program category, the "elite genre," which accounted for 20 percent of the total offering.

In 2002, the Second Authority also adopted special rules for commercial radio broadcasts in Arabic. Of the twelve commercial radio regions in the country, one was dedicated to broadcasting in Arabic and was carved out of noncontiguous natural geographical regions where the majority of Palestinian Israelis reside. Cross-ownership barriers were lifted in order to expand the pool of operators eligible for this license.

In its annual reports that provide information on how franchise holders have complied with the terms of their licenses and other regulations since 1999, the Second Authority reported that the only sanction taken against franchise holders who failed to meet the quota of programming in Arabic in 2002 and 2004 was that they were required to increase the number of hours they broadcast in Arabic the following year.

THE IBA

The Beresheet Committee, which was formed by a Labor-led government in 2000, proposed a major overhaul of broadcasts to Palestinian Israelis, which included introducing affirmative action hiring policies at the IBA, appointing Palestinian Israelis to management positions in the organization, and providing the Palestinian-Israeli population with proportional representation on the IBA's board. The committee advocated designing broadcasts that express the "national Arab minority's" society and culture while eliminating the propaganda content of such programs (Caspi 2005).

These recommendations notwithstanding, the IBA remained loyal to its traditional credo of broadcasting largely propaganda to the Palestinian minority, and the government supported this practice. In August 2001, yet again, the IBA announced plans to launch another satellite channel to enhance its Arabic and English broadcasts and to compensate for the decline in terrestrial broadcasting in Arabic. (This was the reason for launching Channel 33 in the 1990s, which was still broadcasting in 2001.) The government announced in a press release that it "took notice" of the IBA's plan, and the minister of communications announced in another press release that the new channel would broadcast in Arabic twelve hours every day. Soon thereafter, the IBA's management announced its plans to eliminate programming in Arabic altogether from its terrestrial channel and to divert all programs to the new channel. In June 2002, the

IBA launched this satellite channel, which ended up targeting Arabic-speaking viewers in neighboring countries.[12] In June 2003, the IBA decided to unite both satellite channels and all existing Arabic-language broadcasting that targeted both local and foreign audiences (Balint 2003c). This decision to deny Palestinian-Israeli audiences the choice of terrestrial-based public television was soon challenged in a petition to the Supreme Court (*Musawa Center for the Rights of Arab Citizens of Israel v. Prime Minister* [2004]). In mid-July 2003, the Supreme Court issued an order nisi to the government and the IBA, demanding that they explain their reasons for eliminating broadcasting in Arabic from public broadcasting's main terrestrial channel. The deputy minister of commerce, industry, and employment notified the Knesset in November 2003 that for the first time since broadcasting was launched in 1968, the new Middle East Channel would provide around-the-clock broadcasts in Arabic to fulfill the needs of "the Arabic-speaking population" and thereby make possible the cessation of broadcasts in Arabic on the IBA's only terrestrial channel (Knesset Records, 11 November 2003).[13]

In January 2004, the Supreme Court announced that it had been informed by the state that as of that month, the satellite channel's broadcasts would be rebroadcast terrestrially for one hour a day and a few more hours on weekends. As a result, the *Musawa* petition was withdrawn and the petitioners were deemed victors. In fact, however, the outcome of this decision was that the IBA began retransmitting into Israel a propaganda channel aimed at enemy countries in order to abide by the legal requirement to provide a *mamlakhti* service to Palestinian Israelis. Neither the petitioners, who were Palestinian Israelis, nor the courts commented on this paradoxical outcome, which virtually categorized citizens of the state as enemies.[14] The *Musawa* case indicates that as far as broadcasting is concerned, the Supreme Court itself has condoned this policy.

Following the *Musawa* case, the public broadcaster began retransmitting the propagandist Middle East channel for a limited number of hours a day over terrestrial channels (since only a small percentage of Israelis had satellite dishes), but it vowed to eventually provide a 24–hour service. Since the petition was consequently withdrawn, the court was exempted from discussing the meaning of the compromise reached. In June 2004, however, the deputy minister announced yet another policy, this one involving the integration of Channel 33 and the Middle East channel. This integration, he argued, would allow the two channels to carry more broadcasts in Arabic than ever before, daily from 4 P.M. to 8 P.M (Knesset Records, 6 June 2004). Although the IBA Web site describes

"Channel 3—the Middle East" as a channel broadcasting in Arabic over satellite for Arabic-speaking viewers in Israel and neighboring countries, the program schedule shows that its content is limited to one hour a day of news and current affairs programs in Arabic and, on occasion, an additional hour of programming in Arabic.[15]

The final attempt to provide for the broadcasting needs of Palestinian Israelis was made by the Dinur Committee, which was appointed in 2003 by the Ariel Sharon government, as described in chapter 5. The committee devoted a number of its recommendations to broadcasting to the Palestinian minority. It recommended maintaining a separate radio station in Arabic and improving its distribution facilities (Dinur 2005, 21) and establishing two public television channels, one in Hebrew and one in Arabic. The committee said that the "Arab population" (and women) should be represented in the new Public Broadcasting Council it was recommending (11). On the other hand, it recommended that the directors of Arabic radio and television, while designated as editors in chief of their respective media, be administratively subordinate to the respective directors of Hebrew radio and television (6).

The committee's paternalistic view of the Palestinian minority also came through in its reference to public broadcasting as a "vital element in a democratic regime" that should "contribute to the preservation and advancement of the Hebrew culture with its many colors, and in addition, provide a decent solution to Arabic speakers" (7). Although it urged the government to undertake a reordering of the IBA's objectives and make maintaining a "broadcasting entity independent of commercial funding" its top priority (9), it found no need to update references to the needs of Palestinian Israelis, repeating the goals set forth in the 1960s, namely "maintaining broadcasts in the Arabic language for the needs of the Arabic-speaking population as well as broadcasts for the advancement of understanding and peace" (ibid.). The committee's recommendations were adopted "in principle" by the government in October 2005.[16] They were introduced as a draft bill in the Knesset in 2008, differentiating once more between the goals of broadcasting to Jews and Arabs, defining the Palestinian population as Arabic speaking, and including the neighboring countries' citizens in the same target group as Israeli citizens.[17]

CABLE AND SATELLITE

Although the designated Arabic-language channel never got off the ground, the CSBC continued to take its cultural role seriously, redrafting local production quota rules and requiring that any new channels in the cable offering obtain its approval. Two incidents relevant to Arabic-language broadcasting should be mentioned. On 1 March 2000, the CSBC approved the retransmission of the Qatar-based Al Jazeera satellite channel to one cable operator of the three operating at the time. The operator, however, was allowed to retransmit the channel only to viewers in the "Arab sector" of this franchise and was not allowed to translate its programs into Hebrew or carry promotional material for the channel on other channels (that might be retransmitted or cablecast in the "Jewish sector"). On 2 May 2000, the council approved a similar arrangement with another operator. Obviously, the consolidation of all cable operators and the launching of the DBS service several years later have made these arrangements obsolete. Still, they reflect the tendency of Israeli media regulators to view Palestinian Israelis as an "enemy within." Only Palestinian Israelis were provided with the viewpoint of an Arabic country's broadcaster, a policy that lumped Palestinians with "Arabs" and separated them from Israeli Jews.

Cross-Media Laws

Broadcasting in Arabic is addressed in other laws that apply to all or selected media. The Television Broadcasts Law (Subtitles and Sign Language), which in 2005 replaced the Deaf Alleviation Law of 1992, requires that a minimum number of programs be broadcast with subtitles in Hebrew, Arabic, and Russian for the benefit of the deaf.[18] Only Hebrew news broadcasts are required to provide sign language. The Television Broadcasts from the Knesset Law of 2003 requires that Knesset channel broadcasts in Hebrew that are not live carry subtitles in Arabic and vice versa.[19] Another relevant law is the Encouragement of Songs in the Hebrew Language Law (1998) which requires that half the songs played on public broadcasting be in Hebrew and that the Second Authority actively encourage local radio stations to broadcast songs in Hebrew.[20] This law set off an emotional debate on the Knesset floor in both its first and second readings, during which many of the underlying ideological biases of its members surfaced.

MK Tamar Gozansky of the left-wing Hadash-Balad alliance[21] said that Israeli-Arab songwriters deserve as much promotion as Hebrew songwriters, setting up a debate on a topic that paralleled the existing dictates regarding quotas on television. MK Anat Maor of the left-wing Meretz party seconded her proposal. MK Ahmed Sa'd of Hadash-Balad stated that the law gives a "50% priority" to Hebrew songs. "How much are you giving to the Arabs?" he asked. "There are a million Arabs living in this country." His implied suggestion that songs in Arabic be proportionately represented was met with across-the-board opposition, as MK Yonah Yahav, who initiated the law, stated: "You don't understand. In the Arabic music programs, 100 percent of the songs are in Arabic, while on Hebrew radio, only 10 percent of the songs are in Hebrew."

MK Yahav did agree, however, that the Arab population was being discriminated against when it came to support for Arabic culture in the general budget. MK Talab El-Sana of the United Arab List Ra'am-Ta'al said that the law represented an attempt to obscure the national identity of Israel's Arab population. He said he would support the law only if proper time was budgeted for Middle Eastern music as well. During the final reading of the law, MK Abdulmalik Dehamshe asked rhetorically whether it would not be preferable to have the law refer to Israeli songs in both Hebrew and Arabic. MK Rechavam Ze'evi replied angrily to his proposition: "You have 21 countries where they sing only in Arabic. . . . We give you programs in Arabic, once I even demanded giving you a channel in Arabic, only in Arabic, so that you wouldn't need to take hours that are inconvenient. . . . You may be discriminated against there, but it is unacceptable that you will introduce your demands that are based on discrimination and providing a means of expression for another language, to the Hebrew programs aimed at the people of Israel[22] whose language is the Hebrew language" (Knesset Records, 2 November 1998).

The Significance of the Laws Regarding Broadcasting to Palestinian Israelis

Two underlying beliefs have influenced the approach Israeli policymakers have taken to providing the country's Palestinian citizens with electronic media services: one, that Palestinians are merely a linguistic minority with linguistic needs, and two, that they are an "enemy within." These characterizations of this minority, which emerge throughout the legal documentation described herein, are rooted in the hegemonic Zionist narrative and have created a two-headed policy, both de jure and de facto, that has effectively driven broadcasts aimed at Palestinian Israelis away from the traditional channels offered to society at large and into seclusion on dedicated channels, most of which are meant to serve as propaganda apparatuses aimed at neighboring countries.

The Implications of Defining Palestinian Israelis as a Linguistic Minority

The characterization of Palestinian Israelis as a linguistic minority allows the Israeli legal system to simultaneously adopt a "liberal" and a "hostile" approach toward them, thus appearing to be "democratic" and preserving the "Jewish" nature of the state. Linguistic rights are widely regarded as a minority right that should be guarded, in accordance with Article 27 of the International Covenant on Civil and Political Rights, to which Israel is party.[23] Palestinian Israelis are consistently defined as an "Arabic-speaking" minority in Israeli media laws and regulations and in most regulatory preparatory work, such as committee reports. Providing Palestinian Israelis with some Arabic content in broadcasts would seem to fulfill an international obligation aimed at linguistic minorities and be in line with the state's democratic ethos. At the same time, it achieves another goal—one implied in the wording of Israeli media laws and many of the accompanying legal documents: It associates this minority with an "Arab" culture and an "Arab" nation, thereby denying the group its self-proclaimed "Palestinian" identity.

Kymlicka and Patten (2003, 5) see a connection between the creation of language rights and the acceptance of the legitimacy of minority nationalism, and Cormack (1998) believes that if there is a connection between language distinction and national aspirations, governments will be inclined to address the needs of these populations more seriously (41). But in the Israeli case, awarding linguistic rights has become a way of restraining a minority group's nationalistic sentiments.

How the Law Has Created an "Enemy Within"

The constant parallels drawn between Israel's Palestinian citizens and the state's enemies abroad is neither accidental, incidental, or archaic. The practice is systematic and repetitious in both law and practice. It is a common thread in all the documentation referring to the Palestinian-Israeli minority that comes out in two ways. First, whenever broadcasting to the Palestinian minority is discussed, it is not described as an obligation the state has toward citizens with equal rights but rather an obligation of the state to citizens with "special needs" who are susceptible to across-the-border propaganda and whose television viewing should be monitored. Second, the law and the policy that has been implemented band together Palestinian Israelis and the citizens of neighboring enemy states, both in the definition of the service and in the actual provision of one service to both audiences. For example, Article 3 of the Broadcasting Authority Law and Article 5 of the Second Authority Law require the IBA and its franchisees to broadcast programs that fulfill the "needs" of the "Arabic-speaking" minority, and in the same breath, they require them to broadcast programs in Arabic that represent the "state's basic goals with regard to neighboring countries." And as the Knesset record and the court decision regarding the retransmission of the Middle East channel demonstrate, as far as the IBA is concerned, the two goals are served by the same broadcasts. In other words, broadcasts that supposedly serve the "needs" of "Arabic-speaking Israelis" in fact serve the propaganda needs of the state.

The Policy's Outcome

The exclusion of Palestinian Israelis from the national discourse has been achieved by eliminating Arabic broadcasts from public channels originally created to serve the entire population, including Arabic speakers, and by creating a media service aimed at Palestinian Israelis and Arabs in other Middle Eastern countries. Arabic programs are no longer broadcast on the *mamlakhti* channel, and on the main commercial channels, the time allotted for Arabic programs has been slashed from 18 percent of the total to a mere 5 percent (all during non–prime time viewing hours). In addition, Arabic speakers are not offered any professional news programs in their own language on television, while Hebrew speakers can choose every night among three. The only Arabic-language news broadcast that remains is one produced for the Middle East channel, which is propagandistic by its very nature. Since the commercial and cable channels are not required to broadcast Arabic newscasts (although regulators were empowered to require such broadcasts), Arabic-speaking viewers are left to choose between Israeli propaganda and propaganda emanating from neighboring Arab countries and transmitted via satellite, the same choice Israel's enemies face.

   In his insightful study, Saban (2004) illustrates the extent of Israel's denial of the collective rights of its Palestinian minority, including the right to preserve its distinct culture, the right to take part in the symbolic order of the state, and the right to fair access to the goods allocated by the state's social institutions. This chapter has demonstrated how these policies have also infiltrated the realm of media.

Conclusion

IS ISRAELI DEMOCRACY MUTED?

"They have mouths, but no voice"
—Psalms 135:16

According to news reports in 2005, as part of their bid for a renewed license, two commercial television license holders promised to include in their program offering for the coming decade two new versions of the IBA's seminal series *The Pillar of Fire:* an ultra-orthodox version and a Mizrahi version.[1] In March 2007, the Democratic Mizrahi Rainbow, a public advocacy group bent on promoting multiculturalism in Israeli society, filed a complaint with the Second Authority, claiming that the franchisees had not yet met their obligation and were not planning to broadcast these programs anytime in the foreseeable future. The Second Authority responded that the programs are part of the new franchisees' obligations and will be broadcast.[2]

The Religious Action Center of Reform Judaism filed a petition with the High Court of Justice in June 2007 against the joint decision of the communications minister and the Second Authority to put out a tender for a regional radio station that would cater to the religious Mizrahi community represented in the Knesset by the party of the minister of communications, Shas. The organization argued that only two more analog frequencies were available and that they should be put to better use by serving a community in greater need of a radio station (the Russian immigrant community, for instance). The Second Authority responded that since all the professional preparatory work for the new station had been completed, it was too late to reverse the decision. The communications ministry's spokesperson claimed that the petition was unfounded, as the new radio station would fulfill the unique needs of the religious Mizrahi community, providing it with content it could not receive elsewhere.[3]

Israelis of all social and cultural groups seem to agree that electronic media, even commercial media, exist to serve cultural needs. Where they disagree is which cultural agenda deserves priority. The overriding consensus about the legitimacy of and justification for broadcast regulation as a form of social regulatory policy is the defining characteristic of Israel's muted democracy.

Broadcast regulations in Israel are designed to mute certain groups and certain forms of speech, to prevent them from engaging in the cultural discourse that contributes to the development of the national culture, while promoting others quite aggressively. Israel has the formal makings of a democracy, as Chief Justice Shimon Agranat noted as far back as 1953. However, the right to take part in building national culture is reserved, at least in the electronic media, for those who subscribe to the hegemonic interpretation of the national narrative, and the system is designed to welcome into the national culture-building effort only those groups it wishes to integrate. The lack of constitutional safeguards in Israel has left these policies unchallenged.

A society's media reflect a system of control that is founded on the basic assumptions and beliefs the society upholds (Siebert, Peterson, and Schramm 1956). The critical legal analysis I employed in this study allowed me to expose the pattern of control of the Israeli political system as created by the legal texts I presented. I have thus penetrated the "ideological curtain" that surrounds these texts (Swirski 1993). Systematic analysis of the legal documentation relevant to a particular issue makes it possible to identify a pattern of control and the motivations that may be legitimate within a specific social order (at least formally) but whose formal justification obscures their real political importance in serving a dominant ideology (Cotterell 1992, 212).

As the previous chapters have demonstrated, Israeli lawmakers and policymakers have been at work for six decades trying to devise policies that would allow them to exploit the electronic media in order to advance their political and cultural agendas. These have included:

- Operating electronic media (radio) as a government entity until 1965
- Designing the Israel Broadcasting Authority in 1965 as a government-controlled institution whose task was to further the *mamlakhti* agenda
- Having the *mamlakhti* agenda serve a Jewish-Ashkenazi-centric interpretation of both the meaning of the state and its history

- Introducing television in 1968 as a means of countering transborder propaganda while engaging in such propaganda at the same time
- Subjecting the IBA to tighter controls after the introduction of television
- Adopting the view that electronic media need to serve the government's cultural and political agendas in the design of commercial television even after political power had shifted into the hands of the economic right
- Designing the cultural goals of the broadcasters (both *mamlakhti* and commercial) with an eye toward change as taking place in the dominant culture
- Launching the commercial broadcasting "experiment" in order to block transborder broadcasts
- Launching cable television with a view to providing a limited and controlled offering of programs
- Prohibiting both commercial television and cable television from operating independent news broadcasts
- Creating a policy based on "cultural ghettos" that replaced the unity-oriented *mamlakhti* ethos in response to the rise to power of special-interest political parties
- Tightening government control of cultural policies in the 1990s and 2000s, including more detailed program quotas for commercial, cable, and satellite television
- Excluding Palestinian Israelis even further from access to electronic media by eliminating broadcasting in Arabic from the *mamlakhti* channels, diminishing such broadcasting on over-the-air commercial channels, and never launching such broadcasting over cable and satellite

How Is Israeli Democracy Muted?

The contribution of Israeli electronic media to the country's image as an open and vibrant democracy has been well documented. It should suffice to mention a few of the scandals that rocked the Israeli political establishment in recent years that were exposed by the electronic media. On 17 November 1995, the IBA's Channel 1 revealed that a close friend of the assassin of Prime Minister Yitzhak Rabin had been an agent of Israel's internal security services, the Shin Bet. Although the police pressured the reporter who broke this story to reveal the source of his information, he was never put on trial (*Eitan Peleg v. The Attorney General* [1997]). In another example, on 22 January 1997, Channel 1 revealed that a cabinet minister under police investigation had orchestrated the appointment of the attorney general—the official who heads the state prosecution apparatus—in return for support for a controversial agreement with the Palestinian Authority (*MK Yona Yahav et al. v. The State Attorney* [1997]). In a final example, in November 2004, Channel 2 publicized the fact that wireless transmissions over a military network that had taken place between soldiers in a border post that purportedly proved that their commander had "verified" the death of Aiman-al-Hamas, a thirteen-year-old Palestinian girl suspected of being an enemy combatant, by emptying a magazine of bullets into her dead body. A Second Authority ombudsman's investigation into the report found it to be accurate and denied any claims that it had been "doctored," even though the officer was eventually cleared by the court of any wrongdoing.[4]

In addition to being the source of these and other exclusive and investigative pieces, Israeli electronic media have never been blocked from following up and reporting on the revelations of the print media regarding wrongdoings of the government and its officials. The Israeli legal corpus as well supports the notion that Israeli media are free to report about government wrongdoings. The *Kol Ha'am* ruling of 1953, which restricted the minister of interior's power to shut down newspapers; the *Schnitzer* case, which limited the power of the military censor; and, in particular, the *Zikhroni* case, which limited the political censorship powers of the IBA itself have all contributed to the ability of Israeli media in general and electronic media in particular to operate quite freely. The *Kirsch* case described in chapter 4 provides further confirmation for this, especially because it pertains to the public's right to choose its sources of information even in times of national emergency.

Almog's (2004) seminal assessment of the transitions in Israeli culture since the 1980s provides a detailed and convincing description of the content of Israel's electronic media. Almog argues that Israel's transition to a capitalist, democratic, and global society is expressed through this new media fare, challenging the old dominant cultural paradigm in a multitude of ways.

How, then, is it possible to argue that Israeli democracy is muted?

Mutedness, as defined is this book, is not synonymous with silence. Muted speakers and forms of speech may find other outlets through which they can articulate their ideas. Indeed, there are many avenues for expression in Israeli society and there are many dissenting voices. What is clear, however, is that the electronic media have been assigned to play an active role in promoting the hegemonic national narrative and that this role has not been contested, even by the purportedly unregulated print media. I contend that it is possible to identify more than one role for the media in a democratic society, and in the case of Israel I identify two roles that run along the "Jewish-Democratic" divide. Clearly, as the examples I just outlined attest, the Israeli electronic media take part in their ascribed role as the government's watchdog. Indeed, as a wide body of literature on Israeli media describes, if this role is not performed to perfection, lapses occur mostly with regard to reporting on sensitive security issues, in which the media have historically collaborated with the government to conceal information from the public in return for being in the know (Lahav 1978; Falloon 1984; Nossek and Limor 2001). However, that practice has decreased over the years because the *Schnitzer* (1989) and *Kirsch* (2003) cases allowed the court to deem such cooperation undemocratic. As I demonstrated in chapter 4, the potential for controlling broadcast news still exists. Nevertheless, no one can deny that the media played a central role in political change in Israel by exposing government corruption, in particular during the two major political upheavals from Labor to Likud in 1977 and vice versa in 1992.

However, when it comes to the "Jewish" half of the dyad, as this book demonstrates, the electronic media are designed to follow the hegemonic line. The danger to democracy inherent in this design is twofold. First, the national culture that is created is exclusive and homogenous. Second, because of the control system and as the participation in statist symbol creation becomes second nature to the electronic media, it acquiesces and participates in the government's propaganda efforts, perhaps even subconsciously unaware that it is playing that role.

Do the electronic media play the role assigned to them? The answer to that is affirmative. Proof of this argument can be found, for example, in a report published in summer 2007 by the Israeli media watchdog Keshev, which reviewed more than 9,000 print and broadcast news items published and broadcast during the month-long war between Israel and the Hezbollah guerilla militia in Southern Lebanon the previous summer. The report concludes that

> except for incidents that can be singled out and are detailed in the report, all major Israeli media have reported about the war in a totally mobilized fashion. . . . The media created a general atmosphere of full and complete support for the war and systematically sidelined all question marks that appeared from the first day of the fighting on. (5)

Additional assessments with similar conclusions have been published by Dor (2003, 2005). Zuckerman (2001) contends that security issues were able to unite the Jewish-Israeli front, as an unquestioned consensus emerged regarding the borders of the debate on the appropriate avenues for society to follow and justify amid external threats. However, the security prism is too narrow to fully explain this media behavior. Indeed, as Yadgar (2004) observes, the Israeli media, including the print media, have played a central role in reflecting and promoting the national narrative for decades, and as Yuran (2001) has noted, the free Israeli press, in particular Channel 2, has been swept into the "national fantasies at the base of the state's ideology, that are on the border of democracy or maybe even beyond it" (11). An editorial published by the liberal daily *Ha'aretz* on 31 July 2007 under the headline "Vanity Fair" underscores this point as it laments the quality of programming on Channel 2. Citing the cultural obligations of the franchisees as stipulated by the Second Authority Law, the editorial charges:

> This is not only a legal matter; this is first and foremost an important social-cultural issue. Israeli citizens en masse are glued to the television screens every evening, perhaps especially on summer nights, and the insulting variety [of programming] they are presented with has the power to mold the face of society, in particular that of the young generation. . . . Since television is a social agent of the first order, there are long-lasting consequences for this. A generation raised on "American Idol" and "Are You Smarter Than a Fifth Grader?" will be a degenerated generation, ignorant and blind to the happenings around it. (*Ha'aretz*, 7/31/2007)

Indeed, as these studies and examples illustrate, Israeli print and broadcast media more often than not subscribe to the nationalistic and hegemonic-cultural agenda of the state. The muteness of Israeli democracy emanates from two of its defining features: the way its electronic media are structured, which provides the government with considerable means for influencing the content of electronic media and puts electronic media owners at the mercy of government, and a massive amount of cultural regulations that are exhausting in their detail.

It appears that the mobilization of content in the electronic media has infected the print media as well. In the past, it was common for information suppressed by military censorship to make its way back into the country through the foreign press. Such was the case, for instance, with Mordechai Va'anunu, the nuclear whistleblower who found a way to publish his revelations concerning Israel's nuclear capabilities in Britain's *Sunday Times*. If a characteristic of muteness is the search for alternative ways to communicate, then this case proves that point. In more recent years, the Internet has become a source of information that the established media refuse to publish or a source of information the established media were coerced into keeping silent about. Indeed, research shows that Israelis are characterized by their straightforward speech, which they call *dugri* (Katriel 1986), and their refusal to be taken for suckers, or *friers*, as the term is known in Hebrew (Bloch 2003). These attributes have created a society of individuals resistant to control who constantly seek ways to express themselves and tell all.

Still, as this book demonstrates, the Israeli electronic media operate in an environment that is designed to control the national culture, as the legislative, judicial, and executive branches regard electronic media as all-powerful and the public interest is equated with the government's interest. The electronic media are structured in a way that ensures a particular cultural discourse that perpetuates a hegemonic interpretation of social reality and history. In order to achieve this goal, no legal stone has been left unturned and no state apparatus has been left unengaged, whether it be the Knesset, the executive branch, the courts, or regulators. All of them have left their mark on media regulation and on the perpetuation of the hegemonic ideological perception of the State of Israel and what it stands for. This comes through not only in the formal legal documentation but also in less formal utterances of lawmakers and policymakers and, eventually, the utterances of journalists.

The muted segments of society have turned to alternative means of communicating, and these alternative means have come to reflect the role in society the dominant majority wishes them to fill. Hence, the state has made it so the only viable Russian-language electronic medium available to Russian immigrants is one laden down with cultural obligations. Russian broadcasts aimed at Israel that do not fulfill these obligations are blocked. Palestinian Israelis are excluded from Israeli electronic media outlets, leaving them exposed to either internal propaganda or external propaganda, since society has branded them a "fifth column."

The state exercises control over programming and programming genres, intervening in the most meticulous details with a view toward promoting the Western-Ashkenazi and Jewish ethos. Mediterranean-style music and Mizrahi religious programming find their way to isolated channels, while the "general interest" major channels broadcast programs that serve the dominant power structure.

Within these underlying assumptions about the effects of media and the scope of the public interest standard, Israeli policymakers believe it is legitimate to structure electronic media so that they serve a national culture that serves the particular interests of a group or groups in society at the expense of others.

The following is evidence of this phenomenon:

- In the 1960s, radio was separated from the government so that it could provide a *mamlakhti* service: in other words, serve as a unifying force in the young country.
- In the late 1960s, television was created to serve the same purpose.

- In the 1970s, commercial television was designed with the same objectives.
- In the 1980s, cable television was designed as a service that would provide little in the way of content to ensure the dominance of the two terrestrial content providers in the cultural arena.
- In the late 1980s and early 1990s, when cable and commercial broadcasting were launched, they were required to fulfill cultural agendas that were exhaustive in their detail and were designed to ensure that these two types of broadcasting would play their role in unifying the nation or in ensuring that the social segmentation they promote is contained and controlled.
- And in the dawning of the twenty-first century, multichannel and digital platforms are constantly controlled to perform the same tasks.

The government did not let up on its attempts to control the electronic media, despite new realities created in the market in the late 1980s when a small number of corporate players gained dominance, despite new technological developments and new political realities. Even as Israeli policymakers began embracing a very powerful neoliberal pro-market ideology in the mid-1980s, they continued to intervene in the electronic media market. What can be said, though, is that while the collective *mamlakhti* ethos was still evident during the early stages of the political shift in power, as Israeli society began embracing individualism at the expense of social cohesiveness, the focus of social-regulatory policy began changing as well, as the following examples indicate:

- While ideologically committed to an "open sky" policy, the government ended up creating "cultural ghettos" in order to find favor with groups who had gained political power and block alternative broadcasting these same groups might enjoy that is not controlled by the official cultural agenda.
- Although the creation of the second commercial channel was designed to create more choice in programming for the public, in fact the scope of content regulation involved in this endeavor was greater than ever before, and eventually control of content genres was handed over to the legislature over the heads of the regulatory body.
- Israel further removed its Palestinian minority from the public sphere by categorizing certain cultural rights of that group as individual rights and by enclosing it in a media ghetto where its only real option is to communicate with Arabs in neighboring states, even though the media consumption patterns of Palestinian Israelis demonstrate that they want to be exposed to Israeli content.

Are Media-Culture Policies That Create
a Muted Democracy Justified?

Israeli policymakers have adopted a narrow and formal interpretation of the concept of democracy. If a "common culture" is to be created, however, all channels of communication should be open to all members of society (Williams 1989, 32). Equal and open communication channels are the ideal for a society free of distortion, and for this reason, the goals of communicative action should include promoting social integration and establishing solidarity (Habermas 1984–1987b, 138). The mass media have played a central role in the transformation of the public sphere's political function (Habermas 1989). As an example, the takeover of the mass media in Europe by the private sector has caused governments to view their citizens as "customers," thereby limiting their participatory role as members of the public. In the case of Israel, the government's control of the media and its intervention in media content has led to a bipolar definition of its citizenry as either vassals (or serfs) or consumers. But they are definitely not participants.

Indeed, it is possible to argue that the social regulatory policies regarding the role of media in culture that Israeli lawmakers and policymakers have adopted are an inevitable outcome of challenges confronting the state, in particular the need to outweigh the effects of cross-border propaganda and the need to build a cohesive society out of a diverse immigrant body. It can also be argued that assigning enculturation roles to the media is a common practice in both developing and developed nations and that the unique circumstances surrounding Israel's creation and existence justify these elements of policy that deviate significantly from the norm in developed Western democracies. The fact that Israel blocks commercial transborder broadcasts that target the local market— something that is not done in Europe, for example (Schejter 2005)—can be justified by the fact that the pan-European ethos of "harmonization" is not a popular Middle Eastern theme. At the same time, policies that exclude Israel's Palestinian minority from access to media can be justified by the fact that creating separate channels for minorities is a common practice worldwide (Browne 2005; Schejter et al. 2007), although the practice has been criticized for offering only a partial solution to minorities, whose voices should be heard in general broadcasting as well (Sreberny 2005).

These mitigating circumstances might excuse Israel's democracy-muting social regulatory policies if indeed a move in the direction of freer media were visible. That, unfortunately, is not the case, as this book demonstrates. Despite advances in media technology, Israeli policymakers have not yet been convinced that the time is ripe to allow culture to develop freely and that their grand culture-engineering aspirations and schemes have become archaic. On the contrary, new media policies that developed in the state's sixth decade of independence have become even more restrictive, including general policies that promote nationalism and media policies that relate to quotas for programming, licensing requirements for all multichannel platform channels, and propaganda broadcasts. It could be said that the Israeli multicultural experience and the inherent contradiction between inclusion in the public sphere and the legitimacy of cultural ghettos as a means for minority expression has led to inequality in the opportunities for cultural expression. Not all social and ethnic groups have an equal opportunity to build walls or tear them down and to choose under what circumstances they wish to be exclusive and autonomous and under what other conditions they are to be able to take part in cultural cross-fertilization across social groups (Gur Ze'ev 2004). Extenuating circumstances can serve as justification for such policies only when the number of available media is limited and a real need for a grand government plan of social cohesion exists, neither of which are the case in Israel anymore. It is time for Israel to move in a different direction.

Is There a Way to Make Israeli Democracy Speak Out?

The inevitable conclusion of this study is that Israeli media policies need to be rewritten with a view to opening free communication channels to allow all Israelis to participate fully and equally in building a national culture. The 1948 Proclamation of Independence says that "Israel will practice full social political equality"—a text preferred over an earlier version that said only that "Israel will award equality" (Tal 2007). The proclamation implies that equality is a natural right of all Israelis, regardless of their religion, race, or gender. Although Israel lacks a constitution that would prevent the enactment of laws restricting speech, the positive elements inherent in its constitutional framework could serve as the guiding light for future regulation designed to promote an egalitarian communication system.

Equality in communications is achieved by combining open communication channels with equal access and by ensuring that the ability to control a specific channel of communications does not spill over into other channels. In practice, this means that in a multichannel world, where the potential for universal access exists, distinctions should be drawn between commercial, governmental, and public channels. The potential for a truly democratic Israeli society lies in providing an equal opportunity for expression over all these channels.

In order to achieve this goal, Israeli media should be organized according to the following principles:

- All citizens should be guaranteed universal access to a multichannel platform: cable, satellite, or over-the-air digital.
- The most important reform is needed with regard to the most important media outlet, the only one with the potential to contribute to an egalitarian form of culture-building—Public Broadcasting. Both inclusive publicly funded channels and special-interest publicly funded channels (that offer types of programming and audiences the market fails to serve) should have a free and unrestricted presence on all platforms—cable, satellite, terrestrial, digital, and Internet—and should be the platform for all noncommercial creativity. Funding schemes for both the infrastructure of such channels and the noncommercial programming they carry should be devised in a way that guarantees their financial viability using sources ranging from a levy on Social Security, electric bills, and car licenses to a charge on the income of cable and satellite operators or the advertising income of commercial broadcasters. The structure of publicly funded broadcasters should guarantee freedom from both government and commercial pressures. First and foremost among "programming the market fails to serve" are news and children's programming. Indeed, the provision of news and children's programming over commercial channels does not obviate the need to create an egalitarian public sphere by electronic means.
- Owners of multichannel platforms (cable and satellite) should not be allowed to have a stake in content providers.
- Programming with commercial content should be transmitted over any or all of the infrastructures based upon free contractual relationships.
- Once viable and independent public and noncommercial media have been guaranteed, commercial channels should be guaranteed editorial independence and should not be subject to any content regulations beyond those mandated by criminal law. Commercial media should operate as an industry and be treated as such. The less members of the commercial media rub shoulders with the political establishment, the better.
- The government may maintain its own channels that provide government information and serve the government educational system so long as they are designated and identified as such.

Final Word

Israel's 59th Independence Day celebrations were kicked off on the night of 23 April 2007.[5] The official national ceremony, held on Mt. Herzl in Jerusalem, focused on the 40th anniversary of the "unification of Jerusalem," underscoring the centrality of "Jerusalem the capital of the Jewish and democratic State of Israel and of the Jewish people," the official theme chosen by the government for celebrations that year.[6] The "unification of Jerusalem" is, however, but a euphemism for Israel's annexation of Palestinian neighborhoods and villages east of the Jewish city of Jerusalem after they were occupied in the 1967 Israeli-Arab war and jurisdiction over them was transferred to the "unified" municipality of Jerusalem. Fourteen individuals, four women and ten men, lit twelve torches during the ceremony, each symbolizing one of the twelve tribes that constituted biblical Israel and representing a different aspect of the official theme. According to the official protocol, the torch-lighters had to represent in their "personal identity, actions, linkage or representation the central theme of the particular year of independence, and Israeli society as a whole—with its linkage to the said theme—and this from as many points of view as possible and from all important dimensions of public importance."[7] Not one Palestinian resident of either side of the city, however, lit a ceremonial torch celebrating the "unification." The only non-Jew among the fourteen Israelis was a Druze police officer from a northern Israeli town that had been heavily hit by Katyusha rockets during the month-long war with the Lebanese Hezbollah the previous summer.[8]

The ceremony was broadcast live for ninety-nine minutes on Israel's three broadcast networks, the *mamlakhti* Channel 1 and the commercial Channels 2 and 10. Thirty percent of Israeli households were tuned into the ceremony—most of them on Channel 2.[9] The blatant contradiction between the theme of the event, which celebrated "unification," and the staging of the event, which provided no representation to those people "unified" into the city, was never mentioned during the broadcasts. The commercial channel carried no commercials during the broadcast, sticking to the script prepared by its organizers, the government's Information Center.[10] Equally noteworthy is the fact that the broadcast was sandwiched between two parts of Channel 2's evening news, enabling the news anchors to introduce it by segueing into the event and following it within the flow of the broadcast as if it was news. I have discussed this event in lectures around Israel and was mostly confronted with either a shrug or an angry reaction.

The average Israeli would not find anything unusual or disturbing in this broadcast. The annual Independence Day ceremony has been carried live by Israeli television for decades. Ever since it was inaugurated in 1968, the *mamlakhti* channel has broadcast the ceremony live, as have the two commercial channels since their inception. Almog (2004) argues that broadcasts of Israel's 50th anniversary celebrations, which were mired in controversy, were an expression of the breakup of Israeli society, a signifier of a change among its elite, and a knee-jerk acceptance of national pride expressed through civil ceremony. However, close to one in three Israelis still tuned in to the anniversary broadcast nine years later, similar to the proportion that watched it nine years earlier. It is still one of the most popular programs of the year, demonstrating that the majority of Israelis are still in tune with the hegemonic cultural form built into the national ceremony. The Israeli television networks, both public and commercial, also join the popular sentiment and take upon themselves the role of willing partners in the state's propaganda efforts on this night of national celebration. This unholy alliance between broadcasting institutions and the political establishment, in which seemingly "free" media take part in the perpetuation of a nationalistic ritual while shedding their traditional role of challenging the establishment, indicates the extent of mutedness of Israeli democracy.

The author of Psalms, believed by many to be King David, was critical of polytheistic idolatry, pointing out to his detractors that silver and gold idols are man-made. Although they have mouths, he noted, they do not have voices; although they have eyes, they cannot see; although they have ears, they cannot listen; and, although they have noses, they cannot breathe. Indeed, man-made idols cannot communicate. But man-made media should be designed to communicate, since free and egalitarian communications are the basis for the development of a free and egalitarian society.

The desire of governments to use the media to exercise control over the minds of their citizen is an evil that may have been necessary and might have been justified under circumstances that no longer exist in Israel. The interest of the public is to have its ears and eyes open and to be able to speak, and the media of mass communication should serve that public need above all.

NOTES

Preface

1. All quotes in this preface are from C. W. Mills, *The Power Elite* (1956; repr., New York: Oxford University Press 2000), 4.

2. Technically, I am not a sabra—Israeli born—but my parents moved back to Israel from the United States when I was two years old, so for all intents and purposes I was considered a sabra.

Introduction: The Makings of a Muted Democracy

1. Freedom House, "Freedom of the Press: Press Freedom Rankings by Region," 5, available at http://www.freedomhouse.org/uploads/Chart90File148.pdf (accessed 2 June 2007); Freedom House, "Freedom of the Press 2006: Global Press Freedoms by Ranking," 2, available at http://www.freedomhouse.org/uploads/Chart89File147.pdf(accessed 2 June 2007).

2. WorldAudit.org: "About Us," available at http://www.worldaudit.org/aboutus .htm 20; "Israel: World Democracy Profile," available at http://www.worldaudit .org/countries/israel.htm; and "Democracy Audit: Political Rights," available at http://www.worldaudit.org/polrights.htm (all accessed 2 June 2007).

3. Reporters Without Borders: "About Us," available at http://www.rsf.org/ rubrique.php3?id_rubrique=280 20; "Israel: Press Freedom," available at http:// www.rsf.org/article.php3?id_article=17231andValider=OK; and "Press Freedom Index 2006: North Korea, Turkmenistan, Eritrea the worst violators of press freedom," available at http://www.rsf.org/rubrique.php3?id_rubrique=639 (all accessed 2 June 2007).

4. Citations for court decisions are located on the reference list.

5. Press Ordinance (1933) 1933 Palestine Gazette, 56. Full citations of laws are provided on the reference list.

6. Defense (Emergency) Regulations (1945), 1945 Palestine Gazette, 855.

Chapter 1: Culture: Features and Institutions

1. The terms "myth" and "ritual" and what they represent do not necessarily appear in non-Western cultures (Obeyesekere 1981).

Chapter 2: The Building Blocks of Official Israeli Culture

1. Some literature refers to *mamlakhtiyut* as "statism." I believe the Israeli term, as described in this chapter and throughout the book, is unique and requires the use of the unique Hebrew term. Its adjective form is *mamlakhti.*

2. Basic Law: Human Dignity and Liberty (1992); Basic Law: Freedom of Occupation (1992). Basic Law: Freedom of Occupation was later replaced by a new version in 1994.

3. Political Party Law (1992); Basic Law: The Knesset (1985).

4. Mamlakhti Education Law (1953).

5. Mamlakhti Education Law (Amendment No. 3) (1980).

6. Mamlakhti Education Law (Amendment No. 5) (2000).

7. Flag and Emblem Law (1949).

8. Flag and Emblem Law (Amendment No. 2) (1986).

9. Flag and Emblem Law (Amendment No. 3) (1997).

10. Flag and Emblem Law (Amendment No. 4) (2004).

11. Independence Day Law (1949).

12. Memorial Day for the Dead of the War of Independence and the Israel Defense Forces Law (1963).

13. As is explained by the chairman of the Knesset Committee, MK Chaim Zadok, when presenting the law for the second and third reading (36 D.K., 1718, 28 March 1963).

14. Yair Sheleg, "The Memorial Day War," *Ha'aretz,* 30 April 2007, available at http://www.haaretz.co.il/hasite/spages/850226.html (retrieved on 4 June 2007).

15. Memorial Day for the Dead of the War of Independence and the Israel Defense Forces Law (Amendment No. 2) (1968).

16. Prohibition over Opening Sites of Enjoyment on Tisha B'Av (Special Authorization) (1997).

17. Communications Regulations (Telecommunications and Broadcasting) (Advertising, Public Service Announcements and Underwriting in Dedicated Channel Broadcasts) (2004); Communications Regulations (Telecommunications and Broadcasting) (Broadcast License Holder) (1987). Although the regulations use the term "Israel's heritage," this is a common reference to the Jewish tradition.

18. Comunication Regulations (Telecommunications and Broadcasting) (Payments for Telecommunications Services) (2005).

19. Law for the Memory of the Holocaust and the Heroism—Yad Vashem (1953).

20. Memorial Day for the Holocaust and the Heroism Law (1959).

21. Matya Kain, "Memoral Day for the Holocaust and the Heroism," Center for Educational Technology Virtual Library Web site, available at http://lib.cet.ac.il/pages/item.asp?item=3155.

22. Prohibition of Denial of the Holocaust Law (1986).

23. Basic Law: Jerusalem (1980).

24. Festival of Unleavened Bread (Forbidden Bread) Law (1986).

25. Culture and the Arts Law (2002).

26. Culture and the Arts Law (Amendment) (2004).

27. Culture and the Arts Law (Amendment, Draft Bill) (2004).

28. Support for Israeli Film Law (1954).

29. The law defined an "Israeli movie" as a feature film of which a minimum of 80 percent had been "filmed, recorded, developed and processed" in Israel; Film Law (1999).

30. Cinematography Films Ordinance (1927).

Chapter 3: Media Space and Political Culture in Israel

1. With the probable exception of the mobile phone. See A. Cohen, D. Lemish, and A. Schejter, *The wonder phone in the land of miracles: Mobile telephony in Israel* (Cresskill, N.J.: Hampton Press, 2008).

2. That 31 percent represented 46 percent of households who had access to cable.

3. Z. Blumenkranz, "22% of Arab population does not watch television," *Ha'aretz*, 23 June 1994; A. Belizovski, "Cable council chairwoman: Allow subscription to part of the channels—Prices are among the highest in the world," *Haaretz*, 19 November 1996. Both available at http://www.haaretz.co.il (retrieved 28 July 2004). The discrepancy in statistics between the Cable Broadcasting Council and the Central Bureau of Statistics is attributable to the fact that the council draws on cable industry data and the Central Bureau of Statistics draws on census data.

4. From 1982 to 2001, the Communications (Telecommunications and Broadcasting) Law was known as the Telecommunications Law.

5. January 2008 study by TGI, a media research company, cited in Yael Gaoni, "TGI: Impressive penetration for 'Israel Today,'" *Globes*, 23 January 2008, available at http://sf.tapuz.co.il/shirshur-1118–111857528.htm.

6. Web site of the Israel Audience Research Board, available at www.midrug-tv.org.il.

7. Second Authority for Television and Radio Law (Amendment No. 29) (2008).

8. It should be noted, however, that these figures were not produced by the objective IARB, but by the Second Authority.

9. "TGI: More readers, less listeners," *NRG*, 29 January 2007, available at http://www.nrg.co.il/online/4/ART1/536/760.html.

10. Midgam Consulting and Research for the Second Authority for Radio and Television, "Poll on listening to national and regional radio station broadcast in Israel," (in Hebrew), December 2006, available at http://www.rashut2.org.il/editor/UpLoadSeker/%20%20%20.pdf.

11. Yossi Nachmias, "Television comes to Israel," *Yediot Aharonot*, 30 August 2007, available at http://www.ynet.co.il/articles/0,7340,L-3443290,00.html (accessed on September 3 2007).

12. The Hebrew acronym for the name "United Arab Republic" translates as "thunder," thus the "Voice of Thunder."

13. Broadcasting Authority Law (1965).

14. Transportation Regulations (1961).

15. Arrangements in the Israeli Economy (Legislative Amendments for the Achievement of the Budgetary Goals and Economic Policy for the Budget Year 2000) (2000).

16. Aviation Regulations (Operation of an Airplane and Rules of Flying) (1981).

17. Water Law (1959).

18. Land Appraisers Law (2001); Regulation of Occupation in Tax Representation Law (2005); Private Investigators and Security Services Law (1972).

19. Law for the Encouragement of Competition and the Diminution of Conflict of Interest in the Israeli Capital Market (Legislative Amendments) (2005).

20. Electricity Industry Regulations (Terms and Procedures for Awarding a License and License Holder Obligations) Regulations) (1997).

21. Tax Ordinance, Laws of the State of Israel [new version] (1957); Prison Ordinance (Amendment No. 8) [new version] (1971); Banking Ordinance (1941), 1941 Palestine Gazette, 69; Water and Sewage Corporations Law (2001).

22. Insurance Business Oversight Law (1981); Banking (Licensing) Law (1981).

23. Museums Law (1983).

24. Telecommunications Law (1982).

25. Telecommunications Law (Amendment No. 12) (1996).

26. Telecommunications Draft Proposal (Amendment No. 12) (1995).

27. Law to Boost Economic Growth, Employment and Achieve the Goals of the 1998 National Budget (Legislative Amendments) (1998).

28. Telecommunications Law (Amendment No. 25) (2001).

29. Economic Policy for Fiscal Year 2004 Law (Legislative Amendments) (2004).

30. Articles 37(8) and 42(1) of Second Authority for Radio and Television Law (1990).

31. Article 87 of Second Authority for Radio and Television Law (1990).

32. Law to Boost Economic Growth, Employment and Achieve the Goals of the 1998 National Budget (Legislative Amendments) (1999).

33. Economic Policy for Fiscal Year 2005 Law (Legislative Amendments) (2005).

Chapter 4: Israeli Electronic Media as a System of Control

1. Wireless Telegraphy Ordinance (1937).

2. Second Authority for Radio and Television Law (1990).

3. Broadcasting Authority Law (Amendment No. 2) (1968).

4. Broadcasting Authority Law (1965).

5. "Announcement of Cabinet Secretary, Attorney Israel Maimon, at the conclusion of the Cabinet meeting of 2 May 2005," available at http://www.pmo.gov .il/NR/rdonlyres/BB913389–649D-423B-92D5–EEA4073A60E1/0/gov020505.doc (accessed 5 July 2007). In 1993, the sitting director-general, who was unpopular with the newly elected government, accepted an appointment with the foreign service in order to clear the way for his quiet removal.

6. Telecommunications Law (Amendment No. 4) (1986). In 1996, the number of council members was raised to thirteen, one new member representing the government and one new member representing artists and creators. See Telecommunications Law (Amendment No. 13) (1996).

7. Currently channels 1, 2, and 10.

8. Telecommunications Regulations (Broadcasts by a Franchise Holder) (1987).

9. Telecommunications Regulations (Broadcasts by a Franchise Holder) (1997); Telecommunications Regulations (Broadcasts by a Franchise Holder) (1998); Telecommunications Law (Amendment No. 25) (2001).

10. Second Network on Television Law Draft (1985); Second Authority for Radio and Television Law Draft (1986).

11. Second Authority for Radio and Television Law (Amendment Nos. 1–5) (1990).

12. Telecommunications Law (Amendment No. 15) (1997).

13. Enhancement of Growth and Employment and Attainment of Budgetary Goals Law (Amendment) (1999).

14. Enhancement of Growth and Employment and Attainment of Budgetary Goals Law (1998).

15. Cable and Satellite Broadcasting Council Decision 2–2/2002 of January 10, 2002, available at http://www.moc.gov.il/new/documents/council1/dec_10.01.02 .pdf (accessed 21 June 2007).

16. They were soon to merge into one.

17. Cable and Satellite Broadcasting Council decision 2–28/2002, 3–28/2002, 4–28/2002 of 1 August 2002, available at http://www.moc.gov.il/new/documets/ council1/dec_11.8.02.pdf (accessed 28 November 2008).

18. Cable and Satellite Broadcasting Council decision 12–09/2003, 13–9/2003, 14–9/2003 of 3 April 2003, available at http://www.moc.gov.il/new/documents/ council1/dec_13.4.03.pdf (accessed 28 November 2008).

19. Cable and Satellite Broadcasting Council Decision 5–13/2007 of October 11, 2007, available at http://www.moc.gov.il/sip_storage/FILES/2/1232.pdf (accessed 6 February 2008).

20. Although the legal name may create the impression the channel was created as a terrestrial broadcaster and although it is regulated by the Second Authority, it was launched, in fact, as a channel distributed by cable and satellite. Policymakers cited spectrum scarcity as the reason for this technological choice.

21. Law for Arrangements in the Israeli Economy (Amendments Geared to Attain Budget and Economic Policy Goals for the Budget Year 2000) (Amendment) (2000).

22. Second Authority for Television and Radio Law (Amendment No. 19) (2003).

23. In the spring of 2009, as the book was going to press, the Knesset Economic Committee determined that Channel 10 has breached its license once too often and has not met its content obligations. The current franchise, decided the committee, should not be extended but should be put out for a new tender by the end of the year. At the same time, owners of Channels 2 and 10 were negotiating a possible merger, which in itself had the potential to bring about the closing down of Channel 10 or a new ownership structure for both Channels 2 and 10.

Chapter 5: Broadcasting

An earlier version of some of the history and analysis of the *Hannah Senesz* case appeared in A. Schejter, "The Cultural Obligations of Broadcast Television in Israel," *International Communication Gazette* 56, no. 3 (1996): 183–200; and A. Schejter, "'The pillar of fire by night, to shew them light': Israeli broadcasting, the Supreme Court, and the Zionist narrative," *Media, Culture & Society* 29, no. 6 (2007): 917–34.

1. Broadcasting Authority Law Draft (1963).

2. Broadcasting Authority Law (1965).

3. The law uses the Hebrew word for "tribe" (*shevet*), in itself alluding to the Zionist narrative's bent on the continuity of the people of Israel. Indeed, even Jewish tradition has mostly written off ten of the original twelve biblical tribes as "lost."

4. Chapter 8 provides a more detailed description and analysis of broadcasting to Palestinian Israelis.

5. *Knesset Records* 1979, 970. The implications of the resolution regarding the role of the director-general of IBA are discussed in chapter 3.

6. Second Authority for Radio and Television Regulations (Television Programs Broadcast by a Franchise Holder) (1992).

7. A distance-learning nonprofit educational venture founded, like Instructional Television, by the Rothschild Foundation.

8. See Second Authority for Radio and Television Regulations (Television Programs Broadcast by a Franchise Holder) (1992), article 8(b)(3).

9. Law for the Encouragement of Original Israeli Production in Television Broadcasting (Legislative Amendments) (1996).

10. Law for Support of Songs in the Hebrew Language (1998).

11. National Authority for Ladino Culture Law (1996); National Authority for Yiddish Culture Law (1996).

12. In 2007, the Knesset enacted two laws that established the National Authority for the Preservation of the Heritage of Jews from Bukhara and the National Authority for the Preservation of the Heritage of Jews from Libya. Neither of these authorities included representatives of the IBA. See The National Authority for the Preservation of the Heritage of Jews from Bukhara Law (2007) and The National Authority for the Preservation of the Heritage of Jews from Libya Law (2007).

13. Originally, Channel 10 was to be operated by two franchise holders (compared with the original three on Channel 2). However, economic realities eventually caused Channel 10 to be operated by one franchise holder and Channel 2 by two.

14. Arrangements in the National Economy Draft Legislation (Legislative Amendments Ensuring Attainment of Budgetary and Economic Policy Goals for the Budget Year 2000) (1999); Second Authority for Television and Radio Regulations (Broadcasting of Television Programs by a Franchise Holder) (2002).

15. See Second Authority for Radio and Television Regulations (Television Programs Broadcast by a Franchise Holder) (1992), footnote 6.

16. Second Authority for Television and Radio Law (Amendment No. 19) (2003).

17. Second Authority for Television and Radio Law (Amendment No. 26) (2005).

18. Minister without Portfolio Ra'anan Cohen, a member of the Ariel Sharon administration between 2001 and 2003, also presented a report.

19. "Announcement of Cabinet Secretary, Attorney Israel Maimon, at the conclusion of the Cabinet meeting of 30 October 2005," available at http://www.pmo.gov.il/NR/rdonlyres/5B733CF9-4447-4AE6-9FAB-768DB3AF5E69/0/govmes301005.doc (accessed 5 July 2007).

Chapter 6: Cable and Satellite

Some of the research in this chapter was published previously in A. Schejter, "From a Tool for National Cohesion to a Manifestation of National Conflict: The Evolution of Cable Television Policy in Israel 1986–1998," *Communication Law and Policy* 4, no. 2 (1999): 177–200.

1. See chapter 3 for a discussion of the Barsela Committee report and the Tele-communications Law of 1986.

2. Telecommunications Law (Amendment No. 4) (1986).

3. The regulations refer only to four channels: a family channel, a movie channel, a sports channel, and a children's channel. The fifth channel, the "science and culture" channel, was imposed on the cable operators' cartel as part of their 1996 agreement with the antitrust commissioner described later in this chapter and thus did not appear in the regulations, which had been created by the CBC earlier.

4. The Administration of Law Ordinance of 1948, the first legislative act of the independent State of Israel, states that the Jewish New Year, Yom Kippur, the first and last days of Succoth (Tabernacles), and Passover, as well as Shavuot (Pentecost) will be the days of rest in Israel. Non-Jews, however, have the right to have their days of rest according to their holidays. The ordinance can be accessed at www.knesset.gov.il/laws/special/neb/law_and_order.htm (accessed 28 November 2008).

5. In 1997, a law creating a national memorial day to commemorate the assassination of Prime Minister Yitzhak Rabin was enacted; Memorial Day for Yitzhak Rabin Law (1997). However, the CBC has refrained from including this day in the regulations stipulating memorial days.

6. Telecommunications Regulations (Broadcasts by a Franchise Holder, reg. 20) (1991).

7. Promotion of Original Television Programs Law (1996).

8. See chapter 5 for the quotas this law mandated for the IBA.

9. Basic Law: The Government (1992).

10. Telecommunications Law (Amendment No. 15) (1997).

11. A further discussion of these channels in the context of transborder broadcasting is found in chapter 7, and in the context of broadcasting for the Palestinian-Israeli minority, in chapter 8.

12. "Mediterranean" is often a euphemism for "Mizrahi."

13. Law to Boost Economic Growth and Employment and Achieve the Goals of the 1998 National Budget (Legislative Amendments) (1998).

14. Telecommunications Law (Amendment No. 25) (2001).

15. This channel, formerly known as the Family Channel, mostly broadcast made-for-TV series sitcoms, soap operas, telenovelas, dramas, and the like.

16. CSBC Policy Decision of 23 March 2000, available at http://www.moc.gov.il/sip_storage/FILES/6/1016.pdf (accessed 28 November 2007).

17. In June 2002, the obligation to sell the movie channel was removed.

18. CSBC decision 3–37/2002 of 14 November 2002, available at http://www.moc.gov.il/sip_storage/FILES/3/933.pdf (accessed 29 November 2007).

19. CSBC decision 7–4/2006 of February 23 2006 (available at http://www.moc.gov.il/sip_storage/FILES/5/835.pdf (accessed 28 November 2007).

20. CSBC decision 2–8/2003 of March 13 2003, available at http://www.moc .gov.il/sip_storage/FILES/0/920.pdf (accessed 29 November 2007).

21. CSBC decision 3–19/2001 of 12 July 2001, available at http://www.moc .gov.il/sip_storage/FILES/1/981.pdf (accessed 29 November 2007).

22. CSBC decision 5–22/2002 of 30 May 2002, available at http://www.moc .gov.il/sip_storage/FILES/8/948.pdf (accessed 29 November 2007).

23. Some of these competitions no longer exist.

24. CSBC decision 1–18/2000 of 24 September 2000, available at http://www .moc.gov.il/sip_storage/FILES/5/1005.pdf (accessed 29 November 2007).

25. CSBC decision 7–10/2001 of 5 April 2001, available at http://www.moc .gov.il/sip_storage/FILES/0/990.pdf (accessed 29 November 2007).

26. CSBC decision 1–30/2002 of 15 August 2002, available at http://www.moc .gov.il/sip_storage/FILES/0/940.pdf (accessed 29 November 2007).

27. Television Broadcasts from the Knesset (Interim Provision) (1997); Television Broadcasts from the Knesset Law (2003).

28. CSBC decision 1–2/2007 of 18 January 2007, available at http://www.moc .gov.il/sip_storage/FILES/5/815.pdf (accessed 29 November 2007).

Chapter 7: Transborder Broadcasting

Parts of this chapter were previously published in A. Schejter, "'The people shall dwell alone': The effect of transfrontier broadcasting on freedom of speech and information in Israel," *North Carolina Journal of International Law and Commercial Regulation* 31, no. 2 (2005): 337–76.

1. Wireless Telegraphy Ordinance (1981), which added articles 5A–5C to the ordinance.

2. Wireless Telegraphy Ordinance Proposed Bill (Amendment) (1981).

3. See European Agreement for the Prevention of Broadcasts Transmitted from Stations Outside National Territories, Council of Europe, European Treaty Series, no. 53, available at http://conventions.coe.int/Treaty/en/Treaties/Html/053.htm (accessed 20 October 2007).

4. Israeli law divides channels transmitted on cable and satellite platforms into several categories. The difference in the rules regarding these different channel groups is particularly relevant to broadcast financing because only a limited number of channels are allowed to sell advertising. While advertising is permitted on over-the-air commercial channels operating under the Second Authority Law, it is not allowed on channels owned by cable operators. However, the minister of communications can grant them permission to do so in a prescribed procedure.

5. *Cable Television Corporations Association in Israel v. The Minister of Communications,* H.C.J. 1413/93 (the petition was retracted). The committee report is in the author's possession along with an affidavit by the chair of the Cable Council affirming that the minister had adopted the policy.

6. Unpublished opinion in author's possession.

7. Decision no. 2444 of the Israeli government, adopted on 8 August 1997, available at www.moc.gov.il/new/documents/peled/government.pdf (accessed 11 June 2007).

8. Law to Boost Economic Growth and Employment and Achieve the Goals of the 1998 National Budget (Legislative Amendments) (1998).

9. For more about METV, see Middle East Television, "METV—Limassol, Cyprus," available at http://www.metv.org/index.cfm/fa/aboutUs (accessed 11 June 2007).

10. Telecommunications Regulations (Broadcasts by a Franchise Holder), 1987; currently named Communications Regulations (Television and Broadcasting) (Broadcasts by a Franchise Holder), 1987.

11. Using the Hebrew term for "conversion," associated with converts to Judaism.

12. The author served as counsel to METV in this petition.

13. Details of the compromise were outlined by the justices in the Gal-Er case (*Natanel Gal-Er v. Minister of Communications and Others*, H.C.J. 388/99, 474/99, court interim decision taken on 10 May 1999); see http://elyon1.court.gov.il/files/99/880/003/l09/99003880.l09.pdf (accessed 29 November 2008).

14. Amharic is an Ethiopian dialect.

15. Communications Regulations (Telecommunications and Broadcasting) (Broadcast License Holder) (Amendment) (2002); and Communications Regulations (Telecommunications and Broadcasting) (Broadcast License Holder) (Amendment No. 2) (2002).

Chapter 8: The Palestinian Minority

Portions of this chapter appear in A. Schejter, "'The stranger that dwelleth with you shall be unto you as one born among you': Israeli media law and the cultural rights of the Palestinian Israeli minority," *Middle East Journal of Culture and Communication* 1 (2008): 256–79.

1. See United Nations General Assembly Resolution 181, 29 November 1947, available at http://www.yale.edu/lawweb/avalon/un/res181.htm (accessed 13 June 2007).

2. "Arab Israelis" is Rubinstein and Medina's terminology.

3. This de facto recognition of a Palestinian people can be traced to the 1978 Camp David Accords, the basis for the peace agreement between Israel and the Republic of Egypt.

4. In Israeli political lingo, the word "explanation" (*hasbara*) is a euphemism for propaganda.

5. Second Authority for Television and Radio Regulations (Television Broadcasts by a Franchise Holder) (1992).

6. Second Authority for Television and Radio Regulations (Television Broadcasts by a Franchise Holder) (Amendment No. 2) (1997).

7. Second Authority for Television and Radio Regulations (Television Broadcasts by a Franchise Holder) (Amendment) (1999).

8. The author was a member of this committee.

9. The Zuckerman Committee used the language "Israeli-Arabs" rather than "Arabic-speaking population."

10. This change in preference can be attributed to the fact that a member of

the opposition party traditionally heads the Knesset Economics Committee. In 1998, the BRA was appointed by the ruling right-wing Likud coalition.

11. Telecommunications Law (Amendment No. 25) (2001).

12. IBA Freedom of Information Report, available at http://dover.iba.org.il/dover/html/DoverFreedomOfInfo.html (accessed 13 June 2007).

13. The deputy minister of commerce, industry, and employment was representing the minister of commerce, industry, and employment, who was in charge of the IBA at the time.

14. This analysis of how the new policy characterizes Palestinian Israelis is not so far fetched. In 2003, a national investigative committee headed by Supreme Court Justice Theodore Orr called for re-educating the national police force so that it would stop regarding Palestinian Israelis as enemies. See Report of the 2003 Mamlakhti Investigative Committee on the Confrontation between Security Forces and Israeli Citizens in October 2000, headed by Justice Theodore Orr, available at http://elyon1.court.gov.il/heb/veadot/or/inside_index.htm (accessed 29 November 2008).

15. In May 2006, this description was available on the IBA Web site, but it has since been removed. Currently, the Web site has no descriptions of the IBA's channels. See www.iba.org.il (accessed 8 September 2006).

16. "Announcement of Cabinet Secretary, Attorney Israel Maiman, at the Conclusion of Cabinet Meeting of 30 October 2005," available at http://www.pmo.gov.il/NR/rdonlyres/5B733CF9–4447–4AE6–9FAB-768DB3AF5E69/0/govmes301005.doc (accessed 5 July 2007).

17. Broadcasting Authority Law (Amendment No. 18) (Draft), available at http://www.Knesset.gov.il/Laws/Data/BillGoverment/353/353.pdf.

18. Television Broadcasts Law (Subtitles and Sign Language) (2005); Deaf Alleviation Law (1992).

19. Television Broadcasts from the Knesset Law (2003).

20. Encouragement of Songs in the Hebrew Language Law (1998).

21. The full name of MK Gozansky's alliance is Democratic Front for Peace and Equality—The National Democratic Covenant.

22. "The People of Israel" is used here in the biblical sense, meaning the Jewish people, not the people of the State of Israel.

23. Linguistic rights are recognized in many other international documents; however only the International Covenant on Civil and Political Rights is part of Israeli law.

Conclusion: Is Israeli Democracy Muted?

1. Yaniv Zach, "Soon on your screen," *NRG*, 14 April 2005, available at http://www.nrg.co.il/online/4/ART/922/280.html (accessed 25 June 2007).

2. Assef Carmel, "The Mizrahi rainbow demands that action be taken against Keshet and Reshet," *Ha'aretz*, 23 March 2007, available at http://www.haaretz.co.il/hasite/spages/842669.html (accessed 25 June 2007).

3. Assaf Carmel, "Petition to High Court of Justice against launching religious-sephardi radio," available at http://b.walla.co.il/?w=/3050/1125624 (accessed 25 June 2007).

4. Gil Salomon, "'Captain R' suing Ilana Dayan for 3 million shekels," *NRG,* 16 May 2006, available at www.nrg.co.il/online/1/ART1/422/634.html (accessed 29 November 2008).

5. Israeli Independence Day is determined each year according to the traditional Hebrew calendar, which is based on a lunar year, hence its celebration on different dates on the Gregorian calendar each year.

6. Decision st/16 of the Ministerial Committee on Symbols and Ceremonies of November 8, 2006, as appended to the Minutes of Cabinet Decisions and accepted as Cabinet Decision 753 (st/16) on November 30, 2006. Available at http://www .pmo.gov.il/PMO/vadot/sig-events/des753.htm (accessed 29 November 2008).

7. Decision st/65 of the Ministerial Committee on Symbols and Ceremonies of May 31, 2005, as appended to the Minutes of Cabinet Decisions and accepted as Cabinet Decision 3772 (st/65) on June 23, 2005 (in author's possession).

8. The ministerial committee recommended to the organizing committee that the previous year's war be commemorated as part of the ceremony as well (see Cabinet Decision 753(st/16), footnote 7).

9. According to the Israel Audience Research Board, 12.5 percent watched the ceremony on Channel 2, 10.9 percent on Channel 1, and 7.3 percent on Channel 10. See http://b.walla.co.il/?w=/3057/1096648 (accessed 2 June 2007).

10. The name of the organizer, "Merkaz Hahasbara," uses the word "hasbara," a euphemism for "propaganda."

REFERENCES

Abbreviations Used in Citations to Laws and Court Cases

A.B.   Ishur Bkhirot: approval process for disqualifying a political party
A.T.   Anti-Trust: anti-trust court proceeding (district court)
C.A.   Civil Appeal: the Supreme Court in its civil appeal capacity
D.K.   *Divrey Haknesset:* the official publication of Knesset Records
H.C.J. High Court of Justice: the Supreme Court in its administrative
        capacity
H.H.   *Hatzaot Hok:* the official publication of draft bills
K.T.   *Kovetz Hatakanot,* the official publication of secondary legislation
P.D.   *Piskey Din,* the official publication of Supreme Court decisions
S.H.   *Sefer Hukim,* the official publication of Israeli laws

Israeli Laws

Arrangements in the Israeli Economy (Amendments Geared to Attain Goals of
   Budget and Economic Policy for the Budget Year 2000) (Amendment) (2000),
   S.H. 1733, 140 (4 April 2000)
Arrangements in the Israeli Economy (Legislative Amendments for the Achieve-
   ment of the Budgetary Goals and Economic Policy for the Budget Year 2000)
   (2000), S.H. 1724, 66 (10 January 2000)
Aviation Regulations (Operation of an Airplane and Rules of Flying) (1981), K.T.
   4276, 8 (1 October 1981)
Banking (Licensing) Law (1981), S.H. 1022, 232 (26 April 1981)
Banking Ordinance (1941) 1941 Palestine Gazette, 85
Basic Law: Freedom of Occupation (1992), S.H. 1387, 114 (12 March 1992)
Basic Law: Human Dignity and Liberty (1992), S.H. 1391, 150 (25 March 1992)
Basic Law: Jerusalem (1980), S.H. 980, 186 (5 August 1980)
Basic Law: The Government (2001), S.H. 1780, 158 (18 March 2001)
Basic Law: The Knesset (Amendment No. 9) (1985), S.H. 1155, 196 (7 August
   1985)
Broadcasting Authority Law (draft) (1963) H.H. 533, 236 (25 February 1963)
Broadcasting Authority Law (1965), S.H. 451, 106 (17 March 1965)
Broadcasting Authority Law (Amendment No. 2) (1968), S.H. 0547 20 (30 De-
   cember 1968)
Broadcasting Authority Law (Amendment No. 18) (2008), H.H. 353, 286 (2 Janu-
   ary 2008)

Cinematography Films Ordinance (1927), 1927 Palestine Gazette, 188, 348

Communications Regulations (Telecommunications and Broadcasting) (Broadcast License Holder) (1987), K.T. 5064, 138 (12 November 1987. Also known as Telecommunications Regulations (Broadcasts by a Franchise Holder) (1987), K.T. 5064, 138 (12 November 1987)

Communications Regulations (Telecommunications and Broadcasting) (Broadcast License Holder) (Amendment) (2002), K.T. 6146, 340 (16 January 2002)

Communications Regulations (Telecommunications and Broadcasting) (Broadcast License Holder) (Amendment No. 2) (2002), K.T. 6169, 764 (22 May 2002)

Communications Regulations (Telecommunications and Broadcasting) (Advertising, Public Service Announcements, and Underwriting in Dedicated Channel Broadcasts) (2004), K.T. 6328, 776 (5 July 2004)

Communications Regulations (Telecommunications and Broadcasting) (Payments for Telecommunications Services) (2005), K.T. 6389, 680 (1 June 2005)

Culture and the Arts Law (2002), S.H. 1874, 64 (20 November 2002)

Culture and the Arts Law (Amendment) (2004), S.H. 1927, 304 (22 February 2004)

Culture and the Arts Law (Amendment, Draft Bill) (2004), H.H. 85, 352 (27 January 2004)

Customs Ordinance, Laws of the State of Israel (1957), 3, 39 (29 July 1957)

Deaf Alleviation Law (1992), S.H 1387, 116 (12 March 1992)

Defense (Emergency) Regulations (1945), 1945 Palestine Gazette, 855

Economic Policy for Fiscal Year 2004 Law (Legislative Amendments) (2004), S.H. 1920, 70 (18 January 2004)

Economic Policy for Fiscal Year 2005 Law (Legislative Amendments) (2005), S.H. 1997, 346 (11 April 2005)

Electricity Industry Regulations (Terms and Procedures for Awarding a License and License Holder Obligations) (1997), K.T. 5859, 40 (2 November 1997)

Encouragement of Competition and the Diminution of Conflict of Interest in the Israeli Capital Market Law (Legislative Amendments) (2005), S.H. 2024, 830 (10 August 2005)

Enhancement of Growth and Employment and Attainment of Budgetary Goals Law (1998), S.H. 1665, 48 (15 January 1998)

Enhancement of Growth and Employment and Attainment of Budgetary Goals Law (legislative amendments) (1999), S.H. 1706, 122 (4 March 1999)

Festival of Unleavened Bread (Forbidden Bread) Law, 1986, S.H. 1191, 220 (August 8, 1986)

Film Law (1999), S.H. 1698, 53 (10 January 1999)

Flag and Emblem Law (1949), S.H. 1949, 37 (24 May 1949)

Flag and Emblem Law (Amendment No. 2) (1986), S.H. 1201, 24 (1 January 1987)

Flag and Emblem Law (Amendment No. 3) (1997), S.H. 1631, 194 (24 July 1997)

Flag and Emblem Law (Amendment No. 4) (2004), S.H. 1961, 6 (17 November 2004)

Independence Day Law (1949), S.H. 5, 10 (13 April 1949)

Insurance Business Oversight Law (1981), S.H. 1021, 208 (23 April 1981)

Land Appraisers Law (2001), S.H. 1799, 436 (24 July 2001)

Law for Arrangements in the Israeli Economy (Amendments Geared to Attain

Budget and Economic Policy Goals for the Budget Year 2000) (Draft Legislation) (1999), H.H. 2824 (25 October 1999)

Law to Boost Economic Growth, Employment and Achieve the Goals of the 1998 National Budget Law (Legislative Amendments) (1998), S.H. 1645, 48, 73 (15 January 1998)

Law to Boost Economic Growth, Employment and Achieve the Goals of the 1998 National Budget Law (Legislative Amendments) (1999), S.H. 1706, 122 (4 March 1999)

Law for the Encouragement of Original Israeli Production in Television Broadcasting (Legislative Amendments) (1996), S.H. 1590, 308 (10 May 1996)

Law for the Encouragement of Songs in the Hebrew Language (Legislative Amendments) (1998) S.H. 1699, 39 (18 December 1998)

Law for the Memory of the Holocaust and the Heroism—Yad Vashem (1953), S.H. 132, 144 (28 August 1953)

Mamlakhti Education Law (1953), S.H. 131, 137 (20 August 1953)

Mamlakhti Education Law (Amendment No. 3) (1980), S.H. 967, 105 (3 April 1980)

Mamlakhti Education Law (Amendment No. 5) (2000), S.H. 1729, 122 (22 February 2000)

Memorial Day for the Dead of the War of Independence and the Israel Defense Forces (1963), S.H. 393, 72 (5 April 1963)

Memorial Day for the Dead of the War of Independence and the Israel Defense Forces (Amendment No. 2) (1980), S.H. 986, 6 (4 November 1980)

Memorial Day for the Holocaust and the Heroism Law (1959), S.H. 28, 112 (8 April 1959)

Memorial Day for Yitzhak Rabin Law (1997) S.H. 1630, 186 (17 July 1997)

Museums Law (1983), S.H. 1084, 113 (30 June 1983)

National Authority for Ladino Culture Law (1996), S.H. 1577, 185 (17 March 1996)

National Authority for Yiddish Culture Law (1996), S.H. 1577, 182 (17 March 1996)

National Authority for the Preservation of the Heritage of Jews from Bukhara (2001), S.H. 2080, 101 (1 February 2007)

National Authority for the Preservation of the Heritage of Jews from Libya (2007), S.H. 2080, 105 (1 February 2007)

Political Party Law (1992), S.H. 1395, 190 (9 April 1992)

Press Ordinance (1933) 1933 Palestine Gazette 1191

Prison Ordinance (Amendment No. 8) (1971), S.H. 1262, 228 (27 July 1988)

Private Investigators and Security Services Law (1972), S.H. 654, 127 (2 April 1972)

Prohibition on Denial of the Holocaust Law (1986), S.H. 1187, 196 (16 July 1986)

Prohibition on Opening of Sites of Enjoyment on Tisha B'Av Law (Special Authorization) (1997), S.H. 1637, 8 (14 November 1997)

Regulation of Occupation in Tax Representation Law (2005), S.H. 1978, 114 (27 January 2005)

Second Authority for Radio and Television Law (Draft) (1986), H.H. 1801, 2 (7 October 1986)

Second Authority for Radio and Television Law (1990), S.H. 1304, 58 (13 February 1990)

Second Authority for Television and Radio Law (Amendment No. 19) (2003), S.H. 1899, 528 (6 August 2003)

Second Authority for Television and Radio Law (Amendment No. 26) (2005), S.H. 2035, 16 (22 November 2005)

Second Authority for Television and Radio Law (Amendment No. 29), S.H. 2133, 192 (10 February 2008)

Second Authority for Radio and Television Law (Amendment) (1991), S.H. 1347, 102 (1 March 1991)

Second Authority for Radio and Television Law (Amendment No. 2) (1992), S.H. 1384, 84 (21 February 1992)

Second Authority for Radio and Television Law (Amendment No. 3) (1992), S.H. 1392, 167 (26 March 1992)

Second Authority for Radio and Television Law (Amendment No. 4) (1992), S.H. 1399, 248 (4 August 1992)

Second Authority for Radio and Television Law (Amendment No. 5) (1993), S.H. 1412, 58 (4 February 1993)

Second Authority for Radio and Television Regulations (Television Broadcasts by a Franchise Holder) (1992), K.T. 5455, 1243 (6 July 1992)

Second Authority for Television and Radio Regulations (Television Broadcasts by a Franchise Holder) (Amendment No. 2) (1997), K.T. 5846, 1070 (8 July 1997)

Second Authority for Television and Radio Regulations (Television Broadcasts by a Franchise Holder) (Amendment) (1999), K.T. 5946, 274 (12 January 1999)

Second Authority for Television and Radio Regulations (Television Broadcasts by a Franchise Holder) (2002), K.T. 6206, 146 (5 November 2002)

Second Network on Television Law (Draft) (1985), H.H. 1752, 309 (2 September 1985)

Support for Israeli Film Law (1954), S.H. 158, 143 (16 July 1954)

Telecommunications Draft Proposal (Amendment No. 12) (1995), H.H. 2349, 244 (16 January 1995)

Telecommunications Law (1982), S.H. 1960, 218 (22 August 1982)

Telecommunications Law (Amendment No. 4) (1986), S.H. 1192, 224 (13 August 1986)

Telecommunications Law (Amendment No. 12) (1996), S.H. 586, 248 (13 March 1996)

Telecommunications Law (Amendment No. 13) (1996), S.H. 1590, 302 (10 May 1996)

Telecommunications Law (Amendment No. 15) (1997), S.H. 1620, 102 (9 April 1997)

Telecommunications Law (Amendment No. 25) (2001), S.H. 1807, 530 (7 August 2001)

Telecommunications Regulations (Broadcasts by a Franchise Holder) (1991), K.T. 5397, 429 (14 November 1991)

Telecommunications Regulations (Broadcasts by a Franchise Holder) (1997), K.T. 5827, 622 (6 May 1997)

Telecommunications Regulations (Broadcasts by a Franchise Holder) (1998), K.T. 5879, 390 (9 February 1998)

Television Broadcasts Law (Subtitles and Sign Language) (2005) S.H. 2026, 956 (10 August 2005)

Television Broadcasts from the Knesset Law (2003), S.H. 1915, 32 (29 December 2003)

Transportation Regulations (1961), K.T. 1128, 1425 (6 April 1961)

Water and Sewage Corporations Law (2001), S.H. 1802, 454 (31 July 2001)

Water Law (1959), S.H. 288, 169 (13 August 1959)

Wireless Telegraphy Ordinance (1937), 1937 Palestine Gazette 1

Wireless Telegraphy Ordinance (Amendment) (1981), S.H. 1981, 2 (30 November 1981)

Wireless Telegraphy Ordinance Proposed Bill (Amendment) (1981), H.H. 1541, 389 (19 May 1981)

Knesset Documents

Knesset records are available online as of 1980. Citations of Knesset plenum debates that took place prior to 1980 are taken from the official *Divrey Haknesset*. Citations from debates that took place after 1980 can be searched on the Knesset's Web site at http://www.knesset.gov.il/Divrey/QForm.asp.

PLENUM RECORDS

18 June 1963
8 March 1965
17 December 1979
27 March 1986
14 February 1994
16 November 1994
4 November 1996
2 November 1998
28 March 2000
25 July 2001
11 November 2003
6 June 2004

KNESSET ECONOMICS COMMITTEE RECORDS

20 March 2001
18 July 2001

KNESSET FINANCE COMMITTEE RECORDS

24 January 2000
3 February 2000

Israeli Court Cases

Adalah, the Legal Center for the Rights of the Arab Minority in Israel v. The Municipalities of Tel Aviv, Ramla, Lod, and Upper Nazareth (1999) (H.C.J. 4112/99, 56[5] P.D. 393)

Central Election Committee v. MK Ahmed Tibi (2002) (A.B. 11280/02, 57[4] P.D. 1)

Eitan Peleg, Attorney, v. The Attorney General (1997) (H.C.J. 6926/97, unpublished decision of 10 September 1998, available at www.takdinet.co.il)

Elias Yaakov v. Chair of the IBA and Others (1998) (H.C.J. 2137/98, unpublished decision of 5 April 1998, available at http://elyon1.court.gov.il/files/98/370/021/i01/98021370.i01.pdf)

Film Studios v. Levi Geri (1962) (H.C.J. 243/62, 16 P.D. 2407)

Gaza Shore Regional Council v. The Knesset of Israel (2005) (H.C.J. 1661/05 and 11 more petitions, available at http://elyon1.court.gov.il/files/05/610/016/a20/05016610.a20.htm)

Gideon Zilberstein v. The Mayor of Haifa Adv. Yona Yahav (A.P. [Haifa] 1160/05, unpublished decision, in author's possession)

Hachayim Book Publishers v. Israel Broadcasting Authority (1979) (C.A. 7/79, 35[2], P.D. 365)

I.C.S. Israel Cable Systems, Ltd. v. The Antitrust Commissioner (1994) (Antitrust case 445, in author's possession)

Idan Cable Corp. Ltd. v. Antitrust Commissioner (1995) (A.T. 466/95, 32[1], Dinim-Mehozi 393)

Israel Instructional Television v. The Second Authority (1999) (H.C.J. 4170/96, 53[1], P.D. 178)

Joseph Brand v. Minister of Communications (1992) (H.C.J. 3472/92, 47[3] P.D. 143)

Kidum Entrepreneurship and Publishing Ltd. v. IBA (1994) (H.C.J. 606/93, 48[2], P.D. 1)

Kol Haam v. Minister of the Interior (1953) (H.C.J. 73/53, 7 P.D. 871)

Mayo Simon Marketing and Public Relations Ltd. v. Second Authority for Radio and Television (1996) (H.C.J. 5118/95, 49[5], P.D. 751)

Media Most Inc. v. Cable and Satellite Broadcasting Council (2004) (H.C.J. 6962/03, 10338/03, 59[3] P.D. 14)

M. E. Television Services Ltd. v. The Minister of Communications (1999) (H.C.J. 474/99, petition retracted on 9/15/99, decision approval in author's possession)

Michael Kirsch v. Chief of Staff of the Israeli Def. Forces (2003) (H.C.J. 2753/03, 2791/03, unpublished decision available at http://elyon1.court.gov.il/files/03/530/027/l09/03027530.l09.pdf)

MK Haim Oron, v. Speaker of the Knesset (2002) (H.C.J. 1030/99, 56[3], P.D. 640)

MK Rabbi Meir Kahane v. Board of the Broadcasting Authority (1987) (H.C.J. 399/85, 40[4] P.D. 255)

MK Yonah Yahav v. The State Attorney (1997) (H.C.J. 2534/97, 2535/97, 2541/97, 51[3] P.D. 39)

Musawa Center for the Rights of Arab Citizens of Israel v. Prime Minister (2003)

(H.C.J. 375/03, unpublished decision available at http://elyon1.court.gov.il/ files/03/750/003/l08/03003750.l08.pdf)

Netanel Gal-Er v. the Minister of Communications (1999) (H.C.J. 388/99, unpublished decision available at http://elyon1.court.gov.il/files/99/880/003/ l09/99003880.l09.pdf)

Omar International, Inc. v. Minister of the Interior (1982) (H.C.J. 644/81, 36[1], P.D. 227)

Organization of IDF Widows and Orphans v. The Prime Minister of Israel (2000) (H.C.J. 3181/00, unpublished decision in author's possession)

Schnitzer v. Chief Military Censor (1989) (H.C.J. 680/88, 42[4], P.D. 617)

Senesz Giora v. Israel Broadcasting Authority (1999) (H.C.J. 6126/94, 6143/94, 53[3], P.D. 817)

Sephardi Community of Jerusalem Council v. Ya'acov Arnon (1977) (C.A. 698/77, 32[2], P.D. 183)

Vicki Shiran v. Israel Broadcasting Authority (1981) (H.C.J. 1/81, 35[3], P.D. 365)

Tamarin Georg Raphael v. The State of Israel (1972) (C.A. 630/70, 26[1], P.D. 197)

Tel'Ad Jerusalem Studios, Ltd. v. The Minister of Communications (1999) (H.C.J. 7051/98, petition retracted, decision approval available at elyon1.court.gov.il/ files/98/510/070/e08/98070510.e08.pdf)

Walid Muhi a-din Asli v. Superintendent of Jerusalem (1983) (H.C.J. 541/83, 37[4], P.D. 837)

Yisrael Ben David vs. the Minister of Communications (1994) (H.C.J. 5950/94, unpublished decision in author's possession)

Yitzhak Fogel v. Israel Broadcasting Authority (1977) (H.C.J. 112/77, 31[3], P.D. 657)

Zichroni v. Board of the Broadcasting Authority (1983) (H.C. 243/82, 37[1], P.D. 757)

Articles, Books, and Government Reports

Aharoni, Y. 1998. The changing political economy of Israel. *Annals of the Academy of Political and Social Sciences* 555:127–46.

Almog, O. 2000. *The sabra: The creation of the new Jew.* Berkeley, Calif.: University of California Press.

———. 2004. *Farewell to "Srulik": Changing values among the Israeli elite.* Haifa and Or Yehuda, Israel: University of Haifa and Zmora Bitan Press. (In Hebrew.)

Althusser, L. 1965/1969. *For Marx.* Trans. B. Brewster. London: Cox and Wynman.

Anderson, B. 1983. *Imagined communities.* London: Verso.

Anderson, S. 2000. Loafing in the garden of knowledge: History TV and popular memory. *Film and History* 30 (1): 14–23.

Andsager, J., R. Wyatt, and E. Martin. 2004. *Free expression in 5 democratic publics: Support for individual and media rights.* Cresskill, N.J.: Hampton Press.

Aronoff, M. 1983. Conceptualizing the role of culture in political change. In *Cul-*

ture and political change, ed. M. Aronoff, 1–18. New Brunswick, N.J.: Trans-action Books.

———. 2001. Radical change in Israel: A review essay. *Political Science Quar-terly* 116 (3): 447–53.

Asheri, E. 1996. Stop the viewers' decline. *Ha'aretz,* 24 April. Accessed online 6 June 2006.

Avraham, E. 2003. *Behind media marginality: Coverage of social groups and places in the Israeli press.* Lanham, Md.: Lexington Books.

Badran, A. R., and C. Badran. 1991. Christian broadcasting in the Eastern Medi-terranean: The case of Middle East television. *International Communication Gazette* 47:33–46.

Balint, A. 2002a. Cable and Satellite Council refuses to expose minutes of de-bate on discontinuance of CNN broadcasts. *Ha'aretz,* 19 September. Accessed online 28 July 2004.

———. 2002b. Cable companies will continue broadcasting CNN. *Ha'aretz,* 24 October. Accessed online 28 July 2004.

———. 2003a. Cable Council authorizes removal of BBC World. *Ha'aretz,* 7 April. Accessed online 28 July 2004.

———. 2003b. Cable companies will resume BBC World Broadcasts. *Ha'aretz,* 15 April. Accessed online 28 July 2004.

———. 2003c. The Middle East Channel will be united with Channel 33. *Ha'aretz,* 11 June. Accessed online 6 June 2006.

Barak-Erez, D. 2001. Collective memory and judicial legitimacy: The historical narrative of the Israeli Supreme Court. *Canadian Journal of Law and Society* 16 (1): 93–112.

Barsela, Yoram. 1982. Report of the Committee on Cable Television. In Hebrew; in author's possession.

Barzilai, G. 2002. Fantasies of liberalism and liberal jurisprudence: State law, politics, and the Israeli-Arab-Palestinian community. *Israel Law Review* 34 (3): 425–51.

Baumel, J. 1996. The Heroism of Hannah Senesz: An exercise in creating collec-tive national memory in the state of Israel. *Journal of Contemporary History* 31 (3): 521–46.

———. 2002. Founding myths and heroic icons: Reflections on the funerals of Theodor Herzl and Hannah Szenes. *Women's Studies International Forum* 25 (6): 679–95.

Ben Bassat, A. 2002. The obstacle course to a market economy in Israel. In *The Israeli economy, 1985–1998,* ed. A. Ben Bassat, 1–58. Cambridge, Mass.: MIT Press.

Bendor, Shmuel. 1965. Report of the interministerial committee on general tele-vision. In Hebrew; in author's possession.

Bennet, W. 1983. Culture, communication, and political control. In *Culture and political change,* ed. M. Aronoff, 39–52. New Brunswick, N.J.: Transaction Books.

Benvenisti, M. 1997. The Hebrew Map. *Theory and Critique* 11:7–29. (In He-brew.)

Ben Yisrael, R. 1994. Labor laws. In *Yearbook on Israeli law 1992–1993,* ed. A. Rosen-Zvi, 433–68. Tel Aviv: The Israel Bar Association. (In Hebrew.)

Beresheet, Haim. 2000. The Public Broadcasting Committee. Quoted in Caspi, 2005.

Bishara, A. 1993. On the question of the Palestinian minority in Israel. In *Israeli society: Critical perspectives,* ed. U. Ram, 203–21. Tel Aviv: Breirot Publishers. (In Hebrew.)

Bloch, L. R. 2003. When the frame takes over: Analyzing *freier* discourse in Israeli communication culture. *Communication Theory* 13:125–59.

Blumler, J. 1992. *Television and the public interest: Vulnerable values in Western European broadcasting.* London: Sage Publications.

Boyd, D. 1991. Lebanese Broadcasting: Unofficial electronic media during a prolonged civil war. *Journal of Broadcasting and Electronic Media* 35:269–87.

———. 1993. *Broadcasting in the Arab world: A survey of the electronic media in the Middle East.* Ames: Iowa State University Press.

Brog, M. 2004. Victims and victors: Holocaust and military commemoration in Israel collective memory. *Israel Studies* 8 (3): 65–99.

Browne, D. 2005. *Ethnic minorities, electronic media, and the public sphere: A comparative study.* Cresskill, N.J.: Hampton Press.

Carey, J. 1992. Political correctness and cultural studies. *Journal of Communication* 42 (2): 56–72.

Caspi, D. 2005. *Due to technical difficulties: The fall of the Israel Broadcasting Authority.* Mevasseret Zion, Israel: Zivonim. (In Hebrew.)

Caspi, D., H. Adoni, A. Cohen, and N. Elias. 2002. The Red, the white and the blue: The Russian media in Israel. *Gazette: International Journal for Communication Studies* 64:537–56.

Caspi, D., and Y. Limor. 1992. *The mediators: The mass media in Israel, 1948–1990.* Tel Aviv: Am Oved. (In Hebrew.)

———. 1999. *The in/outsiders: Mass media in Israel.* Cresskill, N.J.: Hampton Press.

Cassirer, Henry, and Talbot Duckmanton. 1961. Educational television in Israel: Report of a UNESCO mission, 31 May–27 June 1961: Recommendations. UNESCO.

Central Bureau of Statistics. 1970. Report to the Israel Broadcasting Authority. In Hebrew; in author's possession.

Central Bureau of Statistics. 1971. *A poll on listening to the radio and watching television.* (In Hebrew; in author's possession.)

———. 1993–2007. *Statistical abstracts of Israel.* Jerusalem: Hemed Publishers. (In Hebrew.)

Chetrit, S. 2004. *The Mizrahi struggle in Israel between oppression and liberation identification and alternative.* Tel Aviv: Am Oved Publishers. (In Hebrew.)

Cohen, A. 1981. People without media: Attitudes and behavior during a general media strike. *Journal of Broadcasting* 25 (2): 171–80.

Cohen, A., and L. Cohen. 1989. Big eyes but clumsy fingers: Knowing about and using technological features of home VCRs. In *The VCR age,* ed. M. Levy, 135–47. Beverly Hills, Calif.: Sage.

Cohen Y., and R. Tukachinsky. 2007. Television and group identity in the age of multichannel television: Local and global viewing patterns among various social groups in Israel. *Israeli Sociology* 8 (2): 241–67. (In Hebrew.)

Comella, Victor Ferreres. 2004. The new regulation of political parties in Spain and the decision to outlaw Batasuna. In *Militant democracy*, ed. Andras Sajo, 133–156. Utrecht, Holland: Eleven International Publishing.

Connerton, P. 1989. *How societies remember.* Cambridge: Cambridge University Press.

Cook, J. 2006. *On the margins: Annual review of human rights violations of the Arab Palestinian minority in Israel 2005.* Nazareth: Arab Association for Human Rights. Available at http://www.arabhra.org/HRA/Pages/Index.aspx?Language=2.

Cormack, M. 1998. Minority language media in Western Europe: Preliminary considerations. *European Journal of Communication* 13 (1): 33–52.

Cotterell, R. 1992. *The politics of jurisprudence: A critical introduction to legal philosophy.* Philadelphia: University of Pennsylvania Press.

Dahan, Y., and G. Levy. 2000. Multicultural education in the Zionist state: The Mizrahi challenge. *Studies in Philosophy and Education* 19:423–44.

Dayan, D., and E. Katz. 1992. *Media events: The live broadcasting of history.* Cambridge, Mass.: Harvard University Press.

Dinur, Ra'anan. 2005. The Committee for Reforming Public Broadcasting. In Hebrew; in author's possession.

Dominguez, V. 1989. *People as subject, people as object: Selfhood and peoplehood in contemporary Israel.* Madison: University of Wisconsin Press.

Dor, D. 2004. *Intifada hits the headlines: How the Israeli press misreported the outbreak of the Second Palestinian Uprising.* Bloomington: Indiana University Press.

———. 2005. *The suppression of guilt: the Israeli media and the reoccupation of the West Bank.* London: Pluto Press.

Doron, G. 1998. The politics of mass communication in Israel. *Annals of the American Academy of Political and Social Science* 555:163–79.

Douglass, L. 2001. *The memory of judgment: Making law and history in the trials of the holocaust.* New Haven, Conn.: Yale University Press.

Dryzek, J., and C. List. 2003. Social choice theory and deliberative democracy: A reconciliation. *British Journal of Political Science* 33:1–28.

Eagleton, T. 1991. *Ideology: An introduction.* London: Verso.

Edsforth, R. 1991. Popular culture and politics in modern America: An introduction. In *Popular culture and political change in modern America,* ed. R. Edsforth and L. Bennett, 1–16. Albany, N.Y.: State University of New York Press.

Eisenstadt, S. 1967. Israeli identity: Problems in the development of the collective identity of an ideological society. *Annals of the American Academy of Political and Social Science* 370:116–23.

Ettinger, Y. 2002. CNN admits mistakes and attempts to undo damage. *Ha'aretz,* 24 June. Accessed online 28 July 2004.

Etziony-Halevy, E. 1987. *National broadcasting under siege: A comparative study of Australia, Britain, Israel and West Germany.* London: Palgrave Macmillan.

European Audiovisual Observatory. 2004. *Transfrontier television in the European Union: market impact and selected legal aspects.* Strasbourg: European Audiovisual Observatory.

European Broadcasting Union. 1965. Report on Israeli television. In Hebrew; in author's possession.

Falloon, V. 1984. Excessive secrecy, lack of guidelines. *Index on Censorship* 13 (4): 32–36.

Farquhar, M., and C. Berry. 2004. Speaking bitterness: History, media and nation in twentieth century China. *Historiography East and West* 2:116–43.

Filc, D. 2006. *Populism and hegemony in Israel.* Tel Aviv: Resling. (In Hebrew.)

Footer, M., and C. Graber. 2000. Trade liberalization and cultural policy. *Journal of International Economic Law* 3 (1): 115–44.

Forgacs, D., ed. 1988. *An Antonio Gramsci reader.* New York: Schocken Books.

Fujitani, T. 1992. Electronic pageantry and Japan's "symbolic emperor." *Journal of Asian Studies* 51 (4): 824–50.

Gandal, Neil 1994. Development of cable television in Israel. *Telecommunications Policy* 18 (4): 342–48.

Gavison, R. 1999. *Can Israel be both Jewish and democratic? Tensions and prospects.* Jerusalem: Van Leer and Hakibutz Hameuchad Publishing House. (In Hebrew.)

Geertz, C. 1973. *The interpretation of culture.* New York: Basic Books.

Ghanem, A. 2001. *The Palestinian Arab minority in Israel, 1948–2000.* Albany, N.Y.: SUNY Press.

Giddens, A. 1979. *Central problems in social theory: Action, structure, and contradiction in social analysis.* London: Macmillan Press, Ltd.

Gil, Z. 1986. *House of diamonds: The history of Israeli television.* Tel Aviv: Sifriyat Poalim. (In Hebrew.)

Gitlin, T. 1980. *The whole world is watching: Mass media in the making and unmaking of the new left.* Berkeley: University of California Press.

Golan-Agnon, D. 2006. Separate but not equal: Discrimination against Palestinian Arab students in Israel. *American Behavioral Scientist* 49 (8): 1075–84.

Gontovnik, G. 2004. The right to culture in a liberal society and in the state of Israel: Living the contradictions. In *Economic, social and cultural rights in Israel,* ed. Y. Rabin and Y. Shany, 619–62. Tel Aviv: Ramot Tel Aviv University Press. (In Hebrew.)

Goren, Dina 1976. *Secrecy, security and freedom of the press.* Jerusalem: Magnes. (In Hebrew.)

Gramsci, A. 1988. [Ethico-political history]. In *An Antonio Gramsci reader,* ed. D. Forgacs, 194. New York: Schocken Books.

Greene, Hugh. 1973. Report to the Minister of Education and Culture. In Hebrew; in author's possession.

Gur-Ze'ev, I. 2004. *Toward a diasporic education: Multiculturalism, post-colonialism and counter-education in a post modern era.* Tel Aviv: Resling. (In Hebrew.)

Habermas, J. 1989. *The structural transformation of the public sphere.* Trans. T. Burger. Cambridge, Mass.: MIT Press.

———. 1984–1987a. *The theory of communicative action.* Vol. 1, *Reason and the rationalization of society.* Trans. T. McCarthy. Boston: Beacon Press.

———. 1984–1987b. *The theory of communicative action.* Vol. 2, *Lifeworld and the system.* Trans. T. McCarthy. Boston: Beacon Press.

Hall, S. 1986. Cultural studies: Two paradigms. In *Media, culture, and society: A critical reader,* ed. R. Collins, J. Curran, N. Garnham, P. Scannell, P. Schlesinger, and C. Sparks, 33–48. London: Sage Publications.

————. 1991. Cultural identity and diaspora. In *Identity: Community, culture, difference*, ed. J. Rutherford, 222–37. London: Lawrence and Wishart.

Hasson, S., and M. Karayanni. 2006. *Arabs in Israel: Barriers to equality.* Jerusalem: Floresheimer Institute for Policy Studies. (In Hebrew.)

Hecht, B. 1961/1997. *Perfidy.* Jerusalem: Milah Press.

Hegland, M. 1983. Ritual and revolution in Iran. In *Culture and political change*, ed. M. Aronoff, 75–100. New Brunswick, N.J.: Transaction Books.

Heilbrun, J., and C. Gray. 1993. *Economics of art and culture: An American perspective.* Cambridge: Cambridge University Press.

Hesmondhalgh, D. 2005. Media and cultural policy as public policy: The case of the British Labour government. *International Journal of Cultural Policy* 11 (1): 95–109.

Hetsroni, A. 2004. The millionaire project: A cross-cultural analysis of quiz shows from the United States, Russia, Poland, Norway, Finland, Israel, and Saudi Arabia. *Mass Communication and Society* 7 (2) 133–56.

Hirschl, R. 1997. The "constitutional revolution" and the emergence of a new economic order in Israel. *Israel Studies* 2 (1): 136–55.

————. 1998. Israel's constitutional revolution: The legal interpretation of entrenched civil liberties in an emerging neo-liberal economic order. *American Journal of Comparative Law* 46 (3): 427–52.

————. 2000. "Negative" rights vs. "positive" entitlements: A comparative study of judicial interpretations of rights in an emerging neo-liberal economic order. *Human Rights Quarterly* 22:1060–98.

Hoskins, A. 2004. Television and the collapse of memory. *Time and Society* 13 (1): 109–27.

Huntington, S. 1991. *The third wave: Democratization in the late twentieth century.* Norman: University of Oklahoma Press.

Hutchinson, J. 1987. *The dynamics of cultural nationalism: The Gaelic revival and the creation of the Irish nation state.* London: Allen and Unwin.

Inglehart, R. 1990. *Culture shift in advanced industrial society.* Princeton, N.J.: Princeton University Press.

Ish-Horowitz, Yitzhak. 1992. Report of the Public Committee on the Issue of Advertising on Cable Channels. In Hebrew; in author's possession.

Jamal, A. 2000. The Palestinian media: An obedient servant or a vanguard of democracy? *Journal of Palestine Studies* 29 (3): 45–59.

————. 2006. *The culture of media consumption among national minorities: The case of Arab society in Israel.* Nazareth: I'lam—Media Center for Arab Palestinians in Israel.

Jamias, J. 1993. The impact of new communication technologies on cultural identity in rural Asia, *Media Asia* 20 (4): 205–7.

Jeffries, L. 2000. Ethnicity and ethnic media use: A panel study, *Communication Research* 27:496–535.

Kahane, R. 1992. Patterns of national identity in Israel. In *Problems of collective identity and legitimation in Israeli society*, ed. R. Kahane and S. Kopstein, 296–314. Jerusalem: Academon. (In Hebrew.)

Kansteiner, W. 2002. Finding meaning in memory: A methodological critique of collective memory studies, *History and Theory* 41:179–97.

Katriel, T. 1986. *Talking straight: Dugri speech in Israeli sabra culture.* Cambridge, Mass.: University of Cambridge Press.

Katz, E. 1971. Television comes to the People of the Book. In *The use and abuse of social science: Behavioral research and social science,* ed. I. Horowits, 249–71. New Brunswick, N.J.: Transaction.

———. 1996. And deliver us from segmentation. *Annals of the American Academy of Political and Social Science* 546:22–33.

Katz, E., and M. Gurevitch. 1973. *The culture of leisure in Israel.* Tel Aviv: Am Oved-Tarbut Vechinuch. (In Hebrew.)

Katz, E., and H. Sella. 1999. *The Beracha report: Culture policy in Israel.* Jerusalem: Van Leer Institute.

Katz, E., and G. Wedell. 1977. *Broadcasting in the Third World: Promise and performance.* Cambridge, Mass.: Harvard University Press.

Katz, E., H. Haas, and M. Gurevitch. 1997. 20 years of television in Israel: Are there long-run effects on values, social connectedness, and cultural practices? *Journal of Communication* 47 (2): 3–20.

Kedar, N. 2002. Ben Gurion's *mamlakhtiyut:* Etymological and theoretical roots. *Israel Studies* 7 (3): 117–33.

Kelman M. 1987. *A guide to critical legal studies.* Cambridge, Mass.: Harvard University Press.

Kertzer, D. 1983. The role of ritual in political change. In *Culture and political change,* ed. M. Aronoff, 53–73. New Brunswick, N.J.: Transaction Books.

Keshev. 2007. *"War to the last minute": Israeli media in the second Lebanon war.* Jerusalem: Keshev. Available at www.keshev.org.il/FileUpload/reportweb .pdf (In Hebrew.)

Kimmerling, B. 2004. *Immigrants, settlers, natives: The Israeli state and society between cultural pluralism and cultural wars.* Tel Aviv: Alma/Am Oved. (In Hebrew.)

Kremnitzer, Mordechai. 2004. Disqualification of lists and parties: The Israeli case. In *Militant democracy,* ed. Andras Sajo, 157–170. Utrecht, Holland: Eleven International Publishing.

Kubersky, Haim. 1979. Report of the Committee to Clarify the Issue of a Second Television Channel in Israel. In Hebrew; in author's possession.

Kymlicka, W., and A. Patten. 2003. Introduction: Language rights and political theory: Context issues and approaches. In *Language rights and political theory,* ed. W. Kymlicka and A. Patten, 1–11. Oxford: Oxford University Press.

Lahav, P. 1978. Governmental regulation of the press: A study of Israel's Press Ordinance. *Israel Law Review* 13: 230–250.

———. 1997. *Judgment in Jerusalem: Chief Justice Shimon Agranat and the Zionist century.* Berkeley: University of California Press.

———. 2001. A "Jewish State . . . to be known as the State of Israel": Notes on Israeli legal historiography. *Law and History Review* 19 (2): 387–433.

Laqueur, W. 2003. *A history of Zionism: From the French revolution to the establishment of the state of Israel.* New York: Schocken.

Lasswell, H. 1948. The structure and function of communication in society. In *Public opinion and communication,* ed. B. Berelson and M. Janowitz, 178–92. New York: The Free Press.

Lehman-Wilzig, S., and A. Schejter. 1994. Mass media in Israel. In *Mass media in the Middle East: A comprehensive handbook,* ed. H. Mowlana and Y. Kamalipour, 109–25. Westport, Conn.: Greenwood Press.

Lemish, D., and C. Tidhar. 2001. How global does it get? The "Teletubbies" in Israel. *Journal of Broadcasting and Electronic Media* 45 (4): 558–74.

Lerner, M. 1995. *The Kasztner trial.* Jerusalem: Israel Broadcasting Authority. (In Hebrew.)

Levi Faur, D. 1998. *The dynamics of liberalization of Israeli telecommunications.* Report 8/98.Center of European and Asian Studies at the Norwegian School of Management.

———. 2000. Change and continuity in the Israeli political economy: Multi-level analysis of the telecommunications and energy sectors. In *The new Israel: Peacemaking and liberalization,* ed. G. Shafir, and Y. Peled, 161–88. Boulder, Colo.: Westview Press.

Levitsky, N. 2006. *The Supremes: Inside the Supreme Court.* Tel Aviv: The New Library. (In Hebrew.)

Liebes, T. 1992. Our war/their war: Comparing the *intifadeh* and the gulf war on U.S. and Israeli television. *Cultural Studies in Mass Communication* 9:44–55.

———. 2003. *American dreams, Hebrew subtitles: Globalization from the receiving end.* Creskill, N.J.: Hampton Press.

Liebes, T., and E. Katz. 1997. Staging peace: Televised ceremonies of reconciliation. *Communication Review* 2 (2): 235–57.

Limor, Y., and H. Naveh. 2008. *Pirate radio in Israel.* Haifa: Pardess Publishers. (In Hebrew.)

Livni, Yitzhak. 1993. Report of the Committee to Examine the Structure and Operation of the Broadcasting Authority. In Hebrew; in author's possession.

Liu, J., and D. J. Hilton. 2005. How the past weighs on the present: Social representations of history and their role in identity politics. *British Journal of Social Psychology* 44:537–56.

Loewenstein, Karl. 1937. Militant democracy and fundamental rights. *American Political Science Review* 31 (3): 417–432; 31 (4): 638–658.

Ma, E. K. 1999. Hong Kong remembers: A thick description of electronic memory. *Social Text* 58:75–91.

Machet, E., and S. Robillard. 1998. *Television and culture: Policies and regulations in Europe.* Dusseldorf: European Institute for the Media.

Maoz, A. 2000. Historical adjudication: Courts of law, commissions of inquiry, and "historical truth." *Law and History Review* 18 (3): 559–606.

Mcguigan, J. 2004. *Rethinking cultural policy.* Maidenhead, UK: Open University Press.

McQuail, D. 1987. *Mass communication theory: An introduction.* 2nd ed. Newbury Park: Sage Publications.

Merelman, M. 1991. *Partial visions: Culture and politics in Britain, Canada, and the United States.* Madison: University of Wisconsin Press.

Minkenberg, Michael. 2006. Repression and reaction: Militant democracy and the radical right in Germany and France. *Patterns of Prejudice* 40 (1): 25–44.

Moglen, E. 2001. Making history: Israeli law and historical reconstruction. *Law and History Review* 18 (3): 613–17.

Napoli, P. 2001. *Foundations of communication policy: Principles and processes in the regulation of electronic media.* Creskill, N.J.: Hampton Press.

Nassar, I. 2002. Reflections on writing the history of Palestinian identity. *Palestine-Israel Journal of Politics, Economics and Culture* 9 (1): 24–37.

Negbi, M. 1998. The enemy within: The effect of "private censorship" on press freedom and how to confront it—an Israeli perspective. Discussion paper D-35. The Joan Shorenstein on the Press, Politics, & Public Policy, John F. Kennedy School of Government, Harvard University. Available at http://www.hks.harvard.edu/presspol/research_publications/papers/discussion_papers/D35%20.pdf.

Nerone, J., and E. Wartella. 1989. Introduction: Studying social memory. *Communication* 11:85–88.

Nissan, Eli. 1997. Report of the Committee on Extending and Reforming of Broadcasting Choice (The Peled Committee). In Hebrew; English summary available at www.moc.gov.il/new/documents/peled/peled.pdf.

Noelle-Neumann, E. 1974. The spiral of silence: A theory of public opinion. *Journal of Communication* 24 (2): 43–51.

Nof, Akiba. 2000. Recommendations regarding community television. Presented to the Minister of Communications by the Public Committee for Studying Community Broadcasts over Cable Television Systems. (In Hebrew; in author's possession.)

Nossek, H., and Y. Limor. 2001. Fifty years in a "marriage of convenience": News media and military censorship in Israel. *Communication Law and Policy* 6 (1): 1–35.

Obeyesekere, G. 1981. *Medusa's hair: An essay on personal symbols and religious experience.* Chicago: University of Chicago Press.

Olick, J., and J. Robbins. 1998. Social memory studies: From collective memory to the historical sociology of mnemonic practices. *Annual Review of Sociology* 24:105–40.

Oren, T. 2004. *Demon in the box: Jews, Arabs, politics, and culture in the making of Israeli television.* New Brunswick, N.J.: Rutgers University Press.

Parsons, Patrick L. 2008. *Blue skies: A history of cable television.* Philadelphia, Pa.: Temple University Press.

Peled, Y., and G. Shafir. 2005. *Being Israeli: The dynamics of multiple citizenship.* Tel Aviv: Tel Aviv University Press. (In Hebrew.)

Peleg, I. 1998. Israel's constitutional order and *Kulturkampf:* The role of Ben Gurion. *Israel Studies* 3 (1): 230–50.

———. 2007. *Democratizing the hegemonic state: Political transformation in the age of identity.* New York: Cambridge University Press.

Peri, Y. 2001. The Rabin myth and the press: Reconstruction of the Israeli collective identity. *European Journal of Communication* 12:435–58.

———. 2004. *Telepopulism: Media and politics in Israel.* Stanford, Calif.: Stanford University Press.

Plessner, Y. 1994. *The political economy of Israel: From ideology to stagnation.* Albany, N.Y.: SUNY Press.

Poster, M. 1999. National identities and communications technologies. *Information Society* 15 (4): 235–40.

Ram, Uri. 1993. Society and social science: Established sociology and critical sociology in Israel. In *Israeli society: Critical perspectives,* ed. U. Ram, 7–39. Tel Aviv: Breirot Publishers. (In Hebrew.)

———. 2006. *The time of the "post": Nationalism and the politics of knowledge in Israel.* Tel Aviv: Resling.

Redford, E. 1969. *The regulatory process.* Austin: University of Texas Press.

Rouhana, N. 1997. *Palestinian citizens in an ethnic Jewish state: Identities in conflict.* New Haven, Conn.: Yale University Press.

Rubinstein, A., and B. Medina. 2005. *The constitutional law of the state of Israel.* 6th ed. Jerusalem and Tel Aviv: Shocken Publishers. (In Hebrew.)

Saban, I. 2004. Minority rights in deeply divided societies: A framework for analysis and the case of the Arab-Palestinian minority in Israel. *New York University Journal of International Law and Politics* 36:885–1003.

Sade, S. 2003a. Arafat, determines the BBC, is a hero made from the materials of which legends are made. *Ha'aretz,* 1 July. Accessed online 28 July 2004.

———. 2003b. Ambassador in London and Jewish leaders criticize boycott of BBC. *Ha'aretz,* 14 July. Accessed online 28 July 2004.

———. 2004. Not broadcasting black and white anymore. *Ha'aretz,* 31 May. Accessed online 28 July 2004.

Sarat, A., and T. Kearns. 1999. *History, memory, and the law.* Ann Arbor: Michigan University Press.

Sassaatelli, M. 2002. Imagined Europe: The shaping of a European cultural identity through EU cultural policy. *European Journal of Social Theory* 5 (4): 435–51.

Schedler, A. 2002. Elections without democracy: The menu of manipulation. *Journal of Democracy* 13 (2): 36–50.

Schejter, A. 1996. The cultural obligations of broadcast television in Israel. *International Communication Gazette* 56 (3): 183–200.

———. 1999. From a tool for national cohesion, to a manifestation of national conflict: The evolution of cable television policy in Israel, 1986–1998. *Communication Law and Policy* 4 (2): 177–200.

———. "The people shall dwell alone": The effect of transfrontier broadcasting on freedom of speech and information in Israel. *North Carolina Journal of International Law and Commercial Regulation* 31 (2): 337–76.

Schejter, A., J. Kittler, M. Lim, M. Balaji, and A. Douai. 2007. "Let's go down, and there confuse their language, that they may not understand one another's speech": Developing a model for comparative analysis and normative assessment of minority media rights. *Global Media Journal* 5 (10). Available at http://lass.calumet.purdue.edu/cca/gmj/sp07/gmj-sp07–schejter-kittler-lim-douai-balaji.htm.

Schejter A., and S. Lee. 2007. The evolution of cable regulatory policies and their consequences: Comparing South Korea and Israel. *Journal of Media Economics,* 20 (1): 1–28.

Schiller, H. 1993. Transnational media: Creating consumers worldwide. *Journal of International Affairs* 47 (1): 47–58.

Schrader, P. 2002. Promoting an international community of democracies. In *Exporting democracy: Rhetoric vs. reality,* ed. P. Schrader, 1–14. Boulder, Colo.: Lynne Rienner Publishers.

Schudson, M. 1994. Culture and the integration of national societies. In *The sociology of culture,* ed. D. Crane, 21–44. Cambridge, Mass.: Basil Blackwell.

Segal, Z. 1990. The military censorship, its authority, judicial review and an alternative proposal. *Iyunei Mishpat (Tel Aviv University Law Review)* 15:311. (In Hebrew.)

Shalit, E. 2004. *The Hero and his shadow: Psychopolitical aspects of myth and reality in Israel.* Dallas, Tex.: University Press of America.

Shapira, A. 2004. Whatever became of "negating exile"? In *Israeli identity in transition*, ed. A. Shapira, 69–108. Westport, Conn.: Praeger.

Sharkansky, I. 1987. *The political economy of Israel.* New Brunswick, N.J.: Transaction Books.

Shaughnessy, H., and C. Fuente Cobo. 1990. *The cultural obligations of broadcasting.* Manchester: European Institute for the Media.

Shavit, Y. 1996. The *Yishuv* between national regeneration of culture and cultural generation of the nation. In *Jewish nationalism and politics: New perspectives*, ed. J. Reinharz, G. Shimoni, and Y. Salmon, 141–58. Jerusalem: The Zalman Shazar Center and Boston: The Tauber Institute. (In Hebrew.)

Shenhav, Y. 2004. *The Arab Jews: Nationalism, religion and ethnicity.* Tel Aviv: Am Oved Publishers. (In Hebrew.)

Shimoni, G. 1996. Jewish nationalism as an ethnic nationalism. In *Jewish nationalism and politics: New perspectives*, ed. J. Reinharz, G. Shimoni, and Y. Salmon, 81–92. Jerusalem: The Zalman Shazar Center and Boston: The Tauber Institute. (In Hebrew.)

Shohat, E. 1988. Sephardim in Israel: Zionism from the standpoint of its Jewish victims. *Social Text* 19/20:1–35.

———. 1989. *Israeli cinema: East/West and the politics of representation.* Austin: University of Texas Press.

———. 1999. The invention of the Mizrahim. *Journal of Palestine studies* 29 (1): 5–20.

Siebert, F., Peterson, T. and Schramm, W. 1956. *Four theories of the press.* Urbana: University of Illinois Press.

Silverstone, R. 1988. Television, myth, and culture. In *Media, myths, and narrative: Television and the press*, ed. J. Carey, 20–47. Newbury Park, Calif.: Sage Publications.

Smooha, S. 1978. *Israel: Pluralism and conflict.* London: Routledge and Kegan Paul.

———. 1990. Minority status in an ethnic democracy: The status of the Arab minority in Israel. *Ethnic and Racial Studies* 13 (3): 389–413.

———. 1993. Class, ethnic and national cleavages and democracy in Israel. In *Israeli society: Critical perspectives*, ed. U. Ram, 172–202. Tel Aviv: Breirot Publishers. (In Hebrew.)

———. 1997. Ethnic democracy: Israel as an archetype. *Israel Studies* 2 (2): 198–241.

Sreberny, A. 2005. "Not only, but also": Mixedness and media. *Journal of Ethnic and Migration Studies* 31 (3): 443–59.

Sternhell, Z. 1998. *The founding myths of Israel: Nationalism, socialism, and the making of the Jewish state.* Princeton, N.J.: Princeton University Press.

Swirski, S. 1993. Comments on the historical sociology of the *Yishuv.* In *Israeli society: Critical perspectives*, ed. U. Ram, 54–82. Tel Aviv: Breirot Publishers. (In Hebrew.)

Tal, I. 2007. The right for equality: A look at the drafts of the Proclamation of Independence. *Ha'aretz*, 23 April. Accessed 29 November 2008.

Tamir, Y. 1993. *Liberal nationalism.* Princeton, N.J.: Princeton University Press.

Tatalovich, R., and B. Daynes, ed. 1988. *Social regulatory policy: Moral controversies in American politics.* Boulder, Colo.: Westview Press.

Thomas, A. 1999. Regulating access to transnational satellite television: Shifting government policies in northeast Asia. *International Communication Gazette* 61 (3–4): 243–54.

Thompson, J. 1995. *The media and modernity: A social theory of the media.* Stanford, Calif.: Stanford University Press.

Throsby, D. 1999. Cultural capital. *Journal of Cultural Economics* 23 (1–2): 3–12.

Tokatly, O. 2000. *Communication policy in Israel.* Tel Aviv: Open University. (In Hebrew.)

Turow, J. 1992. *Media systems in society: Understanding industries, strategies, and power.* New York: Longman.

Weddel, G., and A. Lange. 1991. Regulatory and financial issues in transfrontier television in Europe. In *Broadcasting finance in transition,* in J. Blumler and T. J. Nossiter, 382–403. Oxford: Oxford University Press.

Weimann, G. 1990. "Redefinition of image": The impact of mass mediated terrorism. *International Journal of Public Opinion Research* 2 (2): 16–29.

———. 1995. Zapping in the Holy Land: Coping with multichannel TV in Israel. *Journal of Communication* 45 (1): 96–102.

Weisman, S. 2005. Under pressure, Qatar may sell Jazeera station. *New York Times,* 30 January, A1.

Weitz, Y. 1996. The Holocaust on trial: The impact of the Kasztner and Eichmann trials on Israeli society. *Israel Studies* 1 (2): 1–26.

Williams, R. 1989. The idea of a common culture. In *Resources of hope: Culture, democracy, and socialism,* ed. R. Gable, 32–38. London: Verso.

Wolffsohn, M. 1987. *Israel, polity, society, and economy 1882–1986.* Atlantic Highlands, N.J.: Humanities Press International.

Wright, C. 1960. Functional analysis of mass communication. *Public Opinion Quarterly* 24:606–20.

Yadgar, Y. 2004. *Our story: The national narrative in the Israeli press.* Haifa: University of Haifa Press. (In Hebrew.)

Yiftachel, O. 2000. Social control, urban planning and ethno-class relations: *Mizrahi* Jews in Israel's "development towns." *International Journal of Urban and Regional Research* 24 (2): 418–38.

Yiftachel, O., and A. Kedar. 2000. Power and land: Real estate policy in Israel. *Theory and Criticism* 16:67–100. (In Hebrew.)

Yuran, N. 2001. *Channel 2: The new statehood.* Tel Aviv: Resling. (In Hebrew.)

Zerubavel, Y. 1996. *Recovered roots: Collective memory and the making of Israeli national tradition.* Chicago: University of Chicago Press.

Zimmerman, M. 2003. *Hole in the camera: Gazes of Israeli cinema.* Tel Aviv: Resling. (In Hebrew.)

Zuckerman, Arnon. 1997. Report of the Committee to Analyze the Structure of Public Broadcasting and Its Legal and Public Status. (In Hebrew; in author's possession.)

Zuckerman, M. 2001. *On the fabrication of Israelism: Myths and ideology in a society at conflict.* Tel Aviv: Resling. (In Hebrew.)

INDEX

AMIT M. SCHEJTER is associate professor of communications and co-director of the Institute for Information Policy at Penn State University. An Israeli-trained attorney specializing in telecommunication and media law, policy, and regulation, Dr. Schejter has held senior executive positions in the media and telecommunications industry in Israel. He has served on and chaired a variety of public committees and has counseled media and telecommunication entities in Israel and the Palestinian Authority. Dr. Schejter's studies have been published in communication journals, law journals, and edited volumes in the United States, France, the United Kingdom, Germany, and Israel, and presented at academic conferences worldwide. He is the co-author of *The Wonder Phone in the Land of Miracles: Mobile Telephony in Israel* (with A. Cohen and D. Lemish), and the editor of *. . . And Communications for All: A Policy Agenda for the New Administration.*

The University of Illinois Press
is a founding member of the
Association of American University Presses.

Composed in 9.5/12.5 Trump Mediaeval
by Jim Proefrock
at the University of Illinois Press
Manufactured by Sheridan Books, Inc.

University of Illinois Press
1325 South Oak Street
Champaign, IL 61820-6903
www.press.uillinois.edu